A Return to Normalcy?

A Return to Normalcy?

The 2020 Election That (Almost) Broke America

Edited by Larry J. Sabato, Kyle Kondik, and
J. Miles Coleman

ROWMAN & LITTLEFIELD
Lanham • Boulder • New York • London

Published by Rowman & Littlefield
An imprint of The Rowman & Littlefield Publishing Group, Inc.
4501 Forbes Boulevard, Suite 200, Lanham, Maryland 20706
www.rowman.com

6 Tinworth Street, London SE11 5AL, United Kingdom

British Library Cataloguing in Publication Information Available

Library of Congress Cataloging-in-Publication Data Available

ISBN: 978-1-5381-4851-8 (cloth)
ISBN: 978-1-5381-4852-5 (paper)
ISBN: 978-1-5381-4853-2 (electronic)

∞™ The paper used in this publication meets the minimum requirements of American National Standard for Information Sciences—Permanence of Paper for Printed Library Materials, ANSI/NISO Z39.48-1992.

Contents

Preface and Acknowledgments

In the 1920 election, Republican Warren G. Harding swept into office promising "A Return to Normalcy." A century later, Democrat Joe Biden did not use the same phrase, but the promise of Biden's candidacy was rooted in the same concept.

The question mark at the end of this volume's title, though, is very important to note—for the return of normalcy is indeed an open question. The first weeks of the Biden presidency featured a second impeachment trial of Donald Trump, the former president; a divisive battle over a coronavirus relief package; and Republican headaches with some new, Trumpish members of their House caucus.

The wheel of American politics never stops turning, but the time immediately following an election represents a good time to take stock. As we do every two years, the University of Virginia Center for Politics has assembled an impressive roster of political scientists, analysts, and reporters to study the most recent national election.

One of us, Larry J. Sabato (chapter 1), provides an overview of the 2020 campaign in the opening chapter. He is followed by veteran political journalist Rhodes Cook (chapter 2) and *Washington Post* elections analyst David Byler (chapter 3). They analyze the voting patterns in the primary season and how Biden won the Democratic presidential nomination, respectively. The primary season, with its impressive turnout despite the disruptions of the COVID-19 pandemic, provided a preview of the supercharged turnout we would see in November.

Then we shift back to analyzing the general election. Alan I. Abramowitz (chapter 4), a political scientist at Emory University and long-time senior columnist for our *Sabato's Crystal Ball* election analysis newsletter, looks at the stark divisions in American life that the 2020 election reconfirmed. He is followed by coeditor J. Miles Coleman (chapter 5), who provides a granular look at the shifts in the November electorate. Co-editor Kyle Kondik (chapter 6) then analyzes the House results, where Republicans made impressive and surprising gains while falling short of winning the majority, and *National Journal*'s Madelaine Pisani (chapter 7) and Mary Frances McGowan (chapter 8) tell the story of 2020's Senate and state-level elections, respectively.

Theodore Johnson (chapter 9) of the Brennan Center provides an in-depth look at the gender gap in the Black electorate. Diana Owen (chapter 10) of Georgetown University follows with an analysis of how the media covered the election—as well as how the candidates pushed out messages themselves through the unfiltered world of social media.

Despite the COVID-19 pandemic, Americans voted in huge numbers in 2020; Grace Panetta (chapter 11) of *Business Insider* describes this turnout and the voting method changes that allowed it to happen. Former Federal Election Commission Chairman Michael Toner and his colleague Karen Trainer (chapter 12) detail the immense amounts of money spent on the election, and Sean Trende (chapter 13) of *RealClearPolitics* ponders whether the Trump experience was worth it for Republicans.

Turning this book around so quickly after an election is no easy task, and we want to thank, in particular, our Center for Politics colleagues Eliot Sperling and Garland Branch as well as interns Hunter Brown and Eva Surovell for their help in editing and formatting the manuscript. We also want to thank the Center's Associate Director, Ken Stroupe, and Chief Financial Officer, Mary Daniel Brown, as well as the team at the book's publisher, Rowman and Littlefield, particularly Jon Sisk and Benjamin Knepp.

Larry J. Sabato, Kyle Kondik, and J. Miles Coleman
University of Virginia Center for Politics
February 2021

1

A Return to Normalcy?

Taking Stock at the End of the Trump Presidency

Larry J. Sabato

Lots of unexpected things have happened in America since Donald Trump was elected president, and among the most unexpected is that the 45th president was so different, so abrasive, and so contemptuous of many cherished traditions and norms that by 2020 an exhausted electorate was ready to revive a slogan from 100 years ago. After World War I's death and destruction during the two terms of President Woodrow Wilson, Americans were prepared for what Republican presidential nominee Warren G. Harding called "a return to normalcy." Harding had read the people's mood accurately, and he won the 1920 election in a landslide. Other than inventing the word "normalcy," Harding made little impact on history in a positive way, becoming better known for the Teapot Dome scandal, his mistress and out-of-wedlock child, and an early death after just two years and five months in the White House.

Comparisons are strained where Donald Trump is involved. That's because Trump is unlike any of his predecessors. From his first day in the White House to his last, the 45th president did it his way, and he won not just the support but also the devotion of tens of millions of his fellow citizens. Those in his "base," as it was often called, backed Trump no matter what, and did so in what can only be described as a near-religious fervor. That Trump was undeniably authoritarian, demagogic, narcissistic, often untruthful, and ignorant of most of the government's functions made not a whit of difference to those in the Trump cult.

Trump's election and style of governance was enough to shake the faith of many people at home and around the world in the U.S. system of government and politics. What kind of system and electorate permits this sort of individual to ascend to the most powerful position, arguably, anywhere? What of the nation's vaunted checks and balances—which failed time and again to rein Trump in? The anti-majoritarian momentum in the United States, fed by the Electoral College that twice in 16 years clashed with the popular vote, as well as the U.S. Senate that heavily overrepresented little-populated rural states, was part of the answer. So too was extreme partisan polarization between Republicans and Democrats, two groups that increasingly appeared to have little in common—all but negating comity in Congress as well as pieces of the Constitution such as the 25th Amendment, ratified in 1967 to remove a dangerous or incapable president via bipartisan actions by the Congress and Cabinet.[1]

All this might have worsened in a second Trump term, which many observers believed was at least an even bet or perhaps probable as the election year dawned. The economy was solid, there were no unpopular foreign wars, and Americans seemed almost numb to the constant chaos, insults, and outrages flowing from Trump's White House.

But then two significant developments changed the equation to Trump's disfavor. First came the pandemic. The COVID-19 public health crisis brought illness and death around the globe, but the Trump administration's mismanagement of the country's response—fed by the president's insistence that the disease wasn't particularly serious and could be obviated by warm weather, bleach, and medications unproven to work—resulted in a death toll considerably higher than it had to be. The damage to the economy was serious as soon as lockdowns began in March 2020, and Trump lost the punch of his main talking point in his reelection bid. The pandemic roared right through the November election (and beyond). The economy in some sectors all but collapsed, despite serious rescue packages at the federal and state levels. The advent of effective vaccines, the only real long-term hope to end the pandemic, did not occur until after the election.

The second election-changing development was the nomination of former Vice President Joseph R. Biden Jr. as the Democratic presidential nominee. While there were quite a few attractive, thoughtful, and reasonably well-qualified candidates in the Democrats' field of nearly 30 contenders, Joe Biden was unquestionably the safest choice. His long 36-year career as a U.S. senator and eight years as President Obama's vice president made him one of the most tested White House nominees in modern times. Like many politicians, Biden evolved ideologically over his decades in public office, but the long view suggests his orientation is essentially moderate-liberal, and his rhetoric is much less heated than most of his younger colleagues. No one could credibly charge that Biden was unprepared to be president. Biden simply did not frighten most people and didn't cut any sort of extreme figure. For Biden, the pandemic eased the burdens of typical campaigning. Vigorous stumping was impossible, the national party conventions were all but virtual, and the chances for verbal gaffes—which had long been a Biden staple—were minimized. As a 77-year-old candidate (who turned 78 just after the election), Biden was spared a great deal of physical stress—and so was Trump, age 74, so the two oldest major-party nominees ever could at least be well rested.

ELECTION RESULTS

The first presidential election held in the midst of a once-a-century global pandemic generated a mountainous voter turnout of nearly 160 million, the largest proportion of eligible adults (about 67 percent) in 120 years.[2] (Back in 1900, of course, the electorate was effectively restricted to white men, with few exceptions.) About 158 million Americans voted in the presidential race, far more than the 137 million recorded in 2016. Some of the increase was due to liberalization of early voting and absentee/mail-in ballot procedures in most states due to the pandemic. Remarkably, 46 percent of all votes cast in 2020 came via the mail and absentee balloting—up from just 21 percent in 2016.[3] Early in-person voting also gained, from 19 percent in the last election to 26 percent this time. For the first time ever in a presidential general election, less than a majority of the votes were cast on Election Day. In 2016, 60 percent of all votes were cast on Election Day; in 2020, only 28 percent were.[4] Will this continue in future elections? Without a pandemic as well as the possible dropping of liberalized rules in some places, probably not. However, many Americans liked the convenience of early voting and will likely stick to it.

The unforeseen pandemic guaranteed that the 2020 contest wouldn't be normal in other ways. The national party conventions, a staple of the quadrennial campaign calendar, were converted from in-person events involving approximately tens of thousands of delegates, dignitaries, and press, to virtual shows, such as a memorable state-by-state nominating roundabout for Biden featuring colorful representatives of each state. Trump brought a large group of Republicans to the White House lawn for his acceptance speech, but otherwise most of the GOP presentations were also virtual. The fall campaign was the first in modern history, perhaps ever, without candidates shaking hands and kissing babies—though again, Trump insisted on maintaining his huge rallies, even though many attendees did not wear masks or practice social distancing. (Some of these gatherings became superspreaders of the coronavirus, according to public health events).[5]

Another sharp break with tradition is deeply worrying. Less than a week after the polls closed, there was a clear-cut result in favor of Joe Biden, yet pandemic-induced slow counting gave Trump an opening to claim—just as he asserted he would do for many months—that "massive" voter fraud had deprived him of a "landslide" victory. This was and is utter nonsense, a monstrous lie that still haunts the country because Trump repeated it so often that his millions of cult followers swallowed it whole. Dozens of GOP members of Congress perpetuated the false claims by doing everything they could to slow or stop the formal Electoral College vote-counting on January 6, 2021, a count disrupted by an angry, pro-Trump mob incited by the president that stormed the Capitol and interrupted the formal vote counting. The attempt failed, but not before setting a dangerous precedent that without question will be used in the future to delegitimize presidents-elect for the opposition party's political gain.

The truth is plain, however. Biden switched the three so-called "blue wall" states that fell to Trump in 2016 (Michigan, Pennsylvania, and Wisconsin), and he narrowly added Arizona and Georgia to the Democratic coalition. Trump did not carry any states he lost in 2016, while losing the five just-mentioned states that he carried four years earlier. Biden also carried Nebraska's Second Congressional District, the stand-alone electoral vote that Trump grabbed in 2016. Trump kept Maine's Second Congressional District, the only other stand-alone electoral vote. (Maine and Nebraska, alone among the states, cast some of their electoral votes by congressional district. Every other state is winner takes all.)

In a bit of irony, Biden accumulated 306 electoral votes—precisely the number Trump had won four years earlier. Trump picked up 232 electoral votes, the same total Hillary Clinton posted.[6] Moreover, while Trump lost the popular vote by almost 3 million to Clinton, Biden secured over 7 million more votes nationwide than Trump, and won the popular vote by 4.5 percent (51.3 percent to 46.8 percent). This was a higher percentage than a Democratic nominee had won since Lyndon B. Johnson in 1964, with the exception of Barack Obama in 2008 (52.9 percent). In a very partisan era, real landslides in the popular vote (55 percent +) are no longer possible under most circumstances. Obama and Biden did about as well as Democrats can do until such time as the party coalitions shift significantly.

Analysts will argue endlessly about how close Biden came to losing the Electoral College. Just as Trump won the College in 2016 by a mere 77,700 votes collectively in the three blue-wall states, so too did Biden win Arizona, Georgia, and Wisconsin by even less, about 43,000 votes total. The loss of those three very close states would have put Biden and Trump at 269-269 in the Electoral College, throwing the presidential choice to the House of Representatives, where Republicans controlled enough state delegations to award the White House to Trump. (Under the Constitution, each state's delegation, regardless of size, gets to cast a single vote, and the winner must receive at least 26 votes to win.) But one can contend that this says more about the unfairness of the anti-majoritarian Electoral College—which now clearly favors Republicans in close contests such as 2000 and 2016. When a candidate can win the popular vote by 7 million, as Biden did, and be decently close to losing an Electoral College majority and thus the presidency, constitutional reform ought to be on the table (but of course is not).

As controversial and unpopular a president as Trump was—to judge by the Gallup poll,[7] he never achieved majority support during his four-year tenure—he still managed to increase his total votes from 63 million in 2016 to 74.2 million in 2020. Of course Biden greatly improved on Clinton's nearly 65.8 million, expanding that to 81.3 million. One considerable change from 2016 that helped Biden was the decline in third-party and independent voting—from 8.5 million (6 percent) four years ago to a much smaller 3 million (1.9 percent) in 2020. Trump may have received far more votes in 2020 than he had in 2016, but his percentage of the vote barely enlarged, going from 45.9 percent to 46.8 percent. Meanwhile, Biden garnered more than three points more than Clinton's proportion of the national popular vote. Nonetheless, as suggested earlier, it is a warning sign for Democrats that it took this large a popular plurality for Biden to scale the 270 electoral votes required to win.

While a handful of states changed sides and the margins within individual states varied somewhat from the final results in 2016, on the whole the regional splits were predictable, quite similar to four years earlier (table 1.1). The South, the Plains, and the interior West were Trump's. The Northeast and the Pacific West were heavily Biden. Only the industrial Midwest, as a region, was truly competitive, with Biden edging Trump, 49.6 percent to 48.5 percent. You can compare the 2016 and 2020 two-party results in the 50 states plus Washington, D.C. (table 1.2). By and large, the 2020 election—in terms of the vote percentages—was basically a rerun of 2016, with Biden doing marginally better than Clinton in many states and Trump lagging his earlier performance slightly. In our very partisan, polarized era, marginal changes make all the difference, determining whether the Democrat or Republican secures 306 electoral votes in 2016 or 2020.

EXIT POLLING

Polling had another bad year in 2020, just as in 2016. Other authors will discuss the pre-Election Day polls later in the volume. But exit polling of those who had voted (by any method) also seemed off, at least to many knowledgeable people in the political community—even after postelection adjustments.

Table 1.1. 2020 Presidential Vote—By Region

	Electoral Vote								Percentage of Total Vote		
	Dem.	*Rep.*	*Total Vote*	*Biden (Dem.)*	*Trump (Rep.)*	*Other*	*Rep.-Dem. Plurality*		*Biden (Dem.)*	*Trump (Rep.)*	*Other*
GREATER SOUTH											
Alabama		9	2,323,282	849,624	1,441,170	32,488	591,546	R	36.6%	62.0%	1.4%
Arkansas		6	1,219,069	423,932	760,647	34,490	336,715	R	34.8%	62.4%	2.8%
Florida		29	11,091,758	5,297,045	5,668,731	125,982	371,686	R	47.8%	51.1%	1.1%
Georgia	16		5,001,160	2,473,633	2,461,854	65,673	11,779	D	49.5%	49.2%	1.3%
Kentucky		8	2,136,768	772,474	1,326,646	37,648	554,172	R	36.2%	62.1%	1.8%
Louisiana		8	2,148,062	856,034	1,255,776	36,252	399,742	R	39.9%	58.5%	1.7%
Mississippi		6	1,314,475	539,398	756,764	18,313	217,366	R	41.0%	57.6%	1.4%
Missouri		10	3,030,748	1,253,014	1,718,736	58,998	465,722	R	41.3%	56.7%	1.9%
North Carolina		15	5,524,804	2,684,292	2,758,775	81,737	74,483	R	48.6%	49.9%	1.5%
Oklahoma		7	1,560,699	503,890	1,020,280	36,529	516,390	R	32.3%	65.4%	2.3%
South Carolina		9	2,513,329	1,091,541	1,385,103	36,685	293,562	R	43.4%	55.1%	1.5%
Tennessee		11	3,053,851	1,143,711	1,852,475	57,665	708,764	R	37.5%	60.7%	1.9%
Texas		38	11,324,007	5,259,126	5,890,347	174,534	631,221	R	46.4%	52.0%	1.5%
Virginia	13		4,460,524	2,413,568	1,962,430	84,526	451,138	D	54.1%	44.0%	1.9%
West Virginia		5	794,731	235,984	545,382	13,365	309,398	R	29.7%	68.6%	1.7%
Total - Greater South	29	161	57,497,267	25,797,266	30,805,116	894,885	5,007,850	R	44.9%	53.6%	1.6%

Arizona	11		3,397,388	1,672,143	1,661,686	63,559	10,457	D	49.2%	48.9%	1.9%
Colorado	9		3,256,980	1,804,352	1,364,607	88,021	439,745	D	55.4%	41.9%	2.7%
Idaho		4	870,343	287,021	554,119	29,203	267,098	R	33.0%	63.7%	3.4%
Kansas		6	1,377,484	570,323	771,406	35,755	201,083	R	41.4%	56.0%	2.6%
Montana		3	603,674	244,786	343,602	15,286	98,816	R	40.5%	56.9%	2.5%
Nebraska	1	4	956,383	374,583	556,846	24,954	182,263	R	39.2%	58.2%	2.6%
Nevada	6		1,405,376	703,486	669,890	32,000	33,596	D	50.1%	47.7%	2.3%
New Mexico	5		923,965	501,614	401,894	20,457	99,720	D	54.3%	43.5%	2.2%
North Dakota		3	361,819	114,902	235,595	11,322	120,693	R	31.8%	65.1%	3.1%
South Dakota		3	422,609	150,471	261,043	11,095	110,572	R	35.6%	61.8%	2.6%
Utah		6	1,505,931	560,282	865,140	80,509	304,858	R	37.2%	57.4%	5.3%
Wyoming		3	276,765	73,491	193,559	9,715	120,068	R	26.6%	69.9%	3.5%
Total - Inner West & Plains	32	32	15,358,717	7,057,454	7,879,387	421,876	821,933	R	46.0%	51.3%	2.7%
NORTHEAST											
Connecticut	7		1,824,456	1,080,831	715,311	28,314	365,520	D	59.2%	39.2%	1.6%
Delaware	3		504,346	296,268	200,603	7,475	95,665	D	58.7%	39.8%	1.5%
Maine	3	1	819,461	435,072	360,737	23,652	74,335	D	53.1%	44.0%	2.9%
Maryland	10		3,037,030	1,985,023	976,414	75,593	1,008,609	D	65.4%	32.2%	2.5%
Massachusetts	11		3,631,402	2,382,202	1,167,202	81,998	1,215,000	D	65.6%	32.1%	2.3%

(continued)

Table 1.1. (*continued*)

	Electoral Vote								*Percentage of Total Vote*		
	Dem.	*Rep.*	*Total Vote*	*Biden (Dem.)*	*Trump (Rep.)*	*Other*	*Rep.-Dem. Plurality*		*Biden (Dem.)*	*Trump (Rep.)*	*Other*
New Hampshire	4		806,205	424,937	365,660	15,608	59,277	D	52.7%	45.4%	1.9%
New Jersey	14		4,564,317	2,608,400	1,883,310	72,607	725,090	D	57.1%	41.3%	1.6%
New York	29		8,629,859	5,244,488	3,251,321	134,050	1,993,167	D	60.8%	37.7%	1.6%
Pennsylvania	20		6,940,449	3,461,221	3,379,055	100,173	82,166	D	49.9%	48.7%	1.4%
Rhode Island	4		517,757	307,486	199,922	10,349	107,564	D	59.4%	38.6%	2.0%
Vermont	3		367,428	242,820	112,704	11,904	130,116	D	66.1%	30.7%	3.2%
Dist. of Col.	3		344,356	317,323	18,586	8,447	298,737	D	92.1%	5.4%	2.5%
Total - Northeast	111	1	31,987,066	18,786,071	12,630,825	570,170	6,155,246	D	58.7%	39.5%	1.8%
PACIFIC WEST											
Alaska		3	359,530	153,778	189,951	15,801	36,173	R	42.8%	52.8%	4.4%
California	55		17,511,515	11,110,250	6,006,429	394,836	5,103,821	D	63.4%	34.3%	2.3%
Hawaii	4		574,469	366,130	196,864	11,475	169,266	D	63.7%	34.3%	2.0%
Oregon	7		2,374,321	1,340,383	958,448	75,490	381,935	D	56.5%	40.4%	3.2%
Washington	12		4,087,631	2,369,612	1,584,651	133,368	784,961	D	58.0%	38.8%	3.3%
Total - Pacific West	78	3	24,907,466	15,340,153	8,936,343	630,970	6,403,810	D	61.6%	35.9%	2.5%

INDUSTRIAL MIDWEST											
Illinois	20		6,048,873	3,471,915	2,446,891	130,067	1,025,024	D	57.4%	40.5%	2.2%
Indiana		11	3,039,369	1,242,498	1,729,857	67,014	487,359	R	40.9%	56.9%	2.2%
Iowa		6	1,690,871	759,061	897,672	34,138	138,611	R	44.9%	53.1%	2.0%
Michigan	16		5,547,186	2,804,045	2,649,864	93,277	154,181	D	50.5%	47.8%	1.7%
Minnesota	10		3,277,171	1,717,077	1,484,065	76,029	233,012	D	52.4%	45.3%	2.3%
Ohio		18	5,932,398	2,679,165	3,154,834	98,399	475,669	R	45.2%	53.2%	1.7%
Wisconsin	10		3,298,041	1,630,866	1,610,184	56,991	20,682	D	49.4%	48.8%	1.7%
Total - Industrial Midwest	56	35	28,833,909	14,304,627	13,973,367	555,915	331,260	D	49.6%	48.5%	1.9%
NATIONAL											
Northeast	111	1	31,987,066	18,786,071	12,630,825	570,170	6,155,246	D	58.7%	39.5%	1.8%
Industrial Midwest	56	35	28,833,909	14,304,627	13,973,367	555,915	331,260	D	49.6%	48.5%	1.9%
Pacific West	78	3	24,907,466	15,340,153	8,936,343	630,970	6,403,810	D	61.6%	35.9%	2.5%
Greater South	29	161	57,497,267	25,797,266	30,805,116	894,885	5,007,850	R	44.9%	53.6%	1.6%
Inner West & Plains	32	32	15,358,717	7,057,454	7,879,387	421,876	821,933	R	46.0%	51.3%	2.7%
National Total	**306**	**232**	**158,584,425**	**81,285,571**	**74,225,038**	**3,073,816**	**7,060,533**	**D**	**51.3%**	**46.8%**	**1.9%**

Source: Dave Leip's Atlas of U.S. Presidential Elections, http://uselectionatlas.org/RESULTS/, as of March 1, 2021.

Table 1.2. The 2016 and 2020 Presidential Votes

	2-Party Vote % – 2016					2-Party Vote % – 2020				Biden Change from Clinton 2016
	Clinton		Trump			Biden		Trump		
State	Votes	Percent	Votes	Percent	State	Votes	Percent	Votes	Percent	
Alabama	729,547	35.6%	1,318,255	64.4%	Alabama	849,624	37.1%	1,441,170	62.9%	1.5%
Alaska	116,454	41.6%	163,387	58.4%	Alaska	153,778	44.7%	189,951	55.3%	3.1%
Arizona	1,161,167	48.1%	1,252,401	51.9%	Arizona	1,672,143	50.2%	1,661,686	49.8%	2.0%
Arkansas	380,494	35.7%	684,872	64.3%	Arkansas	423,932	35.8%	760,647	64.2%	0.1%
California	8,753,792	66.1%	4,483,814	33.9%	California	11,110,250	64.9%	6,006,429	35.1%	–1.2%
Colorado	1,338,870	52.7%	1,202,484	47.3%	Colorado	1,804,352	56.9%	1,364,607	43.1%	4.3%
Connecticut	897,572	57.1%	673,215	42.9%	Connecticut	1,080,831	60.2%	715,311	39.8%	3.0%
Delaware	235,603	56.0%	185,127	44.0%	Delaware	296,268	59.6%	200,603	40.4%	3.6%
Florida	4,504,975	49.4%	4,617,886	50.6%	Florida	5,297,045	48.3%	5,668,731	51.7%	–1.1%
Georgia	1,877,963	47.3%	2,089,104	52.7%	Georgia	2,473,633	50.1%	2,461,854	49.9%	2.8%
Hawaii	266,891	67.4%	128,847	32.6%	Hawaii	366,130	65.0%	196,864	35.0%	–2.4%
Idaho	189,765	31.7%	409,055	68.3%	Idaho	287,021	34.1%	554,119	65.9%	2.4%
Illinois	3,090,729	59.0%	2,146,015	41.0%	Illinois	3,471,915	58.7%	2,446,891	41.3%	–0.4%
Indiana	1,033,126	39.9%	1,557,286	60.1%	Indiana	1,242,498	41.8%	1,729,857	58.2%	1.9%
Iowa	653,669	44.9%	800,983	55.1%	Iowa	759,061	45.8%	897,672	54.2%	0.9%
Kansas	427,005	38.9%	671,018	61.1%	Kansas	570,323	42.5%	771,406	57.5%	3.6%
Kentucky	628,854	34.3%	1,202,971	65.7%	Kentucky	772,474	36.8%	1,326,646	63.2%	2.5%
Louisiana	780,154	39.8%	1,178,638	60.2%	Louisiana	856,034	40.5%	1,255,776	59.5%	0.7%
Maine	357,735	51.6%	335,593	48.4%	Maine	435,072	54.7%	360,737	45.3%	3.1%
Maryland	1,677,928	64.0%	943,169	36.0%	Maryland	1,985,023	67.0%	976,414	33.0%	3.0%
Massachusetts	1,995,196	64.7%	1,090,893	35.3%	Massachusetts	2,382,202	67.1%	1,167,202	32.9%	2.5%
Michigan	2,268,839	49.9%	2,279,543	50.1%	Michigan	2,804,045	51.4%	2,649,864	48.6%	1.5%
Minnesota	1,367,825	50.8%	1,323,232	49.2%	Minnesota	1,717,077	53.6%	1,484,065	46.4%	2.8%
Mississippi	485,131	40.9%	700,714	59.1%	Mississippi	539,398	41.6%	756,764	58.4%	0.7%

Missouri	1,071,068	40.2%	1,594,511	59.8%	Missouri	1,253,014	42.2%	1,718,736	57.8%	2.0%
Montana	177,709	38.9%	279,240	61.1%	Montana	244,786	41.6%	343,602	58.4%	2.7%
Nebraska	284,494	36.5%	495,961	63.5%	Nebraska	374,583	40.2%	556,846	59.8%	3.8%
Nevada	539,260	51.3%	512,058	48.7%	Nevada	703,486	51.2%	669,890	48.8%	−0.1%
New Hampshire	348,526	50.2%	345,790	49.8%	New Hampshire	424,937	53.7%	365,660	46.3%	3.6%
New Jersey	2,148,278	57.3%	1,601,933	42.7%	New Jersey	2,608,400	58.1%	1,883,310	41.9%	0.8%
New Mexico	385,234	54.7%	319,667	45.3%	New Mexico	501,614	55.5%	401,894	44.5%	0.9%
New York	4,556,142	61.8%	2,819,557	38.2%	New York	5,244,488	61.7%	3,251,321	38.3%	0.0%
North Carolina	2,189,316	48.1%	2,362,631	51.9%	North Carolina	2,684,292	49.3%	2,758,775	50.7%	1.2%
North Dakota	93,758	30.2%	216,794	69.8%	North Dakota	114,902	32.8%	235,595	67.2%	2.6%
Ohio	2,394,169	45.7%	2,841,006	54.3%	Ohio	2,679,165	45.9%	3,154,834	54.1%	0.2%
Oklahoma	420,375	30.7%	949,136	69.3%	Oklahoma	503,890	33.1%	1,020,280	66.9%	2.4%
Oregon	1,002,106	56.2%	782,403	43.8%	Oregon	1,340,383	58.3%	958,448	41.7%	2.2%
Pennsylvania	2,926,458	49.6%	2,970,742	50.4%	Pennsylvania	3,461,221	50.6%	3,379,055	49.4%	1.0%
Rhode Island	252,525	58.3%	180,543	41.7%	Rhode Island	307,486	60.6%	199,922	39.4%	2.3%
South Carolina	855,373	42.5%	1,155,389	57.5%	South Carolina	1,091,541	44.1%	1,385,103	55.9%	1.5%
South Dakota	117,466	34.0%	227,731	66.0%	South Dakota	150,471	36.6%	261,043	63.4%	2.5%
Tennessee	870,695	36.4%	1,522,925	63.6%	Tennessee	1,143,711	38.2%	1,852,475	61.8%	1.8%
Texas	3,877,868	45.3%	4,685,047	54.7%	Texas	5,259,126	47.2%	5,890,347	52.8%	1.9%
Utah	310,676	37.6%	515,231	62.4%	Utah	560,282	39.3%	865,140	60.7%	1.7%
Vermont	178,573	65.2%	95,369	34.8%	Vermont	242,820	68.3%	112,704	31.7%	3.1%
Virginia	1,981,473	52.8%	1,769,443	47.2%	Virginia	2,413,568	55.2%	1,962,430	44.8%	2.3%
Washington	1,742,718	58.8%	1,221,747	41.2%	Washington	2,369,612	59.9%	1,584,651	40.1%	1.1%
West Virginia	188,794	27.8%	489,371	72.2%	West Virginia	235,984	30.2%	545,382	69.8%	2.4%
Wisconsin	1,382,536	49.6%	1,405,284	50.4%	Wisconsin	1,630,866	50.3%	1,610,184	49.7%	0.7%
Wyoming	55,973	24.3%	174,419	75.7%	Wyoming	73,491	27.5%	193,559	72.5%	3.2%
Dist. of Col.	282,830	95.7%	12,723	4.3%	Dist. of Col.	317,323	94.5%	18,586	5.5%	−1.2%
Total	**65,853,677**	**51.1%**	**62,985,153**	**48.9%**	**Total**	**81,285,571**	**52.3%**	**74,225,038**	**47.7%**	**1.2%**

Source: Dave Leip's Atlas of U.S. Presidential Elections, http://uselectionatlas.org/RESULTS/.

So I want to warn readers to take these exit numbers as estimates rather than a precise accounting. I will avoid use of exact percentages except in those cases where the margin achieved by one candidate or the other was large enough to generate confidence in a conclusion. Here we use Edison exit polls since they are used in previous volumes of this series. Yet the sample size for Edison is 15,590 while the other exit poll, AP VoteCast, surveyed a much larger group of 110,485 voters—though sample size alone does not indicate degree of accuracy. The two exit polls conflicted on quite a number of breakdowns. For example, in measuring Catholic voters, Edison found Biden had won them, 52 percent to 47 percent. AP VoteCast, however, had Trump narrowly ahead, 50 percent to 49 percent. Catholics comprised 25 percent of the total vote nationally in Edison, 22 percent in AP VoteCast. So which is it? Should we average the two exit polls? Prefer one over the other? It isn't at all clear.[8]

As you go down the column of exit poll questions and answers in table 1.3, you will probably find yourself nodding in basic agreement. There are small surprises, but the picture the poll paints is almost entirely recognizable, and again, it resembles the Trump-Clinton contest. Here is a sampling of the exit poll findings (and you will find a great deal more in the table at the end of this chapter):

- In this highly partisan era, Trump won 94 percent of Republicans and Biden won 94 percent of Democrats. The independents, a quarter of the total vote, went decisively for Biden, unlike in 2016 when Trump won them.
- Men favored Trump by 53-45 percent and women chose Biden by a larger 57-42 percent. Women are a majority of the voting electorate (52 percent) so that fact aided Biden. Keep in mind the racial dimension of the vote is hidden by the umbrella gender categories. For example, 61 percent of white men and 55 percent of white women voted for Trump—so while gender is still visible here, the more important point is that both white men and white women were decisively in Trump's camp.
- The younger the voter, the more likely he or she was to vote for Biden, who received 60 percent of the votes of those under age 30 but only 47 percent of senior citizens (roughly Clinton's proportion with seniors).
- Those who thought the American economy was "excellent"—just 13 percent of the total—gravitated in droves to Trump, but those who branded the economy as "poor" (19 percent of the electorate) were overwhelmingly in Biden's column.
- As usual, race was one of the best predictors of the vote, though there were subtle changes. Two-thirds of those who voted were white, and Trump won this group easily, 58 percent to 41 percent. Blacks were heavily for Biden, 87 percent to 12 percent, yet Trump gained four

percentage points with Blacks since 2016. Trump slightly increased his share among Hispanics/Latinos (+4 percent) and Asians (+6 percent), though Biden secured large majorities of both ethnic groups—65 percent with Latinos and 61 percent with Asians. Trump's marginal increase with Latinos helped deliver both Florida and Texas to him.

- Military veterans, 15 percent of all voters, were pro-Trump (54 percent), but not as much as in 2016 (60 percent).
- With a polarizing president such as Trump, voters saw the incumbent as one of the main motivators of their choice. Trump won by seven points among the 71 percent of voters who said they were casting their vote mainly for their preferred candidate, but Biden won by 38 points among the quarter of voters who said they were mainly voting against their candidate's opponent.
- White born-again or evangelical Christians chose Trump by massive margins in both years, 80 percent in 2016 and 76 percent in 2020—but note the small drop in Trump backing this time around.

AN UNCERTAIN FUTURE IN A POST-TRUMP WORLD

One is tempted to say that Donald Trump was a fluke, just an interlude that will be obscured by the "normalcy" that returns with the Biden presidency. Perhaps that will turn out to be true with the perspective of time. Yet Trump has rearranged the way politicians do business and changed what Americans look for in a president. You don't have to like Trump or his ways to understand that officeholders will never communicate again in the same ways they did pre-Trump. Twitter, rallies, off-the-cuff remarks, fewer formal briefings and press conferences, and possibly, unfortunately, less concern about accuracy, truth, and media commentary—all these things will be central parts of White Houses to come.

We can debate whether these shifts are good or bad, but there is one aspect of the Trump presidency that is undeniably disturbing—how it ended. There were times in the last three months of Trump's tenure when serious questions about the Republic itself were asked. For the first time in America's modern history, the incumbent president refused to concede despite a clear-cut defeat. Even worse, he delayed the beginning of the transition out of pure spite, putting the Biden team at a serious disadvantage without access to transition funding and informational briefings, including for the president-elect. Almost to the very end, Biden's staff reported difficulties in finding out background on the domestic and international challenges they would be facing. It is an understatement to say this was not in the nation's interests, and it was contrary to all recent transitions, including President Obama's generous accommodation of Trump and his appointees (despite obvious dismay by the outgoing Obama team that Trump was elected). In other words, President Trump was his petty, egomaniacal self to the day he left Washington.

As distressing as all this was, it didn't compare to Trump's open encouragement of a made-up claim of massive vote fraud that supposedly deprived him of a second term. Dozens of judges, including some appointed by Trump, rejected these outrageous, unsupported claims. Yet much of the Trump base and a sizable majority of all Republicans actually believed this fiction because Trump was so insistent and many GOP members of Congress coddled Trump and refused to contradict him—though they knew better. There was never a doubt that Biden had won the election. Multiple recounts confirmed it, and no widespread chicanery was backed by the evidence. Still, Trump's emphatic assertions of wrongdoing and his open encouragement of his personal followers and loosely affiliated white supremacist groups and conspiracy organizations such as QAnon came close to sedition in the streets and elsewhere. A recording of Trump browbeating the Republican secretary of state in Georgia to "find" him enough additional votes to win emerged in early January, and bordered on criminal. Republicans in Congress made fools of themselves trying to throw out legitimate electoral votes in order to overturn the election on January 6 even after a deadly riot engulfed the Capitol, embarrassing the nation. Throughout Trump's chaotic presidency, all but a handful of Republican officeholders were the president's lackeys, profiles in cowardice with only a few exceptions, such as Utah Senator Mitt Romney, the only Republican senator to vote in favor of the first impeachment effort against Trump in early 2020, and Republican Representative Adam Kinzinger of Illinois, just to mention two prominent voices of dissent. Kinzinger was one of 10 House Republicans to vote in favor of impeaching Trump following the Capitol insurrection.

A lesson that should not be lost is that our long-held, firm confidence in the American system was misplaced. In the end, our institutions and processes of government and politics held together, but their survival was not guaranteed. A truly close election would almost certainly have led Trump and Republicans to attempt more drastic actions to preserve Trump's presidency, with consequences that are hard to predict. Should Americans ever elect another authoritarian-minded president with flagrant disregard for facts and truth, contempt for our norms and traditions, as well as a cynical focus on self instead of the country, we may not be as fortunate as we were in 2020-2021. The discouraging reality is that tens of millions of Americans do not even recognize this critical lesson, and appear to have no interest in applying it in elections to come. This disturbing conclusion may be more important to remember going forward than any other finding in this volume.

Table 1.3. U.S. President Election Results—National Exit Poll

	Trump		Biden
Total	*2020*	*2016*	*2020*
Vote by Age			
18-29 (17%)	36%	36%	60%
30-44 (23%)	46%	41%	52%
45-64 (38%)	50%	52%	49%
65 and older (22%)	52%	52%	47%
Vote by Age			
18-24 (9%)	31%	34%	65%
25-29 (7%)	43%	38%	54%
30-39 (16%)	46%	39%	51%
40-49 (16%)	44%	49%	54%
50-64 (30%)	52%	52%	47%
65 and older (22%)	52%	52%	47%
Family's Financial Situation Today:			
Better than four years ago (41%)	72%	23%	26%
Worse than four years ago (20%)	20%	77%	77%
About the Same (39%)	34%	45%	65%
Life for the Next Generation of Americans Will Be:			
Better than today (54%)	44%	38%	55%
Worse than today (20%)	45%	63%	52%
About the same (21%)	58%	38%	40%
Vote By Marital Status			
Married (56%)	53%	52%	46%
Not married (44%)	40%	37%	58%
Condition of Nation's Economy			
Excellent (13%)	84%	16%	16%
Good (36%)	75%	18%	24%
Not good (31%)	22%	53%	76%
Poor (19%)	10%	79%	87%
Vote By Party ID			
Democratic (37%)	5%	8%	94%
Republican (36%)	94%	88%	6%
Independent (26%)	41%	46%	54%
Vote by Ideology			
Liberal (24%)	10%	10%	89%
Moderate (38%)	34%	40%	64%
Conservative (38%)	85%	81%	14%

(*continued*)

Table 1.3. (*continued*)

Total	*Trump* 2020	*Trump* 2016	*Biden* 2020
Vote by Race			
White (67%)	58%	57%	41%
Black (13%)	12%	8%	87%
Latino (13%)	32%	28%	65%
Asian (4%)	34%	27%	61%
Other (4%)	41%	36%	55%
Vote by Region			
East (20%)	41%	NA	58%
Midwest (23%)	51%	NA	47%
South (35%)	53%	NA	46%
West (22%)	41%	NA	57%
Vote by Gender			
Male (48%)	53%	52%	45%
Female (52%)	42%	41%	57%
Area Type			
Urban Area (29%)	38%	34%	60%
Suburban Area (51%)	48%	49%	50%
Rural Area (19%)	57%	61%	42%
Work Full Time?			
Yes (58)	51%	NA	47%
No (42%)	42%	NA	57%
Vote for US House			
Democratic candidate (51%)	4%	5%	95%
Republican candidate (48%)	95%	87%	4%
Condition of Nation's Economy			
Excellent/good (49%)	78%	18%	22%
Not good/poor (50%)	17%	62%	80%
Abortion Should Be:			
Legal in all cases (25%)	18%	NA	80%
Legal in most cases (26%)	30%	NA	68%
Illegal in most cases (25%)	72%	NA	27%
Illegal in all cases (17%)	81%	NA	18%
US Military veteran?			
Veterans (15%)	54%	60%	44%
Non-veterans (85%)	45%	44%	53%

	Trump		Biden
Total	*2020*	*2016*	*2020*
Vote by Income			
Under $50K (35%)	44%	41%	55%
$50K or more (65%)	47%	49%	51%
Vote for President mainly:			
For your candidate (71%)	53%	NA	46%
Against his opponent (24%)	30%	NA	68%
Vote by Income			
Under $100K (74%)	43%	45%	56%
$100K or more (26%)	54%	47%	42%
White Born-Again or evangelical Christian?			
Yes (28%)	76%	80%	24%
No (72%)	36%	34%	62%
How Confident That Votes will be Counted Accurately?			
Very confident (47%)	47%	27%	52%
Somewhat confident (40%)	42%	61%	56%
Not very confident (8%)	61%	68%	34%
Not at all confident (4%)	66%	57%	31%
How Confident That Votes will be Counted Accurately?			
Confident (86%)	45%	42%	54%
Not confident (12%)	63%	65%	33%
Abortion should be:			
Legal (51%)	24%	NA	74%
Illegal (42%)	76%	NA	23%
Gender by Marital Status			
Married men (30%)	55%	57%	44%
Married women (26%)	51%	47%	47%
Unmarried men (20%)	45%	44%	52%
Unmarried women (23%)	36%	32%	63%
Parents			
Men with children (17%)	49%	NA	48%
Women with children (17%)	43%	NA	56%
Men no children (34%)	51%	NA	47%
Women no children (33%)	44%	NA	55%

(continued)

Table 1.3. (*continued*)

Total	*Trump* 2020	*Trump* 2016	*Biden* 2020
Sex by Race			
White men (35%)	61%	62%	38%
White women (32%)	55%	52%	44%
Black men (4%)	19%	13%	79%
Black women (8%)	9%	4%	90%
Latino men (5%)	36%	32%	59%
Latino women (8%)	30%	25%	69%
All others (8%)	38%	31%	58%
Age by Race			
White 18-29 (8%)	53%	47%	44%
White 30-44 (14%)	57%	54%	41%
White 45-59 (19%)	61%	NA	38%
White over 60 (26%)	57%	NA	42%
Black 18-29 (3%)	10%	9%	89%
Black 30-44 (4%)	19%	7%	78%
Black 45-59 (3%)	10%	NA	89%
Black over 60 (3%)	7%	NA	92%
Latino 18-29 (4%)	28%	26%	69%
Latino 30-44 (4%)	34%	28%	62%
Latino 45-59 (3%)	30%	NA	68%
Latino over 60 (2%)	40%	NA	58%
All Others (8%)	38%	31%	57%
Income			
Under $50K (35%)	44%	41%	55%
$50K-$99K (39%)	42%	49%	57%
$100K or more (26%)	54%	47%	42%
Age			
18-44 (40%)	42%	39%	56%
45 and older (60%)	51%	52%	48%
Education			
College graduate (41%)	43%	42%	55%
No college degree (59%)	50%	51%	48%
Education by Race			
White voters, college degree (32%)	48%	48%	51%
White voters, no degree (35%)	67%	66%	32%
Voters of color, college degree (10%)	27%	22%	70%
Voters of color, no college degree (24%)	26%	20%	72%

Total	*Trump* 2020	*Trump* 2016	*Biden* 2020
Is this the first year you voted?			
Yes (14%)	32%	38%	64%
No (86%)	49%	47%	49%
Importance of recent rise in coronavirus cases to presidential vote			
The most important factor (23%)	38%	NA	61%
An important factor (37%)	51%	NA	47%
A minor factor (18%)	86%	NA	13%
Not a factor at all (16%)	91%	NA	7%
Have any children under 18?			
Yes (33%)	46%	NA	52%
No (67%)	48%	NA	51%
Importance of recent rise in coronavirus cases to presidential vote			
Important (61%)	46%	NA	52%
Not important (34%)	88%	NA	10%
Importance of recent rise in coronavirus cases to presidential vote			
A factor (79%)	56%	NA	43%
Not a factor (16%)	91%	NA	7%
Union Household?			
Yes (20%)	40%	42%	56%
No (80%)	49%	48%	50%
Is climate change a serious problem?			
Yes (67%)	29%	NA	69%
No (30%)	84%	NA	15%
Race			
White voters (67%)	58%	57%	41%
Voters of color (33%)	26%	21%	71%
View of Federal Government			
Enthusiastic (13%)	81%	19%	18%
Satisfied (27%)	70%	19%	29%
Dissatisfied (32%)	31%	48%	67%
Angry (26%)	24%	75%	74%
View of Federal Government			
Enthusiastic/satisfied (40%)	74%	19%	25%
Dissatisfied/angry (57%)	28%	57%	70%

(continued)

Table 1.3. **(continued)**

Total	Trump 2020	Trump 2016	Biden 2020
Are You Gay, Lesbian, Bisexual, or Transgender?			
Yes (7%)	27%	14%	64%
No (93%)	48%	47%	51%
View of Donald Trump			
Favorable (46%)	95%	95%	4%
Unfavorable (52%)	5%	15%	93%
View of Mike Pence			
Favorable (46%)	91%	NA	8%
Unfavorable (48%)	8%	NA	91%
View of Joe Biden			
Favorable (42%)	4%	NA	94%
Unfavorable (46%)	95%	NA	4%
View of Kamala Harris			
Favorable (48%)	8%	NA	91%
Unfavorable (47%)	89%	NA	9%
In vote for president, Supreme Court appointments were:			
The most important factor (13%)	51%	56%	47%
An important factor (47%)	45%	46%	54%
A minor factor (18%)	48%	40%	51%
Not a factor at all (19%)	49%	37%	49%
In vote for president, Supreme Court appointments were:			
Important (60%)	46%	49%	52%
Not important (37%)	48%	39%	50%
Decided on presidential vote:			
In the last few days (3%)	47%	43%	49%
In the last week (2%)	64%	49%	31%
In October (8%)	49%	51%	48%
In September (11%)	45%	48%	52%
Before that (73%)	48%	45%	51%
Decided on presidential vote:			
In the last month (13%)	51%	48%	46%
Before that (83%)	47%	45%	51%
Decided on presidential vote:			
In the last week (5%)	54%	45%	42%
Before that (91%)	47%	46%	51%

Total	Trump 2020	Trump 2016	Biden 2020
Education by Gender Among White Voters			
White college grad women (14%)	45%	44%	54%
White non-college women (17%)	63%	61%	36%
White college grad men (17%)	51%	53%	48%
White non-college men (18%)	70%	71%	28%
Non-whites (33%)	26%	21%	71%
Opinion of Donald Trump as President			
Strongly approve (38%)	96%	NA	4%
Somewhat approve (12%)	75%	NA	20%
Somewhat disapprove (10%)	7%	NA	89%
Strongly disapprove (39%)	1%	NA	97%
Opinion of Donald Trump as President			
Approve (50%)	91%	NA	8%
Disapprove (49%)	3%	NA	96%
Vote By Education			
Never attended college (19%)	54%	51%	46%
Some college (23%)	47%	51%	51%
Associate's degree (16%)	50%	NA	47%
Bachelor's degree (27%)	47%	NA	51%
Advanced degree (15%)	37%	37%	62%
2016 presidential vote?			
Clinton (40%)	4%	NA	95%
Trump (43%)	92%	NA	7%
Someone else (5%)	25%	NA	60%
Did not vote (11%)	39%	NA	58%
Income			
Under $30K (15%)	46%	40%	54%
$30K-$49,999 (20%)	43%	41%	56%
$50K-$99,999 (39%)	42%	49%	57%
$100K-$199,999 (20%)	58%	48%	41%
$200K or more (7%)	44%	NA	44%
Most important issue to your vote?			
Racial inequality (20%)	7%	NA	92%
Coronavirus (17%)	15%	NA	81%
The economy (35%)	83%	41%	17%
Crime and safety (11%)	71%	NA	27%
Health care policy (11%)	37%	NA	62%

(continued)

Table 1.3. *(continued)*

	Trump		*Biden*
Total	*2020*	*2016*	*2020*
Which candidate quality mattered most?			
Can unite the country (19%)	24%	NA	75%
Is a strong leader (33%)	72%	NA	28%
Cares about people like me (21%)	50%	34%	49%
Has good judgment (24%)	26%	25%	68%
Voting in your state is:			
Very easy (69%)	50%	NA	48%
Somewhat easy (25%)	39%	NA	60%
Somewhat difficult (4%)	46%	NA	52%
Very difficult (2%)	NA	NA	NA
Voting in your state is:			
Easy (94%)	47%	NA	51%
Difficult (6%)	45%	NA	52%
Better handle the economy?			
Biden (49%)	2%	NA	96%
Trump (49%)	92%	94%	6%
Which is more important to do now?			
Contain coronavirus (52%)	19%	NA	79%
Rebuild the economy (42%)	79%	NA	20%
On Obamacare, should the Supreme Court:			
Keep it as is (51%)	18%	NA	80%
Overturn it (44%)	78%	NA	21%
Feelings if Biden elected president:			
Excited (22%)	3%	NA	97%
Optimistic (28%)	7%	NA	91%
Concerned (23%)	92%	NA	5%
Scared (23%)	93%	NA	6%
Feelings if Biden elected president:			
Excited/optimistic (50%)	5%	NA	94%
Concerned/scared (46%)	93%	NA	5%
Feelings if Trump re-elected president:			
Excited (24%)	99%	97%	1%
Optimistic (21%)	86%	95%	12%
Concerned (17%)	20%	33%	78%
Scared (33%)	2%	2%	96%

Total	Trump 2020	Trump 2016	Biden 2020
Feelings if Trump re-elected president:			
Excited/optimistic (45%)	93%	NA	6%
Concerned/scared (50%)	8%	NA	90%
Does Biden Have the Temperament to serve as President?			
Yes (54%)	7%	NA	92%
No (44%)	94%	NA	3%
Does Trump Have the Temperament to serve as President?			
Yes (44%)	95%	94%	4%
No (53%)	9%	19%	89%
Who has the physical/mental health to serve effectively as president?			
Only Biden does (41%)	2%	NA	98%
Only Trump does (41%)	98%	NA	1%
Both do (8%)	46%	NA	54%
Neither does (8%)	27%	NA	62%
Does Biden have the physical/mental health to serve effectively as president?			
Yes (49%)	9%	NA	90%
No (49%)	86%	NA	11%
Does Trump have the physical/mental health to serve effectively as president?			
Yes (49%)	89%	NA	10%
No (49%)	6%	NA	92%
Favorable opinion of:			
Biden and Trump (3%)	49%	NA	43%
Only Biden (49%)	2%	NA	97%
Only Trump (43%)	98%	NA	1%
Neither of them (3%)	52%	NA	35%
Favorable opinion of:			
Harris and Pence (6%)	50%	NA	46%
Only Harris (43%)	2%	NA	97%
Only Pence (40%)	97%	NA	2%
Neither of them (7%)	40%	NA	53%
View of Black Lives Matter:			
Favorable (57%)	20%	NA	78%
Unfavorable (86%)	86%	NA	14%
More important to presidential vote?			
Candidate's positions on issues (74%)	53%	NA	47%
Candidate's personal qualities (23%)	31%	NA	64%

(continued)

Table 1.3. **(continued)**

Total	Trump 2020	Trump 2016	Biden 2020
Better handle the coronavirus pandemic?			
Biden (53%)	6%	NA	92%
Trump (43%)	95%	NA	4%
Has the coronavirus pandemic caused you:			
Severe financial hardship (16%)	29%	NA	69%
Moderate financial hardship (39%)	39%	NA	59%
No financial hardship at all (44%)	60%	NA	38%
Has the coronavirus pandemic caused you:			
Financial hardship (55%)	36%	NA	62%
No financial hardship (44%)	60%	NA	39%
US efforts to contain coronavirus are going:			
Very well (18%)	86%	NA	13%
Somewhat well (33%)	78%	NA	21%
Somewhat badly (15%)	24%	NA	74%
Very badly (32%)	4%	NA	94%
US efforts to contain coronavirus are going:			
Well (51%)	81%	NA	18%
Badly (48%)	11%	NA	78%
Is wearing a face mask in public more of a:			
Personal choice (30%)	73%	NA	24%
Public health responsibility (67%)	35%	NA	64%
Does the country's criminal justice system:			
Treat all fairly (40%)	84%	74%	14%
Treat Blacks unfairly (53%)	17%	22%	82%
Racism in the US is:			
The most important problem (18%)	11%	NA	87%
An important problem (51%)	37%	NA	61%
A minor problem (18%)	81%	NA	18%
Not a problem at all (10%)	91%	NA	8%
Racism in the US is:			
An important problem (69%)	30%	NA	68%
Not an important problem (28%)	84%	NA	14%

Source: Edison Research Exit Polls, "National Results 2020 President Exit Polls," CNN Politics, https://www.cnn.com/election/2020/exit-polls/president/national-results

NOTES

1. Herbert L. Abrams, "Shielding the President from the Constitution: Disability and the 25th Amendment," *Presidential Studies Quarterly* 23, no. 3 (Summer 1993), 533-53, http://www.jstor.org/stable/27551112.

2. Michael P. McDonald, "2020 November General Election Turnout Rates," United States Elections Project, http://www.electproject.org/.

3. Charles Stewart III, "How We Voted in 2020: A First Look at the Survey of the Performance of American Elections," MIT Election Science and Data Lab, December 15, 2020, http://electionlab.mit.edu/sites/default/files/2020-12/How-we-voted-in-2020-v01.pdf.

4. Ibid.

5. Sanjay Gupta and Andrea Kane, "From the Rose Garden to Rallies: What Large Gatherings Can Teach Us about the Spread of Coronavirus," CNN, October 6, 2020, https://www.cnn.com/2020/10/06/health/rose-garden-rallies-coronavirus-spread/index.html.

6. In 2016, Donald Trump carried states and districts with 306 electoral votes, while Hillary Clinton carried 232. However, seven faithless electors—five Clinton electors and two Trump electors—voted for different candidates in the formal Electoral College vote count, meaning that technically Trump won 304-227 over Clinton. There were no faithless electors in 2020.

7. Trump got to 49 percent a few times but never 50 percent. Jeffrey M. Jones, "Last Trump Approval 34%; Average is Record-Low 41%," *Gallup*, January 18, 2021, https://news.gallup.com/poll/328637/last-trump-job-approval-average-record-low.aspx.

8. Edison Research Exit Polls, "National Results 2020 President Exit Polls," CNN Politics, https://www.cnn.com/election/2020/exit-polls/president/national-results; AP VoteCast conducted by NORC at the University of Chicago, "How We Voted in the 2020 Presidential Election," *Wall Street Journal*, https://www.wsj.com/graphics/votecast-2020/.

2

The Off-Kilter Presidential Primaries of 2020

Rhodes Cook

If there is a term to describe the 2020 presidential primary season, it would be off-kilter. From its start in early February, the whole nominating process defied belief. Oddities ranged from the first-in-the-nation Iowa caucuses, with its botched vote count, through a pandemic-altered primary season, to conventions that culminated with a potential coronavirus-spreader event on the South Lawn of the White House (the Republicans) and a car-honking fireworks display in a parking lot in Wilmington, Delaware (the Democrats). The whole 2020 presidential nominating process was quirky, unusual, and in the alleged words of Huey Long, *sui generis* (one of a kind).

It also required considerable improvisation to finish once the coronavirus took hold across the country in the middle of March. The opening six weeks of primaries and caucuses went off without a hitch (the Iowa vote count notwithstanding). Candidates crisscrossed the country raising money, meeting voters, and holding debates at regular intervals.

After the Ides of March, though, there was no campaigning and no debates, and primaries scheduled for the early spring were moved back to the late spring or summer. Voting in these later primaries was altered to reflect the changed conditions, with voting by mail accented over the traditional primary day in-person voting. It was a preview of how the presidential election would be conducted in the fall.

Still, even with all the dislocation, the parties got nominees with whom they were comfortable. President Donald Trump breezed through the Republican primaries, winning all of them easily over nominal competition. On the Democratic side, voters spent nearly all of February taking a look at candidates such as Senator Bernie Sanders of Vermont and former South Bend, Indiana Mayor Pete Buttigieg, among others.

Finally, they settled on former Vice President Joe Biden, who all along made his main theme his electability against Trump. He proved an ideal candidate for the times. Democrats in 2020 did not want a champion of the left or center to be their standard-bearer, but someone who could oust the brash and controversial incumbent. Even approaching 80 years old, "average Joe" Biden fit the bill.

In the end, Democrats held 44 primaries from February to August, the most by either party in the nation's history. Biden swept 39 of them, including all those held after Super Tuesday on March 3. In the process, he received more than 18.8 million primary votes, the most garnered by any presidential nominee

Table 2.1. The Growth of Presidential Primaries Since 1968

Since the presidential nominating process was overhauled in the early 1970s to transfer power from party leaders in their "smoke-filled rooms" to voters in the primaries, the number of such contests has steadily grown from a corporal's guard to nearly the entire country. There were a record 44 Democratic primaries (43 states and the District of Columbia) in 2020 plus 39 Republican primaries that involved more than 55 million voters. The total represented about 35 percent of the number who cast ballots in the fall presidential election. The most votes cast for each party came in 2008 for the Democrats, 2016 for the Republicans, and 2016 again for the combined total. In addition, in all but three of the 14 presidential elections starting with 1968, there have been more voters in the Democratic primaries than the Republican contests. The exceptions were 1996, 2000, and 2012, with Democratic presidents running virtually unopposed for renomination in 1996 (Bill Clinton) and 2012 (Barack Obama).

	Democracts		*Republicans*		
Year	*Number of Primaries*	*Voters*	*Number of Primaries*	*Voters*	*Combined Party Totals*
1968	15	7,535,069	15	4,473,551	12,008,620
1972	21	15,993,965	20	6,188,281	22,182,246
1976	27	16,052,652	26	10,374,125	26,426,777
1980	34	18,747,825	34	12,690,451	31,438,276
1984	29	18,009,217	25	6,575,651	24,584,868
1988	36	22,961,936	36	12,165,115	35,127,051
1992	39	20,239,385	38	12,696,547	32,935,932
1996	35	10,996,395	42	14,233,939	25,230,334
2000	40	14,045,745	43	17,156,117	31,201,862
2004	37	16,182,439	27	7,940,331	24,122,770
2008	38	36,848,285	39	20,841,211	57,689,496
2012	26	9,206,764	36	18,770,036	27,976,800
2016	39	30,805,885	38	30,186,654	60,992,539
2020	44	36,143,136	39	19,267,898	55,411,034

Sources: Vital Statistics on American Politics 2015-2016 (CQ Press, an imprint of SAGE) for the number of presidential primaries and primary votes for 1968 through 2004; *America Votes* 28, 30, and 32 (CQ Press, an imprint of SAGE) for similar information for 2008, 2012, and 2016. Presidential primary data for 2020 is based on official returns from state election websites, with the exception of Georgia, where the primary results were nearly complete but unofficial.

in the nation's history. As for Trump, he easily swept all 39 Republican primaries with a near-unanimous 94 percent of the vote. That was based on more than 18.1 million Trump votes, the most ever received by any GOP presidential nominee as well as the highest total for a president seeking renomination.[1]

Voter turnout for the primaries was impressive, given the pandemic and the absence of significant competition for Trump at all and for Biden after mid-March. The combined two-party turnout for the 2020 presidential primaries reached 55.4 million, the third-highest total in the nation's history. It trailed only 2016 (61 million) and 2008 (57.7 million). Fully 36 million primary votes were cast on the Democratic side in 2020, the second-highest total ever for either party, behind only the Democratic total in 2008 (36.8 million).

With Trump as a catalyst, millions of voters on both sides showed that they were not only ready to vote, but badly wanted to vote, even in an off-kilter primary season.

Table 2.2. The All-Time Leading Presidential Primary Vote-Getters: Biden on Top, Trump Number Two

Joe Biden began 2020 as a two-time loser for the Democratic presidential nomination, unable to get out of the starting blocks on either previous occasion (1988 and 2008). Yet he ended the long 2020 nominating season as the all-time leading primary vote-getter, with nearly 18.9 million votes. President Donald Trump finished the primary season right behind Biden in the aggregate tally with more than 18.1 million votes, the most for any Republican presidential candidate, the highest total for any president running for renomination, and the second-highest single-year total behind Biden among all candidates who have ever competed in presidential primaries since they began in earnest in 1912.

Rank	*Candidate*	*Election*	*Primary Votes*	*Nomination Outcome*	*General Election Outcome*
1	Joe Biden (D)	2020	18,864,707	Won	Won
2	Donald Trump (R)*	2020	18,128,395	Won	Lost
3	Hillary Clinton (D)	2008	17,714,899	Lost	—
4	Barack Obama (D)	2008	17,423,314	Won	Won
5	Hillary Clinton (D)	2016	17,121,492	Won	Lost#
6	Donald Trump (R)	2016	13,757,319	Won	Won#
7	Bernie Sanders (D)	2016	13,210,266	Lost	—
8	George W. Bush (R)	2000	10,844,129	Won	Won#
9	Al Gore (D)	2000	10,626,645	Won	Lost#
10	Bill Clinton (D)	1992	10,482,411	Won	Won

Note: An asterisk (*) indicates an incumbent. A pound sign (#) denotes the election was an Electoral College "misfire," with the Democratic nominee taking the popular vote and the Republican nominee winning the all-important electoral vote.

Sources: Race for the Presidency: Winning the 2004 Nomination (CQ Press) for presidential primary vote data through 2000; *America Votes* 28 and 32 (CQ Press, an imprint of SAGE) for similar data for the 2008 and 2016 primaries. Presidential primary results for 2020 are from state election websites (and the District of Columbia) and are official except for Georgia, where returns were nearly complete but unofficial.

LAUNCHING THE PROCESS: NO LONGER "THE INVISIBLE PRIMARY"

In the mid-1970s, a perceptive author named Arthur Hadley wrote a valuable book called *The Invisible Primary.* It explained the vital importance of what transpired during the pre-primary stage of a presidential campaign, when candidates back then operated largely under the radar screen to do the consequential work of preparing for a successful candidacy—such as raising funds, building an organization, and seeking endorsements.[2]

More than four decades later, this initial stage of the nominating process has gone public and become as determinative as the primaries themselves. Candidates that used to delay announcing their presidential candidacies until a few weeks before the voting was to begin now formally enter the race a year or more earlier, often in the wake of the previous midterm election. Nowadays what Hadley called the "Invisible Primary" is very much visible. And the candidates compete not for votes per se, but to be seen as serious candidates capable of winning their party's nomination and the general election to follow.

During the long pre-primary period, they compete against their rivals in several different ways: raising money, drawing sizable crowds for their events, standing out in debates, and ultimately running well in the polls. A failure in one of these areas can make their ability to survive even to the start of the primary season highly problematic.

By May 2019, more than 20 candidates had joined the Democratic field. It was a diverse array, led by Biden, universally known after 36 years in the Senate and eight years as Barack Obama's number two. He was widely liked and respected within his party. But he would be 78 years old at the time of his inauguration, much older than any previous president. Polls tended to tout Biden's electability, buttressing his argument that he would be the Democrat best able to beat Trump. But to many progressive activists that gave energy to the Democratic Party, he was too much the centrist.

Senator Bernie Sanders of Vermont was more their cup of tea. Also in his late 70s, he tended to project more vigor than Biden. His persona was of a rumpled-looking, crusty old uncle, but he was beloved by his followers on the left for his passionate support of progressive causes.

Other candidates tended to line up with Biden or Sanders in the centrist or progressive lanes. Among the candidates identified with the former were the youthful-looking Buttigieg, Senator Amy Klobuchar of Minnesota, and former New York City Mayor Michael Bloomberg, a billionaire who was willing to sink hundreds of millions of dollars of his own money into a presidential campaign should Biden falter. He did not enter the race until November 2019, when Biden appeared vulnerable.

Competing on the Sanders "track" was another group that included most prominently Senator Elizabeth Warren of Massachusetts, a long-time consumer advocate who was arguably the sharpest debater during the Democratic primary season.

In its entirety, the Democratic field reflected the broad diversity of the party and the country. There was a wide gap in age, from Buttigieg in his late 30s to Biden and Sanders in their late 70s.

There was gender diversity, with six female candidates running for president. Four were senators: Kirsten Gillibrand of New York, Kamala Harris of California, Klobuchar, and Warren. One of the women candidates was a representative, Tulsi Gabbard of Hawaii. Another, Marianne Williamson, was a best-selling self-help author who was sometimes referred to as "Oprah's spiritual adviser."[3]

There was racial diversity in the Democratic field. Senator Cory Booker of New Jersey boasted African-American heritage. Former Housing and Urban Development Secretary Julian Castro had Hispanic roots. Tech entrepreneur Andrew Yang was the son of Taiwanese immigrants. Harris' father was Jamaican, while her mother was from India.

The Democratic candidates also provided sexual diversity, as Buttigieg became the first openly gay candidate to ever run for a major party presidential nomination. The youthful-looking "Mayor Pete," who had campaign signs that spelled out his last name as "Boot Edge Edge," was a former Rhodes Scholar and Afghanistan war veteran.

His campaign took off like no other in early 2019, pairing fund-raising success with an articulate message of generational change. It fueled a perceptible rise in the polls for Buttigieg that took him from nowhere to a spot in the top tier of candidates.[4]

As the year unfolded, a few other candidates surged forward in the polls to challenge Biden and Sanders. One was Harris, who gained attention in a mid-year debate in which she skewered Biden for his past positions on race. But she could not maintain her gains, and by the end of the year was out of the race. (Harris, though, was to collect a valuable "consolation prize" the following summer, when Biden named her as his vice presidential running-mate.)

Warren made her move in the fall of 2019, surpassing Sanders for a time for second place in polling of the Democratic field. She was arguably the Democrats' leading debater as well as a feisty advocate of progressive causes. But her momentum stalled after she was unable to clearly explain how she would fund her proposed expansion of health coverage. She stayed in the race until March 5, two days after Super Tuesday, but was unable to win a single primary or caucus.

Table 2.3 Aggregate 2020 Democratic, Republican Presidential Primary Vote

Neither contest for the Democratic or Republican presidential nomination in 2020 was particularly suspenseful. As expected, President Donald Trump had no problems at all on the GOP side against light opposition. He swept all but one of the 39 Republican primaries with at least 80 percent of the vote, the exception being the last primary of the year on August 11 in Connecticut, where the president drew 78 percent. Meanwhile, the Democrats started with a crowded field of candidates, but voters quickly coalesced behind former Vice President Joe Biden after he scored a breakthrough victory in South Carolina in late February. Biden ended up winning all but five of the 44 Democratic primaries in 2020, including every single one held after Super Tuesday, March 3. For the year, Biden drew an aggregate of nearly 18.9 million votes in the Democratic primaries while Trump received 18.1 million in the Republican primaries. The Biden and Trump totals represent all-time highs for each party in terms of presidential primary votes for a single contender in a single year. Candidates in each party who received at least 100,000 votes in the 2020 presidential primaries are listed below.

DEMOCRATIC PRIMARIES

Candidate (Home State)	*Office*	*Primaries on Ballot*	*Primaries Won*	*Primary Vote*	*% of Primary Vote*	*Delegates*	*Best Primary Showing*
Joe Biden (Delaware)	Ex-Vice President	44	39	18,864,707	52.2%	2,739	Delaware (89%)
Bernie Sanders (Vermont)	U.S. Senator	44	5	9,502,934	26.3%	1,119	Vermont (51%)
Elizabeth Warren (Mass.)	U.S. Senator	40	—	2,778,752	7.7%	53	Mass. (21%)
Michael Bloomberg (New York)	Ex-New York City Mayor	29	—	2,491,433	6.9%	46	Colorado (19%)
Pete Buttigieg (Indiana)	Ex-South Bend Mayor	32	—	862,534	2.4%	15	New Hampshire (24%)
Amy Klobuchar (Minnesota)	U.S. Senator	30	—	500,768	1.4%	5	New Hampshire (20%)
Tulsi Gabbard (Hawaii)	U.S. House Member	39	—	273,397	0.8%	2	New Hampshire (3%)
Tom Steyer (California)	Financial investor	32	—	254,920	0.7%	—	South Carolina (11%)
Uncommitted	—	16	—	169,931	0.5%	—	Kentucky (11%)
Andrew Yang (New York)	Technology maven	35	—	169,102	0.5%	—	New Hampshire (3%)
Others	—	—	—	274,768	0.8%	—	—
TOTAL VOTE				36,143,136			
Biden Plurality				9,361,773			

REPUBLICAN PRIMARIES

Candidate (Home State)	*Office*	*Primaries on Ballot*	*Primaries Won*	*Primary Vote*	*% of Primary Vote*	*Delegates*	*Best Primary Showing*
Donald Trump (New York)	Incumbent	39	39	18,128,395	94.1%	2,358	D.C., Georgia, Maine, New Jersey, Ohio (All 100%)
William Weld (Mass.)	Ex-Governor	23	—	453,977	2.4%	1	Maryland (13%)
Uncommitted	—	14	—	260,919	1.4%	—	Conn. (14%)
Joe Walsh (Illinois)	Ex-U.S. House Member	13	—	173,171	0.9%	—	Oklahoma (4%)
Roque "Rocky" De La Fuente (California)	Car dealer, real estate developer	18	—	108,357	0.6%	—	Delaware (12%)
Others	—	—	—	143,079	0.7%	—	—
TOTAL VOTE				19,267,898			
Trump Plurality				17,674,418			

Sources: Presidential primary vote totals are based on official results from state election authorities in all states and the District of Columbia, with the exception of Georgia, where the tally was nearly complete but unofficial. The Democratic and Republican delegate counts are from NBC News (as of August 14, 2020), just before each party's national conventions was held in the latter part of August.

TIME OUT FOR THE REPUBLICANS

Meanwhile, on the Republican side, President Trump was able to glide to renomination without breaking a sweat. The GOP race may have drawn some attention if Larry Hogan had mounted a challenge. Hogan had fashioned an appealing image as governor of bright blue Maryland and had clashed with Trump by calling for more bipartisanship and civility in politics. But Hogan announced that he would not run against the incumbent in June 2019, citing his need to focus on Maryland and his upcoming job as head of the National Governors Association.

Hogan could also read the numbers, showing Trump with a presidential approval rating among Republicans of around 90 percent. The chance of any presidential challenger actually capturing the GOP nomination was virtually nil. Former Representative Mark Sanford of South Carolina, who Trump had helped oust in the 2018 congressional primaries, dipped his toe in the waters around Labor Day 2019 before bowing out before Thanksgiving.[5]

Table 2.4. Trump, the Primaries, and Presidents Seeking Renomination

Since the presidential nominating process became primary dominated in the 1970s, a general rule of thumb has been that the better a president seeking reelection runs in his party's primaries, the better he fares in the general election. But that pattern was broken in 2020, when Donald Trump rolled up nearly 95 percent of the vote in the Republican primaries, only to lose the fall presidential vote by a decisive margin of more than four percentage points. Trump's aggregate share of his party's primary vote in 2020 was higher that what Barack Obama (D) received in 2012, Bill Clinton (D) in 1996, and Richard Nixon (R) in 1972 before they were all reelected. But unlike the others who built broader-based coalitions, Trump's nearly unanimous support among Republicans was more than offset by the nearly universal antipathy he generated among Democrats.

Election	*Incumbent President*	*President's % of Primary Vote*	*General Election Outcome*
1984	Ronald Reagan (R)	99%	Won
2004	George W. Bush (R)	98%	Won
2020	**Donald Trump (R)**	**94%**	**Lost**
2012	Barack Obama (D)	92%	Won
1996	Bill Clinton (D)	89%	Won
1972	Richard Nixon (R)	87%	Won
1992	George H.W. Bush (R)	72%	Lost
1976	Gerald Ford (R)	53%	Lost
1980	Jimmy Carter (D)	51%	Lost

Sources: Race for the Presidency: Winning the 2004 Nomination (CQ Press) for presidential primary percentages through 2000; *America Votes* 26 and 30 (CQ Press, a division of SAGE) for similar data for 2004 and 2012. The presidential primary percentage for 2020 is based on official returns from state election authorities (including the District of Columbia), except for Georgia, where the results were nearly complete but unofficial.

Former Representative Joe Walsh of Illinois, a one-term "Tea Party" Republican, had also announced plans to run, but quickly bowed out after the first-in-the-nation Iowa caucuses. That left former Massachusetts Governor William Weld to challenge the incumbent in the party's presidential primaries. Weld, whose previous claim to fame came in 2016 as the Libertarian Party's vice presidential candidate, embraced a brand of moderate Republicanism that was visibly offended by Trump.

But Weld had a small fraction of the resources that the president did and received hardly any attention from the media. For good measure, a number of Republican state parties pitched in by canceling their primary or caucus (among them, Arizona, New York, South Carolina, and Virginia), smoothing the way for Trump to gain quick control of their delegations.

In the months that followed, Trump swept 18.1 million of the 19.3 million Republican primary votes cast, or 94 percent. He drew the highest number of primary votes ever cast for either a Republican candidate or a sitting president, and swept all 39 GOP primaries with at least 78 percent of the vote. The contests served as a testing ground for the Trump campaign, with the incumbent swooping into some states on the eve of the primary or caucus to spur turnout.[6]

The non-Trump vote, as it was, surpassed 10 percent in nine primaries, including much of the Democratic Northeast, Mormon Utah, and Kentucky. The latter was a bit of a puzzle because it was bright red and Senate Republican leader Mitch McConnell's home state.

FEBRUARY EVENTS: VOTING BEGINS WITH A THUD

The Iowa caucuses have kicked off the voting part of the Democratic presidential nomination for nearly a half century. But never before was the event such a debacle as it was in 2020. It produced a caucus night meltdown in the vote counting that extended for days, and prevented the ultimate winner (Buttigieg) from gaining much momentum from the outcome.

The problem was largely created by Democratic Party rules changes prior to 2020. Over the years, the Iowa vote tally focused on measuring candidate strength in terms of a unique and complex measurement called state delegate equivalents. To increase transparency in the process in 2020, though, caucus states were required to add two more tabulations to the vote count: the first to measure presidential preferences as voters entered each precinct caucus; the second to record the vote after participants realigned in each precinct behind candidates that had reached the needed 15 percent support. That was in addition to the traditional compilation in Iowa of state delegate equivalents.

However, on Iowa caucus night (February 3), the technology employed to deal with the new system was overwhelmed. Many precinct leaders could not get their tallies into state headquarters. Participants milled around caucus sites waiting for something to happen, many of them looking on national television like stranded travelers at a bus station. And media commentators, who showed up to analyze results that were not coming in, instead turned their ire on the debacle that was happening before them.

No results at all were reported on caucus night, and initial returns from Iowa did not appear until late the following afternoon. They revealed a confusing set of numbers. Sanders handily led the two popular votes—the entrance poll by more than 6,000 over Buttigieg, and the post-alignment vote by more than 2,500. But Buttigieg ended up winning the all-important count of state delegate equivalents over Sanders by the narrowest of margins, 562.954 to 562.021 (according to a posting on the website of the Iowa Democratic Party as of March 1). Finishing in their wake were Warren, Biden, and Klobuchar.[7]

The snafus that occurred were a black eye for the party, both state and national, with the Iowa Democratic chair an immediate casualty of the event. Meanwhile, the national party worked feverishly with Democrats in the next caucus state, Nevada, to try to prevent a similar Iowa-style disaster from happening. They largely succeeded, helped in part by the one-sided nature of the Nevada vote; Sanders won in a landslide. Still, the Nevada count on February 22 was slow to unfold, and by the next morning, the day after the caucuses, half the vote was still not tallied.

In between the two early caucuses was the New Hampshire primary on February 11, which produced a close result similar to Iowa, but with Sanders and Buttigieg swapping spots at the top. Klobuchar ran a strong third after a notable performance in a primary-eve debate. Warren and Biden trailed with less than 10 percent of the vote.

At this point, Biden's chances of winning the Democratic nomination did not look good. It appeared as though he had gone off the rails with fourth- and fifth-place finishes in Iowa and New Hampshire—mediocre showings in the first two events that no previous presidential nominee had ever overcome. A distant second-place finish followed in Nevada, which did little more than give him life for the final February event in South Carolina.

But then, with Biden widely viewed as down to his last chance, he began one of the most amazing one-week turnarounds in the history of American presidential politics. Just days before the February 29 primary in South Carolina, he received a full-throated endorsement from the state's leading Democrat, House Majority Whip James Clyburn (the highest-ranking Black member of Congress).

Table 2.5. Iowa, New Hampshire: Not the "Kingmakers" in 2020 That They Usually Are

Since the presidential primaries became the sole route to a party's nomination in the 1970s, every nominee has finished at least second in one of the lead-off states, Iowa or New Hampshire. That is until 2020. In his circuitous path to the Democratic nomination, Joe Biden registered a fourth-place finish in the Iowa caucuses followed by an even more distant fifth-place result in the New Hampshire primary. In normal years, Biden would have been on the path to oblivion after his weak showing in the first two states. Instead, in 2020, he was able to quickly reclaim his footing and effectively nail down the Democratic nomination just weeks after his poor Iowa and New Hampshire showings.

	DEMOCRATS Order of Finish			*REPUBLICANS Order of Finish*		
Election	*Nominee*	*Iowa*	*New Hampshire*	*Nominee*	*Iowa*	*New Hampshire*
1972	G. McGovern	3	2	Richard Nixon*	—	1
1976	Jimmy Carter	2#	1	Gerald Ford*	1#	1
1980	Jimmy Carter*	1	1	Ronald Reagan	2	1
1984	Walter Mondale	1	2	Ronald Reagan*	—	1
1988	M. Dukakis	3	1	G. H.W. Bush	3	1
1992	Bill Clinton	4	2	G. H.W. Bush*	—	1
1996	Bill Clinton*	1	1	Bob Dole	1	2
2000	Al Gore	1	1	G. W. Bush	1	2
2004	John Kerry	1	1	G. W. Bush*	—	1
2008	Barack Obama	1	2	John McCain	4	1
2012	Barack Obama*	1	1	Mitt Romney	2	1
2016	Hillary Clinton	1	2	Donald Trump	2	1
2020	Joe Biden	4	5	Donald Trump*	1	1

Note: A dash (-) denotes the years there was no vote in the Iowa Republican precinct caucuses, basically when GOP presidents were running without significant opposition for renomination. An asterisk (*) designates an incumbent. A pound sign (#) indicates that Jimmy Carter is often credited with winning the Democratic precinct caucuses in Iowa in 1976, although in actuality he finished behind "Uncommitted." On the Republican side in 1976, results from Iowa are based on the vote in a sampling of precincts.

Sources: Race for the Presidency: Winning the 2004 Nomination (CQ Press) for Iowa and New Hampshire results through 2000; *America Votes* 26, 28, 30, and 32 (CQ Press, a publication of SAGE) for similar results for 2004 through 2016; the Iowa Democratic and Republican parties and New Hampshire election authorities for 2020 results.

As Obama's vice president, it was assumed that Biden had the inside track among Black voters in 2020, but Clyburn's support solidified it within a state Democratic electorate that was majority Black. The immediate result: a blowout Biden victory in South Carolina that reshaped the Democratic race in a matter of hours.

With a slim prospect of winning many minority votes in the myriad of states directly ahead, Buttigieg and Klobuchar both withdrew from the race in favor of Biden. Even then, there was some doubt that the former vice president had enough time to transform these favorable events into a wave of

Table 2.6. Results from the Competitive Stage of the 2020 Democratic Primaries

The competitive stage of the 2020 Democratic presidential primaries lasted from February to early April, and ended with about half the primaries remaining to be held. Bernie Sanders was the last major candidate to drop his active challenge to Joe Biden, suspending his campaign the day after the scheduled date (April 7) for the Wisconsin primary. Sanders, though, did leave his name on the ballot in later primaries in order to win as many delegates as he could in advance of the party's national convention. The Democratic race, though, was essentially over on Super Tuesday (March 3), when Biden swept 10 of the day's 14 primaries. He would not lose a single one the rest of the primary season, as his margins over Sanders tended to widen. Candidates are included in the chart below who drew at least 500,000 votes over the course of the 2020 Democratic primaries. For reference, Pete Buttigieg and Amy Klobuchar stopped publicly campaigning for the nomination after South Carolina, and Elizabeth Warren and Michael Bloomberg dropped out after Super Tuesday.

						Other Candidates			
State	*Date*	*Turnout*	*Biden*	*Sanders*	*Winner (Margin)*	*Warren*	*Bloomberg*	*Buttigieg*	*Klobuchar*
NH	Feb. 11	298,337	8%	26%	Sanders + 2%	9%	2%*	24%	20%
SC	Feb. 29	539,263	49%	20%	Biden + 29%	7%	—	8%	3%
AL	March 3	452,093	63%	17%	Biden + 46%	6%	12%	0%	0%
AR	March 3	229,122	41%	22%	Biden + 19%	10%	17%	3%	3%
CA	March 3	5,784,364	28%	36%	Sanders + 8%	13%	12%	4%	2%
CO	March 3	960,128	25%	37%	Sanders + 12%	18%	19%	—	—
ME	March 3	202,520	34%	33%	Biden + 1%	16%	12%	2%	1%
MA	March 3	1,414,119	34%	27%	Biden + 7%	21%	12%	3%	1%
MN	March 3	744,198	39%	30%	Biden + 9%	15%	8%	1%	6%

NC	March 3	1,332,382	43%	24%	Biden + 19%	11%	13%	3%	2%
OK	March 3	304,281	39%	25%	Biden + 14%	13%	14%	2%	2%
TN	March 3	516,250	42%	25%	Biden + 17%	10%	15%	3%	2%
TX	March 3	2,094,428	35%	30%	Biden + 5%	11%	14%	4%	2%
UT	March 3	220,582	18%	36%	Sanders + 18%	16%	15%	8%	3%
VT	March 3	157,652	22%	51%	Sanders + 29%	13%	9%	2%	1%
VA	March 3	1,323,509	53%	23%	Biden + 30%	11%	10%	1%	1%
ID	March 10	108,650	49%	42%	Biden + 7%	3%	2%	1%	1%
MI	March 10	1,587,679	53%	36%	Biden + 17%	2%	5%	1%	1%
MS	March 10	274,631	81%	15%	Biden + 66%	1%	3%	0%	0%
MO	March 10	666,112	60%	35%	Biden + 25%	1%	1%	0%	0%
WA	March 10	1,558,776	38%	37%	Biden + 1%	9%	8%	4%	2%
AZ	March 17	536,509	50%	37%	Biden + 13%	7%	—	5%	—
FL	March 17	1,739,214	62%	23%	Biden + 39%	2%	8%	2%	1%
IL	March 17	1,674,133	59%	36%	Biden + 23%	1%	2%	1%	0%
WI	April 7	925,065	63%	32%	Biden + 31%	2%	1%	1%	1%

Note: An asterisk (*) indicates a write-in vote.

Source: 2020 Democratic presidential primary results are based on official returns posted on state election websites, with the exception of results from Georgia, which were nearly complete but unofficial.

momentum on Super Tuesday March 3, when 14 primaries were to be held from Maine to California. As it turned out, he did.

Before South Carolina, Sanders had looked as though he might do quite well on Super Tuesday. His victories in New Hampshire and Nevada plus a popular vote win in Iowa was enough to convince many observers that Sanders could use superior organization and a passionate base to build a large lead in the cross-country delegate race on March 3.

Yet it did not happen. Altogether, Biden swept 10 of the 14 primaries that day, taking Maine and Massachusetts in Sanders' New England backyard, Klobuchar's Minnesota, and seven Southern states (including Texas). In only one of the seven (Texas) was Biden's margin over Sanders less than a dozen percentage points, even though Biden won some states with only a hint of advertising and organization.

Meanwhile, Sanders could win only his home state of Vermont and three Western states (Colorado, Utah, and California) on Super Tuesday. It might have gone better for Sanders if media outlets had awarded California to him on primary night, even though. By the end of the evening, he had a lead of more than 250,000 votes over Biden in the nation's most populous state.

But roughly half the vote remained to be counted in California. As the tally proceeded over the next few weeks, Sanders' lead in the Golden State grew beyond 460,000 votes. Yet by the time the ultimate acknowledgment of his California victory came, it was too late for him to receive anywhere near full credit for it. As it was, California was one of two states that Sanders had lost to Hillary Rodham Clinton in 2016 but carried in 2020. The other was Nevada.

In the wake of Super Tuesday, two more candidates quit the Democratic race, Bloomberg—who immediately threw his support to Biden—and Warren. Bloomberg had spent hundreds of millions of dollars of his own money to establish himself as a "mainstream" alternative to a faltering Biden, skipping the February events in order to focus on Super Tuesday. But by then, Biden was back on his feet, and Bloomberg could muster victory only in American Samoa.[8]

Like Sanders, Warren had her own passionate cadre of supporters. But she was unable to win anywhere, including her home state of Massachusetts, where she ran third.

By March 5, barely a week after Clyburn's endorsement, the Democratic nomination for all practical purposes was Biden's. In the primaries that followed, he continued to demonstrate his broad acceptability to the Democratic electorate, while Sanders' coalition from 2016 steadily shrank in size. With defeat heaped upon defeat, Sanders stopped actively campaigning in early

April. But he still sought to maintain a role for himself at the party's national convention, by continuing to accept the delegates that his dwindling share of the primary vote qualified him for.

Yet, over the course of March when the Democratic race was still vaguely competitive, the party's primary voters made it abundantly clear that even approaching 80 years of age, Biden was their preferred choice for president. Many greeted his restoration to front-runner status with an almost audible sigh of relief. They viewed Sanders and his "democratic socialist" agenda as too risky for a party whose number one goal in 2020 was not a revolutionary overhaul of health care or an attack on income inequality, but the defeat of Donald Trump.

CORONAVIRUS OVERWHELMS THE PRIMARIES

It was probably good for the Democrats that Biden nailed down the Democratic nomination as quickly as he did. By mid-March, the coronavirus had pushed everything else, including presidential politics, to the side. And given its nationwide breadth and deadliness, the pandemic left a cloud of uncertainty hanging over the nation that extended the rest of the election.

Public campaigning was stopped cold by mid-March; debates were cancelled. And primaries scheduled for late March, April, and May were moved back virtually en masse to June, July, and August.[9]

To say the least, the nation was in an unusual, even ominous, place, both in terms of public and economic health. As of May 1, more than 1 million cases of the virus had been reported across the United States. The death toll had surpassed 60,000 (higher than the number of Americans killed in the entire Vietnam War). The economy had gone into "sleep" mode, with roughly 30 million workers filing jobless claims. And the unemployment rate began to spike dramatically, with nationwide levels reaching double digits percentage wise for at least four consecutive months for the first time since 1983.[10]

For all practical purposes, the 2020 presidential primary season just petered out. Those Americans who did want to vote in the remaining primaries often found fewer polling places and long lines, while the increased numbers who tried to cast their ballots by mail did not always find that to be an easy process.

Yet even with all the problems posed in 2020 for voting, 55.4 million Americans still cast ballots in the year's presidential primaries, the third-highest total since the current primary-dominated era of presidential

Table 2.7. Comparing Democratic Presidential Primary Turnouts, 2016–2020: Coronavirus Affects 2020 in a Big Way

One of the ways to divide the 2020 presidential primary season is between those primaries held before the coronavirus took hold and those held afterwards. Generally, the demarcation point was mid–March, roughly the midway point in 2020 in terms of the number of primaries. By and large, those contests held through March 10 were conducted normally, while those that took place from March 17 on were subject to postponement or changed state rules on voting that accented mail–in ballots. Democratic primary turnout in the former group of states was almost universally higher than in 2016 in terms of the number of ballots cast (down only in Oklahoma). The aggregate increase was 26 percent. After the ides of March, Democratic primary turnout was mixed: In some states, the volume of the vote was higher than 2016, in some states lower. In the aggregate, the turnout was down 5 percent from four years earlier. That made sense, since the Democratic race was essentially over by the time the pandemic had arrived in force and the means of voting no longer accented traditional in–person voting.

Pre–coronavirus primaries (through March 10)						*Primaries affected by coronavirus (March 17 and after)*					
State	*2020 Date*	*2016 Vote*	*2020 Vote*	*Change in Votes*	*Change in % Points*	*State*	*2020 Date*	*2016 Vote*	*2020 Vote*	*Change in Votes*	*Change in % Points*
NH	Feb. 11	253,062	298,377	+45,315	+18%	AZ	March 17	466,235	536,509	+70,274	+15%
SC	Feb. 29	370,904	539,263	+168,359	+45%	FL	March 17	1,709,183	1,739,214	+30,031	+2%
AL	March 3	399,889	452,093	+52,204	+13%	IL	March 17	2,056,047	1,674,133	−381,914	−19%
AR	March 3	221,020	229,122	+8,102	+4%	WI	April 7	1,007,600	925,065	−82,535	−8%
CA	March 3	5,173,338	5,784,364	+611,026	+12%	OH	April 28	1,241,478	894,383	−347,095	−28%
CO	March 3	Caucus	960,128	—	—	NE	May 12	80,436	164,582	+84,146	+105%
ME	March 3	Caucus	202,520	—	—	OR	May 19	641,595	618,711	−22,884	−4%

MA	March 3	1,215,970	1,414,119	+198,149	+16%	DC	June 2	97,763	110,688	+12,925	+13%
MN	March 3	Caucus	744,198	—	—	IN	June 2	638,779	497,927	−140,852	−22%
NC	March 3	1,142,916	1,332,382	+189,466	+17%	MD	June 2	916,763	1,050,773	+134,010	+15%
OK	March 3	335,843	304,281	−31,562	−9%	MT	June 2	126,376	149,973	+23,597	+19%
TN	March 3	372,222	516,250	+144,028	+39%	NM	June 2	216,075	247,880	+31,805	+15%
TX	March 3	1,435,895	2,094,428	+658,533	+46%	PA	June 2	1,681,427	1,595,508	−85,919	−5%
UT	March 3	Caucus	220,582	—	—	RI	June 2	122,458	103,982	−18,476	−15%
VT	March 3	134,838	157,652	+22,814	+17%	SD	June 2	53,006	52,661	−345	−1%
VA	March 3	785,190	1,323,509	+538,319	+69%	GA	June 9	765,366	1,086,731	+321,365	+42%
ID	March 10	Caucus	108,650	—	—	WV	June 9	242,539	187,482	−55,057	−23%
MI	March 10	1,205,552	1,587,679	+382,127	+32%	KY	June 23	454,565	537,905	+83,340	+18%
MS	March 10	227,164	274,631	+47,467	+21%	NY	June 23	1,954,236	1,618,932	−335,304	−17%
MO	March 10	629,425	666,112	+36,687	+6%	DE	July 7	93,640	91,682	−1,958	−2%
WA	March 10	802,754	1,558,776	+756,022	+94%	NJ	July 7	894,305	957,597	+63,292	+7%
						LA	July 11	311,776	267,286	−44,490	+14%
						CT	Aug. 11	328,255	264,416	−63,839	−19%
Comparable Primaries (2016–2020)		14,705,982	18,533,038	+3,827,056	+26%	Comparable Primaries		16,099,903	15,374,020	−725,883	−5%

Note: The term "Comparable Primaries" refers to states that held primaries in both 2016 and 2020. A dash (–) indicates that the state held a caucus, and not a primary, in 2016, and that consequently a turnout comparison between the two elections cannot be reasonably made.

Sources: 2016 Democratic primary turnout numbers are from *America Votes* 32 (CQ Press, an imprint of SAGE). Corresponding data for 2020 are based on official returns from state election authorities (including the District of Columbia), with the exception of Georgia, where results were nearly complete but unofficial.

nominations began in the 1970s. The strong turnout under the circumstances was a hopeful indicator that the electoral system, even under duress, could fairly and accurately handle a high-turnout, high-stakes election in the fall when a record 158.4 million votes for president were cast.

The pandemic aside, conditions were not particularly ripe for a large primary turnout in 2020. In 2008 and 2016, when the total primary vote approached 57.7 million and 61 million, respectively, there was no incumbent gliding to renomination and the Democrats and Republicans both had long, competitive primary seasons. In 2016, the primary turnout for each major party surpassed 30 million votes apiece. But in 2020, with an incumbent in President Trump facing only token opposition, the GOP primary turnout fell below 20 million.

On the Democratic side, the number of primary ballots cast in 2020 surpassed 36 million, even with the opposition to Biden quickly collapsing. That was not the case four years earlier when Sanders mounted an unexpectedly strong challenge to Hillary Rodham Clinton that extended through the whole primary season and on to the Democratic national convention. Sanders that year carried 22 states—10 primaries and 12 caucuses—and drew more than 13 million primary votes (compared to Clinton's 17 million). What energy there was in the 2016 Democratic race was almost exclusively with Sanders and his backers who were "Feeling the Bern."

The Sanders campaign showed signs of that same verve in the opening trio of events in 2020. But just when there was talk of Sanders' unstoppable juggernaut, he began to lose, and lose badly. With a landslide victory in South Carolina in late February, Biden overnight became a satisfactory alternative for Democrats wanting to stop the Vermont senator. Enough of the remaining field of Democratic candidates rallied behind Biden to put him on a glide path to nomination. By early April, Sanders was no longer an active candidate.

Altogether, he carried only seven states in 2020—five primaries, one caucus, and one party-run primary. His aggregate primary vote for the year was just over 9.5 million, more than 3.5 million short of his total against Clinton. Then, Sanders swept much of the northern tier of the country—upper New England, the upper Midwest (including Michigan and Wisconsin), and virtually the entire western half of the country north of the Sun Belt.

In 2020, Sanders' triumphs were scattered and few—his New England backyard (Vermont and New Hampshire), North Dakota, and a collection of western states (California, Colorado, Nevada, and Utah).

As an inactive candidate after early April, Sanders showed little residual support. He reached a modest 20 percent of the vote in only two of the final 19 Democratic primaries held from late April to August (Oregon and South

Dakota). In most of the later events, he was in the teens, percentage wise, or less.[11]

Not surprisingly, voter turnout for the Democratic primaries was higher in the first half of the process, when the race was still competitive and campaigning was normal, than in the second half, when Biden had the nomination in hand and the campaign was disrupted by the pandemic. In the primaries held before mid-March, the number of ballots cast in the Democratic contests was up by 3.8 million votes from 2016, or 26 percent (comparing states that held Democratic primaries in both 2016 and 2020).

In contrast, in the primaries held after mid-March 2020, the number of votes cast in the Democratic events was down by 725,000, or 5 percent. The drop in the Democratic turnout could have been much worse. But there is a sense in this corner that many voters took the disruptions and lack of incentives for voting as a personal challenge. They went out of their way to cast their ballots, which maybe was due to their fuller appreciation of the act of voting.

LOOKING AHEAD: IS IT TIME FOR THE CAUCUSES TO GO?

Since the presidential nominating process was overhauled a half century ago to increase citizen participation, the states have had two basic choices when it comes to selecting their national convention delegates. One is through primary elections, where voters can cast their ballot at a time of their choosing on primary election day (if not before). The other option is through caucuses, neighborhood events in states such as Iowa and Nevada where voters meet at a certain time to express their presidential preferences and sometimes stay for hours to align themselves into viable groups, which among Democrats is at least 15 percent of the vote.

Over the years, far more states have chosen to hold primaries than caucuses. The former is run by the states, who keep the voting lists, open the polling places, tally the vote, and bear the expense. The latter is operated by the state parties, and can require the volunteer-dependent organizations to spend time, money, and energy to put on an event they are not always well suited to administer.

Still, caucuses have long maintained an honored place in the nominating process. That is until 2020, when they appeared after Iowa to be on a slide into oblivion. At their worst, the caucuses are complicated, time-consuming, and prone to vote-tallying delays and errors, all of which were evident in 2020. In the process, they have lost a lot of their luster and more than a few of their defenders.

Doubts about the Iowa caucuses began to appear in 2012, when the Republican event produced two different winners. On caucus night, former Massachusetts Governor Mitt Romney finished ahead of former Senator Rick Santorum of Pennsylvania by eight votes and was widely heralded as the nominal winner, even though there were precincts still outstanding. When the last votes trickled in over the next few weeks, Santorum emerged on top by 34 votes, with a few precincts that never reported. At this point, the Iowa GOP threw up its hands and said no winner could be definitively declared. It expressed congratulations to both candidates.

In 2016, it was the Democrats' turn for angst in Iowa. Caucus night produced a nip-and-tuck affair between Clinton and Sanders that ended with Clinton narrowly ahead in state delegate equivalents, 700.47 to 696.92. The latter is the novel—and complex—measurement of choice employed in Iowa Democratic caucus politics. The Sanders forces cried foul with the result, arguing there was a lack of transparency magnified by the absence of a popular vote.[12]

After the election, national party leaders took note of the problem and adopted rules for 2020 encouraging states to hold primaries, in which more voters would participate and the results were simpler to tally. Many of the dozen or so caucus states in 2016 made the change, leaving a corporal's guard in 2020 holding caucuses, a number that included Iowa and Nevada, plus Alaska, Kansas, and North Dakota (among others) that hold "firehouse" or party-run primaries. There are usually fewer polling places and shorter polling hours in this type of event than in a traditional, state-run primary.

While primaries draw a number of casual voters, the caucuses often have the advantage of serving as a recruiting tool for the state party, drawing activists who become the backbone of party activities. And while the primaries have frequently been expensive affairs for the candidates, requiring extensive advertising campaigns to reach large audiences, caucus campaigns can often be run on the cheap by candidates—outside the expensive lead-off events in Iowa (and Nevada), that is.

The caucuses nowadays, though, have few public supporters in high places. The Democratic National Committee Chair in 2020, Tom Perez, was critical of them. So too was former Senate Majority Leader Harry Reid, who saw no place for the caucuses in the party's future, even in his home state of Nevada. "I believe it's time for the Democratic Party to move to primaries everywhere," he wrote in a statement following the last Nevada vote.[13]

Whether there will be any caucuses around in 2024 is an open question. And if they are, will Iowa retain its accustomed leadoff spot? Caucuses are under attack like never before, as there is little doubt that a long-accepted part of the presidential nominating process has become virtually persona non grata.

NOTES

1. Harold W. Stanley and Richard G. Niemi, *Vital Statistics on American Politics 2015-2016* (Thousand Oaks, CA: CQ Press, an imprint of SAGE Publications, 2015), for presidential primary data from 1968 through 2004. *America Votes* 28, 30, and 32 (Thousand Oaks, CA: CQ Press, an imprint of SAGE) for similar information for 2008, 2012, and 2016. Presidential primary data for 2020 was based on official returns from state election websites, with the exception of Georgia, where the primary results were nearly complete but unofficial.

2. Arthur T. Hadley, *The Invisible Primary* (Englewood Cliffs, NJ: Prentice-Hall, 1976).

3. Marina Pitofsky, "Williamson Campaign Pushes Back On 'Oprah's BFF' Title," *The Hill*, June 25, 2019, https://thehill.com/blogs/blog-briefing-room/news/450249-williamson-campaign-pushes-back-on-oprahs-bff-title.

4. Trip Gabriel, "Pete Buttigieg (It's 'Boot-Edge-Edge') Is Making Waves in the 2020 Race," *New York Times*, March 28, 2019, https://www.nytimes.com/2019/03/28/us/politics/buttigieg-2020-president.html; Jeremy W. Peters and Shane Goldmacher, "As Buttigieg Builds His Campaign, Gay Donors Provide the Foundation," *New York Times*, April 30, 2019, https://www.nytimes.com/2019/04/30/us/politics/pete-buttigieg-gay-donors.html.

5. Emily Bohatch, "Former SC Gov. Mark Sanford Drops Out of 2020 Presidential Race After Two Months," *The State*, November 12, 2019, https://www.thestate.com/news/politics-government/article237280524.html.

6. Julia Manchester, "Trump Holds New Hampshire Campaign Rally on the Eve of Primary," *The Hill*, February 10, 2020, https://thehill.com/homenews/campaign/482456-trump-holds-campaign-rally-on-the-eve-of-the-new-hampshire-primary.

7. Vandana Rambaran, "Buttigieg Wins Iowa After Caucus Recount, State Dem Party Says," Fox News, February 27, 2020, https://www.foxnews.com/politics/buttigieg-wins-Iowa-caucus-recount-delegates-unchanged.

8. Michael Bloomberg reportedly spent more than $500 million of his personal fortune of around $60 billion on his campaign for the 2020 Democratic presidential nomination. Blanket TV advertising and a massive staff drew much of his campaign resources. Bloomberg contested none of the February events, only the 14 primary states that voted on Super Tuesday (March 3). A day later he quit the race and endorsed Joe Biden. Yelena Dzhanova, "How Mike Bloomberg's Very Expensive Presidential Run Turned Into an Epic Failure," CNBC, March 4, 2020, https://www.cnbc.com/2020/03/04/mike-bloombergs-expensive-presidential-run-turns-into-epic-failure.html.

9. Joey Garrison, "As Coronavirus Pandemic Delays 2020 Primaries, Is It Time To Worry About The November Election?" *USA Today*, March 17, 2020, https://www.usatoday.com/story/news/politics/elections/2020/03/17/coronavirus-pandemic-delays-primaries-time-worry-2020-november-election/5057930002/.

10. Because of the effect of the coronavirus on the economy, the nationwide, seasonally adjusted, monthly unemployment rate spiked from 4.4 percent in March 2020

to 14.7 percent in April 2020. It was by far the highest monthly unemployment rate since before 1948. United States Department of Labor, Bureau of Labor Statistics, "Labor Force Statistics from the Current Population Survey" (table), http://data.bls.gov/pdq/SurveyOutputServlet.

11. Rhodes Cook, "2020 Democratic Presidential Primary, Caucus Results by State: Biden's Long Mop-Up Stage," *Rhodes Cook Letter*, October 2020.

12. Jennifer Jacobs, "Iowa Dems Fix Errors in Caucus Results, Say Clinton Still Winner," *Des Moines Register*, February 7, 2016, https://www.desmoinesregister.com/story/news/elections/presidential/caucus/2016/02/07/iowa-dems-fix-errors-caucus-results-say-clinton-still-winner/79967552/.

13. Steve Sebelius, "Harry Reid: Switch to Primaries Everywhere, Make Nevada First," *Las Vegas Review-Journal*, February 23, 2020, https://www.reviewjournal.com/news/politics-and-government/nevada/harry-reid-switch-to-primaries-everywhere-make-nevada-first-1964638/.

3

Was Joe Biden's Primary Win Inevitable or Accidental?

David Byler

Presidential primaries have *so many strange features*. Unlike the typical two-candidate race, primaries often feature a dozen or more competitors who fight each other tooth and nail—despite agreeing on almost every issue—and seem to drop in and out of the race without warning. The process takes more than a year and features more debates than any sane person could sit through. To top it all off, candidates compete for delegates (not votes) on a series of Election Days (rather than just one).

In my mind, the strangest—and most important—feature of primaries is "path-dependency." In normal elections, voters don't have a very long memory. A candidate who stumbles in a debate recovers within days, and partisanship covers over a multitude of gaffes.[1] But in primaries, one bad debate, a single miscalculation in a platform, or a series of good news cycles can change the trajectory of the race. Macro level forces like the economy and partisanship take a backseat, and the journey—or "path" of events—shapes the destination.

For that reason, primaries can't be explained like normal elections. There's no way to pinpoint a demographic trend or a geographic pattern that explains the result. To understand how Biden won, we need to instead trace the twists and turns of the process, embrace contingency, and try to separate Biden's skill-based victories from his lucky breaks.

To that end, I've broken the primary into four phases: the preseason, the long slog, the early states, and the finale. I'll examine these phases one by one, pointing out the moments where Joe Biden's skill drove his victories, as well as moments when chance (or other forces out of Biden's control) shaped the outcome. In taking this approach, I hope to paint a realistic picture of the primary: one that gives Biden credit for his smart moves, but is honest about the moments when he simply got lucky.

PHASE ONE: BIDEN LAYS OUT A GREAT PLAN AND WINS THE PRESEASON

The first phase of the primary takes place long before debates, early state primaries, or any of the flashier parts of the campaign. We'll call it the preseason: the multi-month period when candidates feel out the electorate, decide if they'll run, plan their strategy, and ultimately announce their campaigns. This is a critical part of the process. Many talented candidates misread the electorate in this phase, craft a bad message, and doom their campaign before it officially starts.

Biden excelled in this part of the primary. He put himself squarely in the party's ideological middle, allied himself with the most popular living Democratic politician (Barack Obama), and portrayed himself as "electable" at a time when Democrats were desperate to unseat Donald Trump. Put simply, he did everything right in these early months—and it set him up for success further down the road.

Biden's first smart preseason move: stay in the ideological middle of the Democratic Party.

Before the Democratic primary started, the conventional wisdom was that the energy was on the left. The number of Democrats who identified as "liberal" was rising.[2] Independent Vermont Senator Bernie Sanders—a self-described Democratic Socialist[3]—earned 43 percent[4] of the Democratic primary vote against Hillary Clinton in the 2016 primary. More recently, high-profile progressive insurgents like New York Representative Alexandria Ocasio-Cortez had successfully primaried powerful establishment Democrats.

But Biden bucked the conventional wisdom and stuck with his time-honored strategy: be the median Democrat. Adopt positions and attitudes that allow every Democrat to vote for you, and by doing so, draw a contrast between yourself and your progressive rivals.

This approach wasn't new to Biden. He spent his entire Senate career tracking the center of his party: when the Democrats moved left or right, he moved with them. As figure 3.1 shows, Biden's DW-NOMINATE score—a measure that uses roll call votes to calculate the ideological "distance" between legislators—frequently put him in the most liberal 20th to 30th percentile of senators. That means that throughout his tenure, he voted to the left of the chamber's moderates and to the right of its progressives.

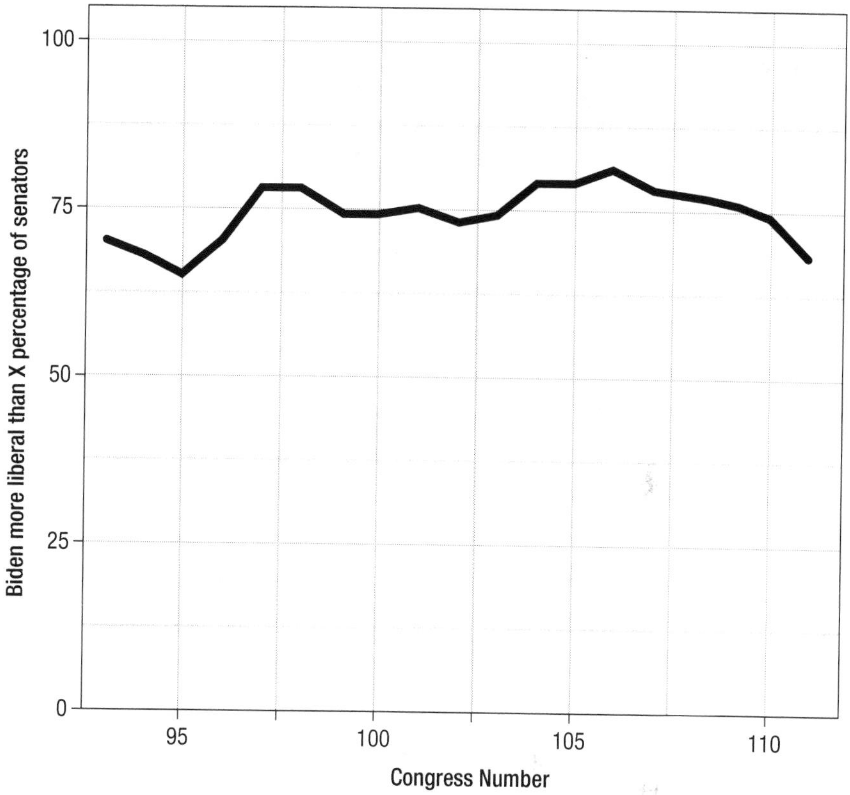

Figure 3.1. Biden DW-NOMINATE Scores During Senate Tenure

By taking this approach, Biden entered a sort of Goldilocks Zone. He made sure he wasn't too far left—he would have gained nothing by competing with Sanders, Massachusetts Senator Elizabeth Warren, New York Senator Kirsten Gillibrand, and so many others for the progressive vote. But he wasn't too conservative either—this posture let him appeal to the oft-forgotten, shrinking, but still powerful "moderate" and "conservative"[5] wings of the party.

Once Biden chose this Goldilocks Zone, his competitors found it hard to dislodge him. Minnesota Senator Amy Klobuchar tried to occupy the same space, but seemed unwilling to take Biden on directly (possibly out of hopes that she'd land a spot on his ticket). Former New York City Mayor Mike Bloomberg tried to oust Biden, but made the mistake of entering the race too late. Meanwhile, promising candidates who might have competed with him for that space—like New Jersey Senator Cory Booker, California Senator Kamala Harris, and former Texas Representative Beto O'Rourke—failed to find their footing, and eventually took positions on reparations for slavery[6] and gun control[7] that made them seem more liberal.

In short, Biden found an ideological niche and dominated it early. In a field of 27 Democrats[8]—each of whom trying to build their own base—that distinctive ideological pitch was a *huge* advantage.

Primaries aren't won on ideology alone, however. Part of success in a primary is picking the right friends—showing voters early and often that you're from the same tribe as politicians they know and love. For Biden, that meant hugging Barack Obama as much as possible.

It's hard to overstate how popular Obama is within the Democratic Party. As CNN analyst Harry Enten pointed out in August 2019, over 90 percent of Democrats rated Obama's presidency as "good" or "excellent," and almost all Democrats held a favorable opinion of Obama.[9] Despite the Democratic Party's purported move toward socialism, the party was roughly evenly divided between those who wanted their candidate to "build on former President Obama's legacy" and one that would take "a new and different approach."[10] Biden, Obama's former vice president, could have tried to evade Obama's shadow and forge his own path—but he did the opposite, and this paid dividends.

As Enten pointed out,[11] 44 percent of voters who said it was very important "to build on Obama's legacy" supported Biden in May 2019, while no other candidate earned more than 15 percent from the group. As the political scientist Michael Tesler demonstrated,[12] Biden enjoyed an "Obama Effect" among Black voters who approved of the former president. Tesler's research[13] shows that politicians who ally themselves with Obama become more popular among Black voters, and those who oppose him (like Hillary Clinton in the 2008 Democratic primary) lose ground with them. Put simply, Biden immediately ingratiated himself with two large (at times overlapping) blocs of the Democratic Party—Obama superfans and Black voters—by choosing to embrace his former boss.

Last but not least, Biden set himself up to be the "electability" candidate—which was an incredibly important advantage in the year 2020.

Some background: throughout the primary, various pollsters asked voters whether they valued strong issue positions over electability—and electability consistently won. For example, a February 2019 Monmouth University Poll asked Democrats to choose between a candidate whom you would "agree with on most issues but would have a hard time beating Donald Trump" or one who "you do NOT agree with on most issues but would be a stronger candidate against Donald Trump."[14] Only 33 percent chose the former, and 56 percent picked the latter. In a September 2019 *FiveThirtyEight*/Ipsos survey,[15] 40 percent of Democrats said "the ability to beat Donald Trump" was the most important issue, and no other issue came close (health care took second place, with one in 10 Democrats saying it was the most important). In February 2020, the Public Policy Institute of California found that 57 percent of California Democrats preferred the candidate who was "most likely to defeat Donald Trump" over one whose "positions on issues come closest to their own."[16]

Biden understood this dynamic and took advantage of it quickly—and gently. He put his campaign headquarters in Philadelphia,[17] the largest city in the key swing state of Pennsylvania. He emphasized his boyhood in another Pennsylvania city, Scranton,[18] a place representative of blue-collar white Obama-to-Trump swing voters. In debates, which we'll discuss more in the next section, he distanced[19] himself from unpopular progressive ideas like Medicare-for-All[20] and the Green New Deal,[21] signaling that he was the sort of moderate who could win swing voters in tough elections. Perhaps most importantly, he benefited passively from public polling, consistently beating Trump[22] in head-to-head polls and often posting larger[23] margins[24] than his top competitors.

Put simply, primary voters were playing pundit, desperately attempting to figure out who was "electable" and who might allow Trump to win another four years. Biden did a great job of nudging them in his direction.

In short, Biden came out of the preseason with the best strategy. Sure, Sanders and Warren came up with eminently reasonable plans (in both cases, build a base on the left and expand from there). Klobuchar smartly positioned herself as the moderate backup—someone who could inherit Biden's voters if he stumbled. Even South Bend Mayor Pete Buttigieg stood up a credible operation in Iowa, hoping to knock out other relative moderates.

But Biden's strategy allowed him to dominate his lane. He was the highest-profile liberal-but-not-far-left candidate, and he held the clearest claim to Obama's legacy. Right or wrong, many voters were convinced that he had the best chance of beating Trump. That made him the early leader in the polls—a position he didn't relinquish for the entirety of the next phase of the race.

PHASE TWO: BIDEN STAYS AHEAD DURING THE LENGTHY MONTHS BEFORE IOWA

After the candidates finish making plans and announcing their runs, they face the second phase of the race: a grueling, months-long slog toward the Iowa caucuses. This period, which stretched from late June 2019 to February 2020, can be treacherous for front-runners. They enter every debate with a target on their back, and bored campaign reporters are on the lookout for any sign of weakness from the front-runner.

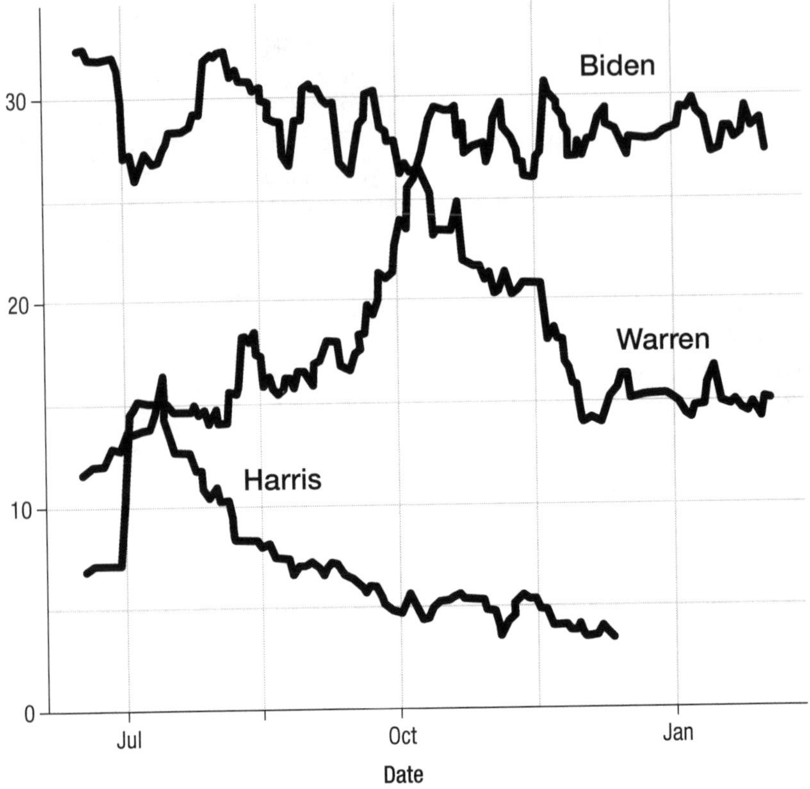

Figure 3.2. 2020 Democratic Primary National Polling Trend
Source: "Election 2020–2020 Democratic Presidential Nomination," *RealClearPolitics*, https://www.realclearpolitics.com/epolls/2020/president/us/2020_democratic_presidential_nomination-6730.html.

Biden wasn't as well-suited to this long march as he was to the preseason. He wasn't the strongest debater in the field. He didn't shine on the campaign stump. And, after spending eight years as vice president and decades in the Senate, Biden wasn't exactly a shiny new object that reporters enjoyed following.

During this phase, Biden almost lost his lead to both Harris and Warren (see figure 3.2). But he managed to get out of those scrapes—and maintain his lead for the rest of the period—through a combination of patience and luck.

The first credible attempt to unseat Biden came from then-California Senator Kamala Harris, now the vice president.

Harris, like Biden, was running as something of a compromise candidate—she didn't start with an unshakable base, but she had the rare potential to satisfy multiple constituencies and generate consensus within the party.[25] Her first step to the nomination was clear: get Biden out of the way so that she could take his "consensus candidate" mantle.

In the first debate, she almost accomplished that initial step. In one of the most memorable moments of the primary, Harris grilled Biden on race. She criticized him for his past stances on busing and school integration, revealing that as a child, she was bused as part of the effort to integrate Berkeley public schools.[26] Biden floundered in his response, and Harris immediately gained ground in the polls.[27]

But, after the debate, Biden benefited from Harris' mistakes. Harris' second debate performance didn't quite match her first, and she didn't have a clear pitch that could keep her new supporters onboard.[28] Put simply, Biden got lucky—if Harris had found a strong second step to her plan, she might have become the nominee. But she stumbled. Biden waited her out, and he regained his lead.

The second significant challenge came from Warren.

Warren's plan of attack was different from Harris': She built a disproportionately white and college-educated base slowly by touring around the country, releasing detailed policy plans, and generating excitement among progressives.[29] It was a solid plan—if Warren had kept expanding, party leaders might have embraced her and made her the new "consensus candidate."

But Biden won his fight with Warren the same way he won with Harris—by benefiting from her missteps. Warren's strategy began to fall apart around October 2019,[30] when her opponents began scrutinizing her health care plan.[31] Up until then, Warren had supported Sanders' plan and emphasized the idea that costs would go down.[32] Multiple opponents became more critical as she became a front-runner, claiming that she would have to raise taxes to make her plan work.[33] The candidate who had a plan for everything suddenly seemed to be caught off guard, and her support began to erode. As an opponent of Medicare-for-All—and the candidate with the most to lose from Warren's rise—Biden happily joined the pile-on.[34]

Put simply, Biden survived his fight with Warren the same way he made it through his tiff with Harris. He defended himself, like all competent politicians do, but he benefited from his opponent's missteps. If Warren had adopted a different strategy on health care, the primary might have turned out very differently. But Warren happened to pick a position that backfired—and Biden was fortunate enough to benefit.

Biden does deserve some credit for what he did well during this phase. Between his fights with Harris and Warren, he managed to avoid making big mistakes. He didn't perform particularly well in debates, but he never catastrophically stumbled. He wasn't a stunning fund-raiser, but he had enough money to stay afloat. And he resisted the temptation to turn left or retool his campaign. This slow and steady approach kept him in the lead—that is, until early states started voting.

PHASE THREE: BIDEN STUMBLES IN THE EARLY STATES, BUT BOUNCES BACK

Biden came the closest to losing in the third stage of the primary season: the early states. In modern presidential primaries, a handful of states vote early, which in theory allows lesser-known candidates to gain steam before the rest of the nation casts their ballots. In 2020, Iowa, New Hampshire, Nevada, and South Carolina voted (in that order) from February 3 to February 29.[35]

The first three states went *horribly* for Joe Biden.

The problems started in the Iowa caucuses. Pre-election polls showed Biden in decent shape heading into the caucuses: according to the *FiveThirtyEight* averages,[36] Sanders led the field at 22.2 percent, Biden was in second at 21 percent, and Buttigieg and Warren sat at 15.4 and 14.7 percent, respectively. But Biden seriously underperformed the polls. In the "first alignment" vote (which, in the byzantine caucus system, is closest to the popular vote), Sanders won 45,652 votes, Buttigieg earned 43,209, Warren took 34,909, and Biden came in a distant fourth at 23,605.[37]

Biden's position only worsened in New Hampshire.[38] Sanders, who represents neighboring Vermont, won the primary with 26 percent of the vote. Buttigieg, Klobuchar, and Warren took second, third, and fourth with 24, 20, and 10 percent of the vote, respectively. Biden came in *fifth*, with a grand total of 9 percent of the overall vote. Biden performed somewhat better in the Nevada caucuses[39]—he took second place—but Sanders still far outpaced him, winning 34 percent to Biden's 18 percent in the first alignment.

For most candidates, that string of losses would have been the end of the line. But Biden had an ace up his sleeve: South Carolina.

South Carolina was a much better fit for Biden than any other early state. Iowa and New Hampshire were flush with Biden-skeptical white liberals.[40] Nevada, a caucus state with a sizable Hispanic population, was also a good fit for Sanders, who performed well with Hispanic voters.[41] But South Carolina was home to a much more Biden-friendly constituency: Black voters (see table 3.1).[42]

Biden always had a strong base with Black voters—many gave him credit for his service as Obama's vice president (see above for more details), and his policy positions were a good fit for a large segment of moderate Black voters. Even after Nevada—his lowest point of the campaign— he maintained a slight lead over Sanders in Palmetto State polls.[44]

Table 3.1. Demographics of Early States

State	*White*	*Black*	*Latino/ Hispanic**	*Very Liberal*	*Somewhat Liberal*
Iowa	91%	3%	4%	25%	42%
New Hampshire	89%	3%	5%	21%	40%
Nevada	65%	11%	17%	31%	36%
South Carolina	46%	49%	3%	22%	33%

Note: *CNN lists Latino as the demographic breakdown in Iowa, but Hispanic in the other three states.[43]
Source: "Exit and Entrance Polls from the 2020 Primaries and Caucuses," *CNN*, 2020, https://www.cnn.com/election/2020/primaries-caucuses/entrance-and-exit-polls/.

In the run-up to voting, Biden again benefited from the missteps of his opponents. According to campaign insiders, Sanders hadn't prepared well for the South Carolina primary. He was late to air TV and radio ads in the state; his class-driven politics didn't always translate to voters who had experienced racism; and it was clear that his focus was on other states.[45] Just as importantly, Sanders's weaknesses were on full display: in the final debate before the primary, Sanders unapologetically defended comments praising Fidel Castro's literacy programs and failed to parry attacks on his electability, his record of "socialism," and his health care plans.[46]

Those mistakes allowed Biden to reassert himself. He earned the endorsement of South Carolina Representative Jim Clyburn—one of the most influential Democrats in the country. He quickly rose from 23 to 38 percent in the polls.[47] Most importantly, he consolidated his base of Black voters—a group that, in 2020, was laser-focused on picking the most electable candidate.[48]

Ultimately, Biden won South Carolina with 48 percent of the vote while Sanders only took 20 percent.[49] Biden had teetered on the brink of collapse—but his toughest opponent stumbled, allowing Biden to reassert himself at the pivotal moment of this race.

PHASE FOUR: BIDEN RALLIES THE PARTY AND WINS THE NOMINATION

After Biden won South Carolina, the last phase of the primary—which I call the "finale"—began. In this segment of the race, the party establishment has one last window to crown a favorite. After that, numerous states vote on "Super Tuesday," and the winner of those contests typically goes on to become the nominee.

In this phase, Biden crushed his remaining opponents.

As soon as Biden won South Carolina, the Democratic establishment decided that Biden was their man. A wave of DNC members and members of the House and Senate—including big names like Virginia Senator Tim Kaine and Illinois Senator Tammy Duckworth—quickly announced their support for Biden.[50] Buttigieg, Klobuchar, and O'Rourke—some of Biden's most prominent moderate rivals—simultaneously endorsed Biden and flew to Dallas to campaign for him (Klobuchar and Buttigieg dropped out right before their endorsements, while O'Rourke had left the contest much earlier in the process).[51] Put simply, the Democratic Party signaled that they both wanted Biden to win *and* believed that he could beat Sanders on Super Tuesday.

Voters picked up on this signal. Biden dominated Sanders on Super Tuesday: he won 10 of the 14 states and picked up over 1,550 delegates—more than 500 more than Sanders. Biden ran up the score in states like Alabama, where Black voters make up much of the Democratic voters, but he also won states that were outside his wheelhouse, such as Massachusetts (Warren's home state) and Minnesota (a state demographically similar to Iowa, where Biden placed fourth). Warren got the third highest tally at 63. And Bloomberg—who might have been able to compete with Biden in South Carolina but instead skipped the early states and spent enormous sums on ads—ended up with only 44.[52]

In short, Democrats from all over the country suddenly, and decisively, chose Biden.

It took some time for the primary to officially wind down: Bloomberg and Warren only endorsed Biden after his Super Tuesday win, and Sanders soldiered on for a few more weeks before conceding. But after Super Tuesday, the trajectory of the race was clear. Biden had crafted a solid strategy, slipped past challenges from Harris and Warren in the long months of 2019, suffered some early losses to Sanders, but rebounded in South Carolina and built a functionally insurmountable lead on Super Tuesday. After Super Tuesday, the "race" became a mere formality.

CONCLUSION: BIDEN TOOK THE PATH MOST-TRAVELED. BUT EVEN HIS RUN SHOWCASED HOW CHAOTIC PRIMARIES CAN BE

From a 30,000-foot view, Biden's victory is wholly unsurprising. He was the vice president to a popular two-term president. He adopted a platform that every faction of his party could live with. And, for the most part, he avoided making the sort of unforced errors that ended so many other White House bids.

But taking this primary apart stage by stage shows that Biden's win was contingent on events he didn't control. If Harris had a better follow-up or if

Warren had written a better health care plan, Biden might have been knocked out before the early states voted. Sanders could have beat Biden out in South Carolina—or at least seriously damaged him—if he had switched gears, made peace with the party, and found a convincing argument for his own electability. And if Bloomberg hadn't skipped South Carolina, he might have displaced Biden as the party's moderate savior. Put simply, this primary was path-dependent. Biden had an excellent strategy—but his fate was ultimately out of his hands. A few tweaks would have made this race much closer, and a few more might have changed the outcome entirely.

NOTES

1. Loosely based on 1 Peter 4:8
2. Lydia Saad, "U.S. Still Leans Conservative, but Liberals Keep Recent Gains," Gallup, January 8, 2019, https://news.gallup.com/poll/245813/leans-conservative-liberals-keep-recent-gains.aspx.
3. "Bernie Sanders: 18 Things the Democratic Front-Runner Believes," BBC, February 28, 2020, https://www.bbc.com/news/magazine-35364868.
4. Richard Berg-Andersson, "Democratic Convention 2016: Nationwide Popular Vote," The Green Papers, https://www.thegreenpapers.com/P16/D.
5. Lydia Saad, "The U.S. Remained Center-Right, Ideologically, in 2019," Gallup, January 9, 2020, https://news.gallup.com/poll/275792/remained-center-right-ideologically-2019.aspx.
6. P. R. Lockhart, "The 2020 Democratic Primary Debate over Reparations, Explained," *Vox*, March 11, 2019, https://www.vox.com/policy-and-politics/2019/3/11/18246741/reparations-democrats-2020-inequality-warren-harris-castro.
7. Kate Sullivan and Eric Bradner, "Beto O'Rourke: 'Hell, Yes, We're Going to Take Your AR-15, Your AK-47'," CNN, September 13, 2019, https://www.cnn.com/2019/09/12/politics/beto-orourke-hell-yes-take-ar-15-ak-47/index.html.
8. Alexander Burns, Matt Flegenheimer, Jasmine C. Lee, Lisa Lerer, and Jonathan Martin, "Who's Running for President in 2020?" *New York Times*, January 21, 2019, https://www.nytimes.com/interactive/2019/us/politics/2020-presidential-candidates.html.
9. Harry Enten, "Democratic Primary Voters May Punish Candidates Critical of Obama," CNN, August 3, 2019, https://www.cnn.com/2019/08/03/politics/democrats-on-obama-legacy/index.html.
10. "Fox News Poll September 15-17, 2019," Fox News, September 18, 2019, https://www.foxnews.com/politics/fox-news-poll-september-15-17-2019.
11. Harry Enten, "Democratic Primary Voters May Punish Candidates Critical of Obama," CNN, August 3, 2019, https://www.cnn.com/2019/08/03/politics/democrats-on-obama-legacy/index.html.
12. Michael Tesler, "Analysis: The Obama Effect Has Helped Joe Biden with Black Voters. Will It Last?" *Washington Post*, October 8, 2019, https://www

.washingtonpost.com/politics/2019/10/08/obama-effect-has-helped-joe-biden-with-black-voters-will-it-last/.

13. Michael Tesler, *Post-Racial or Most-Racial?: Race and Politics in the Obama Era* (Chicago, IL: University of Chicago Press, 2016).

14. Patrick Murray, "Dems Prefer Electability in 2020," Monmouth University Polling Institute, February 4, 2019, https://www.monmouth.edu/polling-institute/reports/monmouthpoll_US_020419/.

15. Sarah Frostenson, "What Issues Should The 2020 Democratic Candidates Be Talking About?" *FiveThirtyEight*, September 18, 2019, https://fivethirtyeight.com/features/what-issues-should-the-2020-democratic-candidates-be-talking-about/.

16. Dean Bonner, "Electability Matters in the Democratic Primary," Public Policy Institute of California, February 27, 2020, https://www.ppic.org/blog/electability-matters-in-the-democratic-primary/.

17. Jonathan Tamari, "Joe Biden Chooses Philadelphia for 2020 Presidential Campaign Headquarters," *Philadelphia Inquirer*, May 16, 2019, https://www.inquirer.com/news/joe-biden-2020-presidential-campaign-philadelphia-headquarters-20190516.html.

18. Jessica Calefati, "Fact-Checking Trump's Frequent Claim That Joe Biden 'Abandoned Scranton,'" *Philadelphia Inquirer*, August 31, 2020, https://www.inquirer.com/politics/election/joe-biden-scranton-roots-trump-fact-check-20200829.html.

19. Tucker Higgins, "Biden Suggests He Would Veto 'Medicare for All' over Its Price Tag," CNBC, March 10, 2020, https://www.cnbc.com/2020/03/10/biden-says-he-wouldd-veto-medicare-for-all-as-coronavirus-focuses-attention-on-health.html.

20. Nate Silver, "Medicare For All Isn't That Popular–Even Among Democrats," *FiveThirtyEight*, July 25, 2019, https://fivethirtyeight.com/features/medicare-for-all-isnt-that-popular-even-among-democrats/.

21. David Roberts, "Fox News Has United the Right against the Green New Deal. The Left Remains Divided," *Vox*, April 22, 2019, https://www.vox.com/energy-and-environment/2019/4/22/18510518/green-new-deal-fox-news-poll.

22. "Election 2020–General Election: Trump vs. Biden," *RealClearPolitics*, https://www.realclearpolitics.com/epolls/2020/president/us/general_election_trump_vs_biden-6247.html.

23. "Election 2020–General Election: Trump vs. Warren," *RealClearPolitics*, https://www.realclearpolitics.com/epolls/2020/president/us/general_election_trump_vs_warren-6251.html.

24. "Election 2020–General Election: Trump vs. Sanders," *RealClearPolitics*, https://www.realclearpolitics.com/epolls/2020/president/us/general_election_trump_vs_sanders-6250.html.

25. Nate Silver, "The 5 Corners of the 2020 Democratic Primary," *FiveThirtyEight*, January 10, 2019, https://fivethirtyeight.com/features/the-5-key-constituencies-of-the-2020-democratic-primary/.

26. Matt Stevens, "When Kamala Harris and Joe Biden Clashed on Busing and Segregation," *New York Times*, July 31, 2019, https://www.nytimes.com/2019/07/31/us/politics/kamala-harris-biden-busing.html.

27. "Election 2020–2020 Democratic Presidential Nomination." *RealClearPolitics*, https://www.realclearpolitics.com/epolls/2020/president/us/2020_democratic_presidential_nomination-6730.html.

28. Perry Bacon Jr., "What Happened to the Kamala Harris Campaign?" *FiveThirtyEight*, October 8, 2019, https://fivethirtyeight.com/features/what-happened-to-the-kamala-harris-campaign/.

29. Thomas Kaplan and Astead W. Herndon, "Elizabeth Warren Gains Ground in 2020 Field, One Plan at a Time," *New York Times*, May 28, 2019, https://www.nytimes.com/2019/05/28/us/politics/elizabeth-warren-2020.html.

30. "Election 2020–2020 Democratic Presidential Nomination," *RealClearPolitics*, https://www.realclearpolitics.com/epolls/2020/president/us/2020_democratic_presidential_nomination-6730.html.

31. Shane Goldmacher and Astead W. Herndon, "Elizabeth Warren, Once a Front-Runner, Drops Out of Presidential Race," *New York Times*, March 5, 2020, https://www.nytimes.com/2020/03/05/us/politics/elizabeth-warren-drops-out.html.

32. Dylan Scott, "Everybody Went after Elizabeth Warren over Medicare-for-All," *Vox*, October 16, 2019, https://www.vox.com/policy-and-politics/2019/10/15/20916531/fourth-democratic-debate-elizabeth-warren-medicare-for-all-cost.

33. Ibid.

34. John Verhovek, Cheyenne Haslett, Molly Nagle, and Sasha Pezenik, "Biden Attacks Warren's Approach to Healthcare as 'Elitism,'" ABC News, November 6, 2019, https://abcnews.go.com/Politics/biden-attack-warren-elitist-amid-health-care-feud/story?id=66801468.

35. "2020 Election Calendar." *NPR*, 2020, https://apps.npr.org/elections20-primaries/.

36. Drumhil Mehta, "Iowa President: Democratic Primary Polls," *FiveThirtyEight*, January 12, 2021, https://projects.fivethirtyeight.com/polls/president-primary-d/iowa/.

37. "Iowa Primary Caucus Results 2020: Live Election Map," NBC News, June 3, 2020, https://www.nbcnews.com/politics/2020-primary-elections/iowa-results.

38. "New Hampshire Primary Results 2020: Live Election Map," NBC News, February 14, 2020, https://www.nbcnews.com/politics/2020-primary-elections/new-hampshire-results.

39. "Nevada Caucus Results 2020," *Las Vegas Review-Journal*, 2020, https://www.reviewjournal.com/nevada-caucus-results-2020/.

40. David Byler, "Opinion: Democrats Wanted Fairer Primaries. But Their Calendar Still Prioritizes White Liberals," *Washington Post*, November 6, 2019, https://www.washingtonpost.com/opinions/2019/11/06/democrats-wanted-fairer-primaries-their-calendar-still-prioritizes-white-liberals/.

41. "Exit and Entrance Polls from the 2020 Primaries and Caucuses," CNN, 2020, https://www.cnn.com/election/2020/primaries-caucuses/entrance-and-exit-polls/nevada/democratic.

42. Ibid.

43. Ibid.

44. Drumhil Mehta, "South Carolina President: Democratic Primary Polls," *FiveThirtyEight*, January 12, 2021, https://projects.fivethirtyeight.com/polls/president-primary-d/south-carolina/.

45. Sean Sullivan, "Insiders Recount How Sanders Lost the Black Vote—and the Nomination Slipped Away," *Washington Post*, March 25, 2020, https://www.washingtonpost.com/politics/insiders-recount-how-sanders-lost-the-black-vote—and-the-nomination-slipped-away/2020/03/24/2b7b8b8e-685e-11ea-b313-df458622c2cc_story.html.

46. Maeve Reston, "Democratic Candidates Try to Put Bernie Sanders in the Hot Seat in Last Debate before Crucial Primaries," CNN, February 26, 2020, https://www.cnn.com/2020/02/25/politics/cbs-democratic-presidential-debate/index.html; Alex Seitz-Wald, "Rivals Pile on Bernie Sanders in South Carolina Debate," NBC News, February 25, 2020, https://www.nbcnews.com/politics/2020-election/rivals-pile-bernie-sanders-south-carolina-debate-n1143026.

47. Drumhil Mehta, "South Carolina President: Democratic Primary Polls," *FiveThirtyEight*, January 12, 2021, https://projects.fivethirtyeight.com/polls/president-primary-d/south-carolina/.

48. Theodore Johnson, "Perspective: Why Do Black Voters Support Biden? They Just Want to Beat Trump," *Washington Post*, May 31, 2019, https://www.washingtonpost.com/outlook/why-do-black-voters-support-biden-they-just-want-to-beat-trump/2019/05/31/74b37ca8-7b33-11e9-8ede-f4abf521ef17_story.html.

49. "South Carolina Democratic Primary Results," *USA Today*, March 2, 2020, https://www.usatoday.com/elections/results/primaries/democratic/south-carolina/.

50. Aaron Bycoffe, "The 2020 Endorsement Primary," *FiveThirtyEight*, April 8, 2020, https://projects.fivethirtyeight.com/2020-endorsements/democratic-primary/.

51. Oliver Laughland and David Smith, "Biden Wins Backing of Former Rivals Klobuchar and O'Rourke at Dallas Rally," *The Guardian*, March 3, 2020, https://www.theguardian.com/us-news/2020/mar/02/joe-biden-rally-amy-klobuchar-beto-orourke.

52. Lenny Bronner and Jason Bernert, "Super Tuesday 2020: Live Results and Exit Polling," *Washington Post*, June 1, 2020, https://www.washingtonpost.com/elections/election-results/super-tuesday/.

4

The Politics of Good versus Evil

Voting in a Polarized America

Alan I. Abramowitz

The 2020 presidential election was actually not very close. Former Vice President Joe Biden defeated President Donald Trump by more than 7 million votes and close to 4.5 percentage points in the popular vote. He won the electoral vote by a decisive margin of 306 to 232. Biden's popular vote margin was larger than that of the two most recently reelected incumbents—George W. Bush in 2004 and Barack Obama in 2012. Yet, somehow, the election felt much closer than either of those contests. Neither Bush nor Obama had to wait four days because of the closeness of the results in several key swing states before being projected as the winner of the election by major news networks. And, of course, neither Bush nor Obama had to deal with an opponent who refused to concede even after the outcome was clear, claimed without evidence that the election had been stolen, and continued to fight to overturn the result for weeks despite numerous setbacks in state and federal courts.

Even after the Electoral College confirmed Biden's victory on December 14, the president continued to claim that he was the rightful winner and attacked Republican officials who dared challenge him, including the Republican governors of Arizona and Georgia.[1] In an unprecedented move, Trump encouraged Republican members of the newly elected Congress and Vice President Pence to challenge the electoral votes of several swing states. On January 6, 2021, as both chambers of the newly elected Congress were preparing to conduct the normally ceremonial electoral vote count, Trump urged an angry crowd of supporters to march on the U.S. Capitol. The result was a violent attack in which the mob occupied the Capitol building for several hours, resulting in considerable property damage, numerous injuries, and several deaths.[2]

Perhaps the most shocking aspect of Trump's effort to overthrow the results of a democratic election was the support that he received from hundreds of Republican elected officials and his success in convincing a substantial majority of Republican voters that the election was rigged and that he and not Joe Biden was the rightful winner.[3] Yet, in some ways, this development can be seen as the logical outgrowth of a long-term trend in American politics: deepening partisan polarization and increasing mistrust and dislike of those on the opposing side. This trend began long before Donald Trump descended the escalator in Trump Tower to declare his candidacy for president in 2015.[4] However, it is now clear that Trump's presidency and his conduct before and after the 2020 election have deepened the division, mistrust, and animosity among supporters of both parties. Indeed, Trump's presidency and conduct during and after the 2020 election have turned party politics, in the minds of many Americans, into a war between good and evil.

A DEEPLY DIVIDED NATION

Whenever a president is seeking a second term in the White House, the election revolves mainly around the performance of the incumbent. In the case of Donald Trump, that was even more true than usual. That is because Donald Trump has been, by almost every measure, the most divisive president in modern American history. Even before the 2020 campaign began, this was evident from public opinion polling data on assessments of his performance in office.

The Gallup poll, which has measured presidential approval since the 1940s, reported that the 82-point average partisan divide in assessments of Trump's performance in 2019 was the largest it had ever recorded for any president for a full year, breaking the record of 79 points set by Trump in 2018.[5] In its final poll prior to the 2020 election, Gallup found that 94 percent of Republicans approved of the president's performance compared with only 4 percent of Democrats—a remarkable 90-point difference. This was the largest difference in approval between Democrats and Republicans in the long history of the Gallup poll. Moreover, Americans' opinions of Trump tend to be very intense. Throughout Trump's presidency, the vast majority of Americans either strongly approved or strongly disapproved of the president's performance, while far fewer either mildly approved or mildly disapproved. In an October 2020 Quinnipiac University poll, for example, 77 percent of likely Republican voters strongly approved of Trump's performance while 89 percent of likely Democratic voters strongly disapproved of his performance.

It is common to describe the differences between the Democratic and Republican electoral coalitions in terms of their social characteristics—and these differences clearly are quite large. The Democratic coalition consists disproportionately of younger voters, racial and ethnic minorities, city-dwellers, the nonreligious and, increasingly, college-educated whites. The Republican electoral coalition consists disproportionately of older, religious, small town and rural white voters without college degrees. In the twenty-first century, however, these differences in the social characteristics of party supporters largely reflect differences in the preferences of voters on major issues. The deep partisan divide over Donald Trump's performance as president largely reflects deep partisan divisions on major issues including the size and role of government, health care, immigration, race relations, climate change, and, perhaps most significantly in the context of the 2020 election, the coronavirus pandemic.

The most fundamental divide between supporters of the two major parties in the United States involves the size and role of the federal government. This divide has existed since at least the New Deal era, but it has perhaps never been as wide as it is today. In September 2019, a Pew Research Center survey of American adults found that 78 percent of Democratic identifiers and leaners felt that "government should do more to solve problems" facing the country versus only 28 percent of Republican identifiers and leaners. In contrast, only 21 percent of Democratic identifiers and leaners felt that "government is doing too many things better left to businesses and individuals" compared with 71 percent of Republican identifiers and leaners.[6]

On the issue of race relations, the same Pew survey found that 84 percent of Democratic identifiers and leaners agreed that white people benefit a great deal or a fair amount from "societal advantages that Black people do not have" compared with only 28 percent of Republican identifiers and leaners. This divide helps to explain the dramatically different responses of Democrats and Republicans to police shootings of unarmed Black citizens and to the Black Lives Matter movement during 2020. Along these lines, a September 2020 Pew Research Center survey of American adults found that 88 percent of white Democratic identifiers and leaners either strongly or somewhat supported the Black Lives Matter movement compared with only 16 percent of white Republican identifiers and leaners. This was an enormous 72-point difference on one of the most salient issues dividing President Trump and the large majority of Republican House and Senate candidates from Joseph Biden and the large majority of Democratic candidates.

Despite fearmongering by President Trump and some members of his administration, attitudes toward immigrants have become more positive among supporters of both parties in recent years. However, the divide between

Democrats and Republicans on this issue has remained very wide. In the September 2019 Pew survey, 79 percent of Democratic identifiers and leaners felt that the growing number of newcomers strengthens American society compared with only 31 percent of Republican identifiers and leaners.

The same September 2019 Pew survey found deep party divides on other issues as well. On the issue of health care, 83 percent of Democratic identifiers and leaners agreed that "it is the federal government's responsibility to make sure all Americans have health care coverage" compared with only 30 percent of Republican identifiers and leaners. On gun control, 86 percent of Democratic identifiers and leaners favored stricter regulations versus only 31 percent of Republican identifiers and leaners. Similarly, on climate change, 77 percent of Democratic identifiers and leaners agreed that the Earth is getting warmer because of human activities such as burning fossil fuels compared with only 23 percent of Republican identifiers and leaners.

On issue after issue, the divide between Democrats and Republicans has grown wider over time. Moreover, on all of these issues, the party divide would undoubtedly be wider among the more politically active supporters of the two parties, including those who give money and vote in primary elections.[7] This widening divide, especially among the politically active, has made it increasingly difficult for political leaders to find any middle ground to arrive at workable compromises to address the serious challenges facing the country.

In recent years, working across party lines has been especially dangerous for Republicans. GOP senators and representatives who cooperated with Democrats have risked being branded as RINOS (Republicans in Name Only) and threatened in a primary by a more conservative challenger. The risk was even greater for those who failed to display sufficient loyalty to President Trump. A critical tweet from the president could put one's political career in jeopardy, as former Trump administration Attorney General Jeff Sessions discovered when he attempted to reclaim his Senate seat in Alabama.[8]

On no other issue has this party divide been more startling and damaging than the coronavirus pandemic. From its onset in January and February through the rest of the year, President Trump consistently sought to downplay the seriousness of the virus' threat to public health. He also consistently refused to adhere to public health guidelines regarding social distancing and mask wearing, regularly appearing unmasked at public events and holding meetings and even political rallies with little or no effort at social distancing. Trump's statements and actions frequently brought him into conflict with Democratic leaders and public health experts, including some within his administration. Yet few Republican officeholders dared to openly challenge the president's leadership on this issue. To a greater extent than in many other democracies, opinions on the seriousness of the threat and support for measures to mitigate the spread of the virus, such as social distancing and mask wearing, divided the American public along party lines.[9] There is little doubt that the reluctance of a large proportion of the American public to practice social distancing and wear masks contributed to substantially higher death rates in the United States than in many other wealthy countries.[10]

A Pew survey between April 29 and May 5, 2020, found that even after millions of Americans had been infected with the virus and tens of thousands had died, only 43 percent of Republican identifiers and leaners versus 82 percent of Democratic identifiers and leaners considered the coronavirus pandemic a major threat to the health of the U.S. population. In the United States, partisanship was actually a stronger predictor of citizens' adherence to public health guidelines than the rate of infection in their surrounding communities.[11]

The growing party divide on issues and on President Trump has fueled growing mistrust and animosity toward the opposing party among rank-and-file Democrats and Republicans. According to the Pew Research Center, between December 2016 and September 2019, the percentage of Democratic identifiers and leaners giving the Republican Party a cold rating on a feeling thermometer scale increased from 56 percent to 79 percent. Over the same time, the percentage of Republican identifiers and leaners giving the Democratic Party a cold rating increased from 58 percent to 83 percent. In 2019, the large majority of both Democrats and Republicans gave the opposing party a "very cold" rating, below 25 degrees on the 0-100 degree scale.[12] Even more concerning, in a Pew survey conducted between September 20 and October 5, 2020, 89 percent of Trump supporters and 90 percent of Biden supporters agreed that a victory by the opposing candidate would not just be a cause for concern but "would lead to lasting harm to the U.S."[13] Is it any wonder, given the level of mutual mistrust and animosity, that millions of President Trump's supporters readily accepted his baseless claims of widespread fraud in the 2020 vote count?

If Democratic and Republican voters increasingly seem to live in two different worlds, that may be because in terms of news and information, they do. Supporters of the two parties increasingly rely on different media outlets that provide very dissimilar perspectives on the news. However, there are important differences in the number and variety of news sources that Democrats and Republicans rely on. According to a Pew survey of American adults conducted between October 29 and November 11, 2019, Democrats and Democratic-leaning independents rely on a variety of what can be described as mainstream media outlets for news and information including CNN, NBC, ABC, CBS, and PBS. No single news source dominates among Democrats. In contrast, Republicans and Republican leaning independents overwhelmingly rely on one media outlet for news and information: Fox News.[14]

Supporters of each party tend to distrust the outlets that Americans on the opposing side of the partisan divide rely on the most. Democrats and Democratic-leaning independents distrust Fox News far more than any other media outlet, while Republicans and Republican-leaning independents distrust all of the leading mainstream media outlets, especially CNN. Thus, media polarization both reflects and reinforces polarization in Americans' views of parties, political leaders, and issues. Republicans and conservatives, especially, live in a media bubble in which media coverage reinforces and amplifies false or misleading messages from conservative political leaders while contradictory information is hard to find. Meanwhile, growing reliance on social media, such as Facebook and Twitter, for political information may be contributing to partisan polarization on both sides by exposing partisans to information that mainly reinforces their predispositions.[15]

HOW PARTISAN POLARIZATION SHAPED THE ELECTION

Four years of Donald Trump's presidency combined with a deadly pandemic left the American people more divided along party lines than at any time in at least half a century. These intense divisions affected the 2020 election in several important ways. Deep partisan polarization contributed to record voter turnout, strong party loyalty, and straight-ticket voting—a very high degree of consistency between the 2016 and 2020 results across states and congressional districts, and a very high degree of consistency between the 2020 presidential results and the 2020 House and Senate results.

The intense partisan polarization among political elites and the public during the Trump years has been described as a threat to the stability or even the survival of American democracy.[16] Deepening partisan polarization has, however, had one positive consequence for democracy: record levels of political engagement and voter turnout. Americans perceived the stakes in the 2020 election as enormous, and they voted accordingly. Turnout in the 2020 presidential election was higher than in any presidential election in over a century. According to political scientist Michael McDonald, 159.6 million Americans, 66.7 percent of those legally eligible, voted in the 2020 election. That compared with 138.8 million, or 60.1 percent of those legally eligible, in the 2016 election.[17]

Voter turnout increased from 2016 to 2020 in every state and the District of Columbia. And it increased by almost as much in states where the outcome was never in doubt as it did in swing states where campaigning was most intense. The fact that this dramatic surge in voter turnout occurred in the midst of a dangerous pandemic was even more impressive. Millions of Americans risked exposing themselves to a deadly virus in order to cast ballots in the 2020 general election as well as the primary elections. The surge in turnout continued into 2021, as voters turned out in record numbers for two runoff elections in Georgia, which determined control of the Senate.[18]

It is true, of course, that many states made changes to their voting rules and procedures to make it easier and safer for voters to cast their ballots. Numerous states made it possible for voters to cast absentee ballots without a special excuse. At the same time, many states expanded early in-person voting opportunities in order to reduce the crush at the polls on Election Day. These changes undoubtedly made voting safer and more convenient and they may have contributed to higher turnout, but they were not the main reason for the dramatic increase in turnout in 2020.

There is little doubt that the main reason why voter turnout soared in 2020 was Donald Trump. It was intense feelings toward the president that drove both Republicans and Democrats to the polls. Republicans were motivated by their desire to support the president and help him to win a second term. Democrats were motivated by their desire to oppose the president and make sure that he did not win a second term.

We know that President Trump was the main reason for higher turnout in 2020, not just because turnout rose in every state regardless of its voting rules, but because we saw the same thing happen in the 2018 midterm election before the pandemic had begun and before states began changing their voting rules. According to McDonald, 118.6 million Americans, or 50 percent of legally eligible voters, went to the polls in the 2018 midterm election. That was an increase from only 83.3 million, or 36.7 percent of legally eligible voters, in the 2014 midterm election. Voter turnout in the 2018 midterm election was the highest in a midterm election in over a century. Not since 1912, before women's suffrage, had midterm turnout reached 50 percent of eligible voters.

Negative partisanship—intense dislike of the opposing party—drove voters to the polls in 2020 just as it had in 2018. It also drove their voting decisions.[19] Supporters of both parties, including independents who leaned toward a party, voted overwhelmingly for their own party's candidates for president and for every other office on the ballot. Party loyalty and straight-ticket voting have been increasing for decades but both reached unprecedented levels in 2020.

According to data from the 2020 national exit poll, Democratic identifiers voted for Joe Biden over Donald Trump by a margin of 94 percent to 5 percent while Republican identifiers voted for Trump over Biden by a margin of 94 percent to 6 percent. Unfortunately, the exit poll data do not break down independent identifiers based on which party they lean toward. Other surveys, however, indicated that leaning independents, who make up the large majority of independent identifiers, voted overwhelmingly for the candidate of their preferred party. For example, a CNN national poll conducted between October 23 and October 26 found that Democratic identifiers and leaners combined favored Biden over Trump by 95 percent to 3 percent while Republican identifiers and leaners combined favored Trump over Biden by 92 percent to 5 percent. The results were almost identical to those for Democratic and Republican identifiers alone.

Levels of party loyalty were very similar in other elections. In the U.S. House elections, for example, according to the national exit poll, Democratic identifiers voted for Democratic House candidates over Republican House candidates by a margin of 95 percent to 5 percent while Republican identifiers voted for Republican candidates over Democratic candidates by a margin of 94 percent to 5 percent. While we do not have national exit poll data on Senate voting preferences, exit polls showed similar rates of party loyalty in most of the key races. In Michigan, for example, Democratic identifiers chose the Democratic incumbent, Gary Peters, over his Republican challenger, John James, by a margin of 95 percent to 3 percent while Republican identifiers chose James over Peters by a margin of 93 percent to 6 percent. In another hotly contested race in North Carolina, Republican identifiers favored the Republican incumbent, Thom Tillis, over his Democratic challenger, Cal Cunningham, by a margin of 94 percent to 4 percent while Democratic identifiers favored Cunningham over Tillis by a margin of 94 percent to 3 percent. Finally, in the two crucial January runoff elections in Georgia, 96 and 97 percent of Democrats voted for Democratic challengers Jon Ossoff and Raphael Warnock, respectively, while 94 and 95 percent of Republicans voted for Republican incumbents David Perdue and Kelly Loeffler, respectively.

In all of these races, as in the presidential contest, there were very few votes for third party candidates. Combined votes for third party candidates fell from 6 percent in the 2016 presidential election to less than 2 percent in 2020. Likewise, third party votes fell from 2.9 percent of the total House vote in 2016 to 1.4 percent in 2020, and there were few significant third party candidates in the Senate elections. Negative partisanship is, once again, the likely explanation. It appears that, even when they had reservations about their own party's nominee, partisans were more reluctant than usual to cast a protest vote for a third party candidate for fear of helping to elect a candidate from the despised opposing party.

Given these extraordinarily high rates of party loyalty, it is not surprising that straight-ticket voting also reached record levels in 2020. According to the national exit poll, 96 percent of Biden voters chose a Democratic candidate for the House of Representatives, while 96 percent of Trump voters chose a Republican candidate. The estimated 4 percent rate of ticket splitting in the national exit poll was identical to that among likely voters in both Senate and House elections according to a Pew survey conducted about a month before Election Day.[20]

These extremely low rates of ticket splitting represent a dramatic change from the behavior of American voters from the 1970s through the 1990s. In that earlier era of candidate-centered elections, it was common to find a quarter to a third or more of voters splitting their tickets between presidential and congressional elections, especially in contests involving House or Senate incumbents. Many incumbents benefited from their ability to add a large "personal vote" to their party's normal base of support. In today's era of polarization and negative partisanship, that is no longer possible. The advantage that incumbents gain from this personal vote is far smaller today than 20 or 30 years ago.[21]

The current era of party competition is characterized by a relatively close balance in strength between the two major parties across the nation—one-party domination of many states and congressional districts, and a high degree of continuity in election results over time. In recent years, swings in the popular vote at the national level have been far smaller than they were in earlier decades due to the strength and stability of party loyalties. Thus, between 2012 and 2020 the Democratic margin in the national popular vote ranged from just over 2 points in 2016 to just under 4.5 points in 2020. The maximum difference in margin between any two elections during this period was only 2.4 points. In contrast, between 1964 and 1972, the Democratic margin in the national popular vote ranged from 22.6 points in 1964 to -23.1 points in 1972. The maximum difference in margin between any two elections during this period was 45.7 points.

The degree of continuity between the results of the 2016 and 2020 presidential elections was truly remarkable. This can be seen in figure 4.1, which displays a scatterplot of the relationship between Joe Biden's margin in the 2020 election and Hillary Clinton's margin in the 2016 election across all 50 states and the District of Columbia. The correlation between Biden's margin and Clinton's margin at the state level is a stunning .993. This means that Clinton's 2016 vote margin explains 99 percent of the variance in Biden's 2020 vote margin. While the degree of continuity between presidential election results in the states has been growing stronger for some time, this is the strongest relationship between the results of two consecutive presidential elections in the modern era. As the regression equation displayed inside the figure indicates, simply adding three points to Clinton's margin yields very accurate predictions of Biden's margin at the state level.

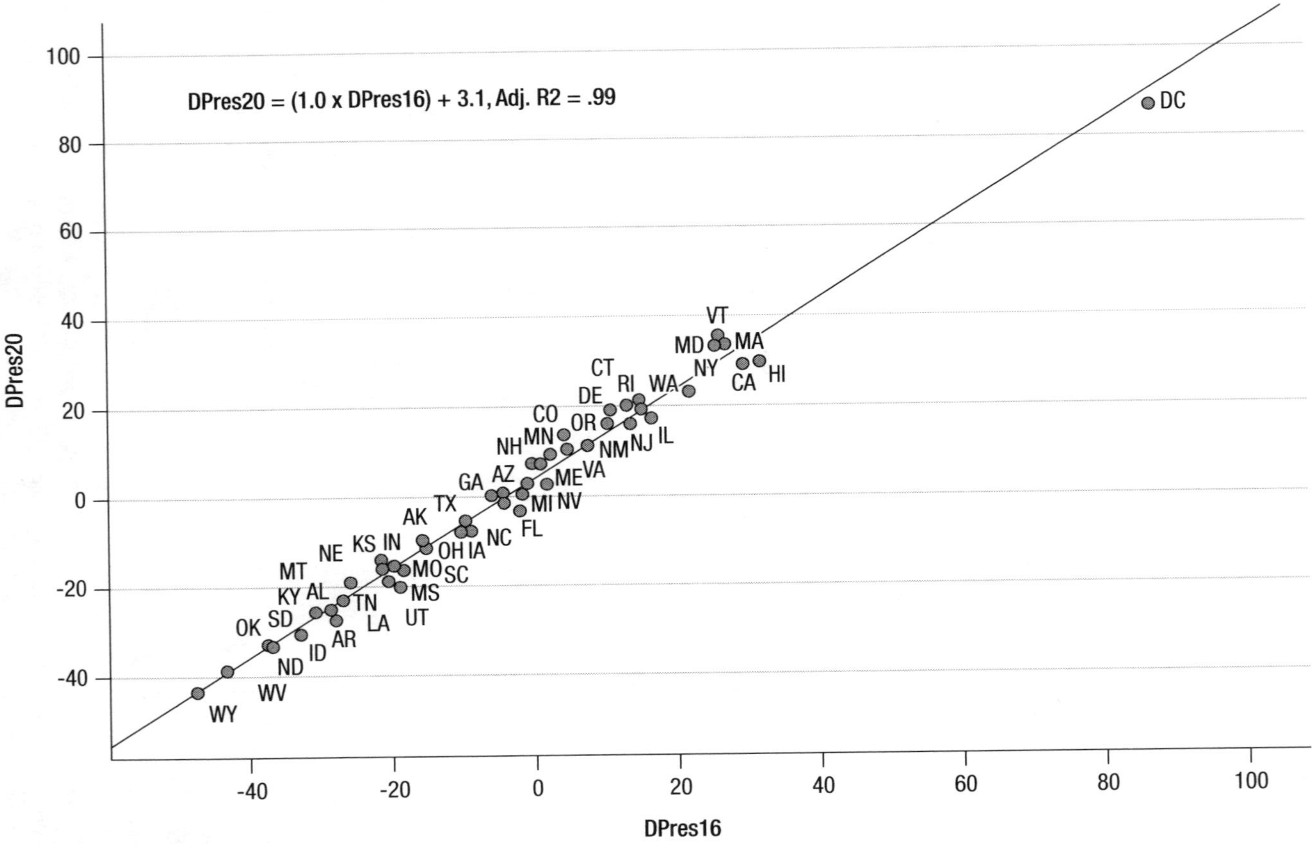

Figure 4.1. Scatterplot of 2020 Biden Margin by 2016 Clinton Margin in the States

The extraordinary degree of continuity between the results of these two elections reflects the durability and strength of partisanship in the Trump era. Another important indicator of the strength of partisan attachments in 2020 is the extraordinary degree of consistency between the results of the presidential election and the results of down-ballot contests, especially U.S. Senate and House contests. The correlation between Biden's margin versus Trump and the margin for Democratic Senate candidates versus their Republican opponents is a remarkable .953, while the correlation between Biden's margin and the margin for Democratic House candidates in 210 contested House races for which presidential results were available at the time of writing is an even stronger .983.

The extremely high levels of straight-ticket voting in 2020 resulted in extremely high levels of consistency between presidential and congressional outcomes. In the case of the Senate elections, the candidate of the winning presidential party won 32 of the 33 contests decided in November as well as both of the runoff elections in Georgia in January. Republicans won all 19 Senate races in states carried by Trump while Democrats won 15 of 16 Senate races in states carried by Biden. The only contest won by a candidate from the losing presidential party was in Maine, where Republican incumbent Susan Collins defied the odds and the polls to win a comfortable victory even as Joe Biden carried the state by nine percentage points.

As a result of record levels of party loyalty and straight-ticket voting, the 117th Congress will have almost no Democratic or Republican members representing constituencies that voted for the opposing party's presidential candidate. Less than 20 of 435 members of the House will represent districts carried by the opposing party's presidential candidate. Only 6 of 100 senators will represent states carried by the opposing party's presidential candidate in 2020.

This alignment of congressional and presidential election results constitutes a dramatic change from the situation for most of the post-World War II era. From the 1950s through the 1990s, a large proportion of members of the Senate and House represented constituencies that voted for the opposing party in presidential elections. Many Democratic members represented rural states and districts that regularly voted for Republican presidential candidates, and many Republican members represented urban states and districts that regularly voted for Democratic presidential candidates. These members had a strong incentive to work across party lines in order to attract support from voters who supported the opposing party in presidential elections. Due to the increasing nationalization of these races, however, those sorts of members have been disappearing from the House and Senate. Today, the vast majority of members represent states and districts that strongly support their own party. Even in the swing states and districts, there is little crossover voting in elections so members have less incentive to reach out to the opposing party, especially since doing so can increase the risk of facing a serious primary challenge. Our polarized Congress reflects our polarized electorate.

WHICH PARTY BENEFITED FROM RECORD TURNOUT?

The remarkable surge in turnout in the 2020 presidential election raises an important question: did this record turnout benefit Democratic or Republican candidates? According to the conventional wisdom about American elections, higher turnout should usually favor Democratic candidates because they receive a disproportionate share of their support from younger voters and racial and ethnic minorities who tend to turn out at lower rates than the older, predominantly white voters who support Republicans. In recent elections, however, Democrats have come to depend more on votes from college-educated whites who typically turn out at relatively high rates and Republicans have come to depend more on votes from whites without college degrees who are less reliable voters. As a result, the partisan consequences of higher turnout have become less clear.[22] The party that benefits from higher turnout now appears to depend on which type of low-propensity voter turns out—young people and minorities or less educated whites.

The data displayed in table 4.1 indicate that higher turnout helped Democratic candidates, at least in the 2020 election. These data show that Biden was much more likely to win states with relatively high turnout than those with relatively low turnout. He won 16 of 20 states with turnout of 70 percent or higher, but only four of 20 states with turnout below 65 percent. Moreover, as the data in table 4.1 shows, the swing in the Democratic presidential margin between 2016 and 2020 was considerably greater in states with relatively high

Table 4.1. Voter Turnout and Presidential Election Results in the States

Estimated Voter Turnout	*States Won by Biden*	*States Won by Trump*	*Average 2016–2020 Swing to Democrats*
50.0-59.9%	1	4	1.2
60.0-64.9%	3	9	2.2
65.0-69.9%	6	8	2.5
70.0-74.9%	9	4	4.1
75.0-80.0%	7	0	5.3
Total	26	25	3.1

Note: Includes all 50 states and the District of Columbia.
Source: Estimated turnout of eligible voters from United States Elections Project. Election results from www.uselectionatlas.org.

turnout than in states with relatively low turnout. The swing to Biden averaged only 1.2 points in low-turnout states vs. 5.3 points in high-turnout states. Controlling for Clinton margin in 2016, the partial correlation between turnout and Biden margin in 2020 is a strong .45, which is significant at the .001 level. This is a remarkably strong relationship considering that the correlation between Clinton margin and Biden margin is .99. Moreover, the relationship between turnout and Democratic success holds for Senate elections as well. Democrats won nine of 13 Senate contests in states with turnout of 70 percent or higher but only one of 12 contests in states with turnout below 65 percent.

Extraordinarily high turnout also appears to have helped Democrats win two crucial Senate runoff elections in Georgia in early January—victories that gave Democrats control of the upper chamber. More than 4.4 million voters turned out for these runoff elections, almost 90 percent of the turnout for the November general election and more than twice the number that voted in the 2008 Senate runoff election in Georgia. In fact, the estimated turnout of 60 percent of eligible voters was greater than the estimated turnout in the 2016 presidential election in Georgia. While turnout was extremely high across the state, it was higher in the most Democratic areas of the state than in the most Republican areas of the state.[23]

CONCLUSIONS AND IMPLICATIONS FOR THE POST-TRUMP ERA

Until January 6, 2021, it appeared that Donald Trump's grip on the Republican Party might extend well beyond the end of his presidency. He was clearly planning to remain a major player in national politics by using baseless challenges to the 2020 election to raise hundreds of millions of dollars to support his future political activities, raising the possibility of another presidential run in 2024 and generally positioning himself to become the leading critic of the incoming Biden administration.[24] Despite widespread condemnation of his behavior in spreading unsubstantiated claims of election fraud, he retained the loyalty of the large majority of Republican voters, most of whom continued to believe that he was the rightful winner of the 2020 election. Even in the aftermath of the violent attack on the U.S. Capitol that occurred on the day members of Congress were set to conduct the official count of the electoral vote and certify the results of the 2020 presidential election, many Republican voters continued to believe the lie that the election was stolen from Donald Trump. Despite this, however, there are reasons to believe that the violent attack on the U.S. Capitol by a mob of Trump supporters may have altered the trajectory of American politics.

On January 6, 2021, thousands of Trump supporters, including some aligned with white supremacist and neo-Nazi organizations, marched on the Capitol and forced their way into the building. They did so with the active encouragement of the president, who had urged the gathered multitude to take action to overturn the results of the presidential election. Police resistance was minimal. The result was an insurrection that resulted in at least five deaths, dozens of serious injuries, and millions of dollars in property damage. Members of Congress, staffers, and the vice president were forced to shelter in place for hours until police reinforcements arrived and were able to clear the building.[25]

The riotous mob failed in its goal of stopping the count. Many of the rioters were subsequently arrested after returning home, identified from videos captured on numerous cameras inside the Capitol building. Others were fired by their employers. Yet the threat of further attacks in Washington and in state capitols around the country remains very real. Democrats and some Republicans in Congress demanded that the president resign or face removal from office by way of the 25th Amendment to the U.S. Constitution or impeachment. Twitter permanently suspended his account, thereby removing his most important means of communicating with millions of his followers.

With only a few days left in his term, it remained unclear what action might actually be taken before the new president was sworn in on January 20. What was clear, however, was that Donald Trump's chances of continuing to play an active role in American politics beyond the end of his term were far dimmer than they had been prior to the events of January 6. At the same time, the chances that Trump would face serious criminal charges after leaving office were clearly far greater than they had been prior to January 6.

Regardless of what happens to Trump himself, the deep divisions that were evident before and after the 2020 election are unlikely to fade away anytime soon. American society is continuing to change in ways that appear threatening to millions of the older, less educated, more religious white citizens who are concentrated in small towns and rural parts of the country. Donald Trump's presidency and his 2016 and 2020 campaigns demonstrated that a message of reactionary conservatism—one emphasizing the dangers of rising immigration, increasing racial and ethnic diversity, and cultural secularization—retains a powerful appeal to a significant segment of the American electorate in the twenty-first century.[26] Even though that Trump base comprises a minority of the electorate, it might be large enough to win back the House of Representatives and the Senate for Republicans in the 2022 midterm election. It might even be large enough, given the uncertainties created by the Electoral College, to win back the presidency in 2024.

One thing that is certain about the next four years is that, despite his attempts to challenge and undermine the results of the 2020 election, Donald

Trump will no longer occupy the White House. That means that his ability to influence events will be greatly diminished. What happens in American politics between now and 2024 will depend far more on the next president than on the ex-president.

Joe Biden will begin his presidency with both important advantages and some extraordinary challenges. The challenges are obvious—a raging pandemic, a battered economy, and a deeply divided electorate including a majority of Republican voters who do not view him as the legitimate winner of the election. He will also begin his presidency with a very narrow Democratic majority in the House of Representatives and a 50-50 Senate with Vice President Kamala Harris as the tie-breaker, giving Democrats control with not a single vote to spare.

Biden's most important advantage may be that he is not Donald Trump. Most Americans will undoubtedly welcome the contrast between the calm, serious, and empathetic Biden and his angry, self-absorbed, and erratic predecessor. This is already evident in strong public approval of the president-elect's handling of his transition. A December Gallup poll found that 65 percent of Americans approved of the way Joe Biden was handling the presidential transition. That compared with only 48 percent who approved of the way Donald Trump was handling his presidential transition in December 2016. Meanwhile, in the aftermath of his ongoing efforts to overturn the results of the presidential election, and even before the assault on the U.S. Capitol by his supporters, Trump's job approval rating as president fell to 39 percent in that December Gallup poll, one of his lowest ratings in his final year in office.

Despite significant ideological divisions, there is broad agreement among Democrats in the House and Senate on a set of ambitious policies that were proposed by Joe Biden during the campaign to address the coronavirus pandemic, climate change, racial injustice, and the economic downturn. The narrowness of the Democratic majorities in the House and Senate may help party leaders keep a lid on policy disagreements between progressives on the left and centrists on the right.

Heading toward 2022, the Senate map offers Democrats some pickup opportunities with 20 of 34 seats at stake held by Republicans, including two seats in states won by Biden in 2020: Pennsylvania and Wisconsin. None of the Democratic seats at stake are in a state won by Trump, although Democrats will have to defend the two senators in narrow Biden states who won special elections in the 2020 cycle: Mark Kelly in Arizona and Raphael Warnock in Georgia. In the House, holding onto a Democratic majority in a midterm election will be difficult. Democrats have very few seats to spare. However, the fact that very few Democratic seats are currently in districts won by Trump could help Democrats, depending on how redistricting during 2021 and 2022 affects the partisan makeup of current Democratic seats.

The most important influence on the outlook for the 2022 and 2024 elections will almost certainly be how the U.S. economy responds to the distribution of vaccines against the coronavirus pandemic in 2021. If mass vaccinations proceed smoothly and the U.S. population achieves something approaching herd immunity, many economic forecasters are projecting a rapid economic recovery during the second half of 2021 and 2022.[27] While perceptions of economic conditions are now heavily influenced by partisanship, a strong economy should help Democrats in both 2022 and 2024. On the other hand, if the vaccines do not prove as effective against the virus as expected and/or the proportion of Americans who get vaccinated is too small to provide herd immunity, economic recovery could be delayed or aborted. That could help Republicans make gains in the 2022 midterm election and, potentially, win back the White House in 2024 despite the failed presidency of Donald Trump and the horrific events of January 6, 2021.

NOTES

1. Seth McLaughlin, "Trump Urges Voters to Oust GOP Governors Kemp, Ducey," *Washington Times*, December 12, 2020, https://www.washingtontimes.com/news/2020/dec/12/trump-urges-voters-oust-gop-governors-kemp-and-duc/.

2. Maggie Haberman, "Trump Told Crowd 'You Will Never Take Back Our Country with Weakness,'" *New York Times*, January 6, 2021, https://www.nytimes.com/2021/01/06/us/politics/trump-speech-capitol.html.

3. Emily Badger, "Most Republicans Say They Doubt the Election. How Many Really Mean It?" *New York Times*, November 30, 2020, https://www.nytimes.com/2020/11/30/upshot/republican-voters-election-doubts.html.

4. See Alan I. Abramowitz, T*he Great Alignment: Race, Party Transformation and the Rise of Donald Trump* (New Haven: Yale University Press, 2018).

5. Jeffrey M. Jones, "Trump Third Year Sets New Standard for Party Polarization," Gallup, January 21, 2020, https://news.gallup.com/poll/283910/trump-third-year-sets-new-standard-party-polarization.aspx.

6. The findings on party differences on issues are from Pew Research Center, "In a Politically Polarized Era, Sharp Divides in Both Partisan Coalitions," December 17, 2019, https://www.pewresearch.org/politics/2019/12/17/in-a-politically-polarized-era-sharp-divides-in-both-partisan-coalitions/.

7. Alan I. Abramowitz, *The Disappearing Center: Engaged Citizens, Polarization and American Democracy* (New Haven: Yale University Press, 2010).

8. David Montgomery, "Will Alabama Take Jeff Sessions Back?" *Washington Post Magazine*, February 6, 2020, https://www.washingtonpost.com/magazine/2020/02/06/jeff-sessions-was-cast-out-by-trump-will-alabama-take-him-back/?arc404=true.

9. Mara Mordecai and Aidan Connaughton, "Public Opinion About Coronavirus is More Divided in U.S. Than in Other Advanced Economies," Pew Research Center, October 28, 2020, https://www.pewresearch.org/fact-tank/2020/10/28/public-opinion-about-coronavirus-is-more-politically-divided-in-u-s-than-in-other-advanced-economies/.

10. Mary Van Beusekom, "U.S. Leads 19 Nations in Covid-19, All-Cause Death Rates," University of Minnesota Center for Infectious Disease Research and Policy, October 12, 2020, https://www.cidrap.umn.edu/news-perspective/2020/10/us-leads-19-nations-covid-19-all-cause-death-rates.

11. Joshua Clinton, Jon Cohen, John Lapinski, and Marc Trussler, "Partisan Pandemic: How Partisanship and Public Health Concerns Affect Individuals' Social Mobility During Covid-19," *Science Advances*, December 11, 2020, https://advances.sciencemag.org/content/7/2/eabd7204.

12. Pew Research Center, "Partisan Antipathy: More Intense, More Personal," Pew Research Center, October 10, 2019: https://www.pewresearch.org/politics/2019/10/10/partisan-antipathy-more-intense-more-personal/.

13. Michael Dimock and Richard Wike, "America is Exceptional in the Nature of Its Political Divide," Pew Research Center, November 13, 2020, https://www.pewresearch.org/fact-tank/2020/11/13/america-is-exceptional-in-the-nature-of-its-political-divide/.

14. Mark Jurkowitz, Amy Mitchell, Elisa Shearer, and Mason Walker, "U.S. Media Polarization and the 2020 Election: A Nation Divided," Pew Research Center, January 24, 2020: https://www.pewresearch.org/pj_19-11-19_mediapolarization_homepage-2/.

15. Damon Centola, "Why Social Media Makes Us More Polarized and How to Fix It," *Scientific American*, October 15, 2020, https://www.scientificamerican.com/article/why-social-media-makes-us-more-polarized-and-how-to-fix-it/.

16. See Jennifer McCoy, Tahmina Rahman, and Murat Somer, "Polarization and the Global Crisis of Democracy: Common Patterns, Dynamics, and Pernicious Consequences for Democratic Polities," *American Behavioral Scientist*, March 20, 2018, https://journals.sagepub.com/doi/10.1177/0002764218759576.

17. Data on voter turnout are from Michael McDonald's United States Elections Project website: http://www.electproject.org/2020g.

18. Tommy Beer, "Record Turnout: More Georgians Voted in Senate Runoffs than 2016 Presidential Election," *Forbes*, January 6, 2021, https://www.forbes.com/sites/tommybeer/2021/01/06/record-turnout-more-georgians-voted-in-senate-runoffs-than-2016-presidential-election/?sh=7b8f8c295853.

19. See Alan I. Abramowitz and Steven Webster, "The Rise of Negative Partisanship and the Nationalization of U.S. Elections in the 21st Century," *Electoral Studies* 41 (2016), 12-22.

20. Pew Research Center, "Large Shares of Voters Plan to Vote a Straight Party Ticket for President, Senate and House," Pew Research Center, October 21, 2020, https://www.pewresearch.org/politics/2020/10/21/large-shares-of-voters-plan-to-vote-a-straight-party-ticket-for-president-senate-and-house/.

21. Gary C. Jacobson, "It's Nothing Personal: The Declining Advantage of Incumbency in U.S. House Elections," *Journal of Politics* 77 (2015), 861-873.

22. See Dhrumil Mehta, " Increased Voter Turnout Could Benefit Republicans or Democrats in 2020," *FiveThirtyEight*, February 21, 2020, https://fivethirtyeight.com/features/increased-voter-turnout-could-benefit-republicans-or-democrats-in-2020/.

23. Nathaniel Rakich, Geoffrey Skelley, Laura Bronner, and Julia Wolfe, "How Democrats Won the Georgia Runoffs," *FiveThirtyEight*, January 7, 2021, https://fivethirtyeight.com/features/how-democrats-won-the-georgia-runoffs/.

24. Josh Dawsey and Michelle Ye Hee Lee, "Trump Raises More Than $170 Million Appealing on False Election Claims," *Washington Post*, December 1, 2020, https://www.washingtonpost.com/politics/trump-raises-more-than-150-million-appealing-to-false-election-claims/2020/11/30/82e922e6-3347-11eb-afe6-e4dbee9689f8_story.html.

25. Julian Borger, "Insurrection Day: When White Supremacist Terror Came to the U.S. Capitol," *The Guardian*, January 9, 2021, https://www.theguardian.com/us-news/2021/jan/09/us-capitol-insurrection-white-supremacist-terror.

26. See Corey Robin, *The Reactionary Mind: Conservatism from Edmund Burke to Donald Trump*, 2nd edition (New York: Oxford University Press, 2017).

27. See for example, Paul Krugman, "Making the Most of the Coming Biden Boom: The Economic Outlook is Probably Brighter Than You Think," *New York Times*, November 19, 2020, https://www.nytimes.com/2020/11/19/opinion/joe-biden-economy.html.

5

A Political Road Trip across the Country

Presidential Trends in Some Swingy, and Not-So Swingy, States

J. Miles Coleman

Much of the focus before, during, and after every presidential election typically falls on an often-recurring cast of swing states. For analysts breaking down 2016's results, it was hard not to mention the states of Michigan, Pennsylvania, and Wisconsin in the same breath. After all, the presidency is won in the Electoral College, and Donald Trump owed his win to razor-close margins in that Rust Belt trio. In 2020, Arizona, Georgia, Pennsylvania, and Wisconsin were, electorally, Joe Biden's Fantastic Four—Biden took less than 50 percent of the vote in each, but his narrow pluralities enabled him to reach, and surpass, 270 electoral votes.

While national political trends play a part in dictating outcomes in swing states, they also materialize in noncompetitive states, too. In other words, just because the margin of a certain state isn't within a few percentage points doesn't mean its results can't be informative. With that in mind, we'll be taking something of a political road trip—while our itinerary includes a few states that were hotly contested, we'll also be driving through several states that are either receding battlegrounds or weren't on either campaign's radar at all. Do blue areas of red states matter? What about the other way around? What pushes some states out of contention? How come this state is always close but stays with the same party? On our trip, we'll be exploring these questions.

THE FIRST DUAL SPLIT-DECISION: MAINE AND NEBRASKA

The 2020 presidential election was unprecedented many ways. Most plainly, it featured a matchup between the two oldest major party nominees in history, and it was held during a pandemic. In terms of electoral math, while 48 states and the District of Columbia award electors on a winner-take-all basis, Maine and Nebraska allocate theirs by congressional district. This election represented the first time that both Maine and Nebraska split their electoral votes simultaneously, and the trends in both states reflected broader voting patterns nationally.

We'll start our road trip in Nebraska, which has been allocating its electoral votes by congressional district since 1992.[1] It has three districts, each carrying one electoral vote, while the statewide winner gets the last two. Though the Cornhusker State is safely Republican, then-candidate Barack Obama carried the Omaha-based Second District in 2008. Roughly 80 percent of its votes come from Omaha's Douglas County, and part of Republican-leaning Sarpy County makes up the rest. While a return of what political analysts Chuck Todd and Sheldon Gawiser dubbed "Obama-ha" eluded Democrats for a few cycles, it showed up again in 2020. Across the board, college-educated whites swung to Biden—this drove the shift in the Omaha area.[2] According to the U.S. Census Bureau's "My Congressional District" tool, 42 percent of the Second District's residents over 25 years old hold a bachelor's degree or higher, putting it on par with Massachusetts, the most educated state in the country (going forward, unless otherwise noted, all demographic information, such as education, economic, and racial data, is from the U.S. Census Bureau).

While no one expected Nebraska's Second District to vote as blue as the Bay State does, it made sense that the Omaha region would move more Democratic given its demographics. This is something we will see frequently in this chapter: comparable demographic groups across geographically disparate states are voting more similarly. Put more concretely, residents in Omaha's wealthier neighborhoods probably have more in common with suburbanites in the Boston metro area than they do with ranchers in Nebraska's High Plains—and this informs voting patterns. In another example of this convergence, House Democrats fared worse than expected in suburban districts around the country. Despite several promising suburban pickup opportunities, they didn't defeat a single incumbent Republican. Nebraska's Second was no exception: despite Biden's clear margin, Republican Representative Don Bacon secured a third term.[3]

Maine, with its two congressional districts, began splitting its electoral votes in 1972. That year, its districts mirrored each other perfectly, as President Nixon carried both—their lines have hardly changed in the decades since then—by 23 percentage points, according to Dave Leip's Atlas of U.S. Presidential elections (unless otherwise noted, this is the primary source for this chapter's electoral data). By 2000, some divergence between the districts was taking hold: as Al Gore won the state by five percentage points, he won the

First District by eight points but came within two points of losing the Second District. Why the drift apart? The contrasting socioeconomic pictures provide clues. The First District takes in the liberal city of Portland, the state capital of Augusta, and the coastal town of Kennebunkport, where the Bush family's summer estate is located. The Second District includes the rugged northern part of the state that is home to a declining logging industry; given the area's economic situation, the forests of northern Maine provide fertile ground for populist candidates—in the 1990s, Reform Party candidate Ross Perot ran especially well there.

After President Obama carried Maine easily twice, Trump held Hillary Clinton to a narrow 48 percent to 45 percent margin in the state in 2016. That year, Maine split its electoral votes, for the first time. Trump carried the Second District by 37,079 votes, but Clinton's 56,852-vote edge out of the First District was enough to carry three of the state's electoral votes. For 2020, the Trumpian tendencies of the Second District meant that it stayed red. Biden won the state 53 percent to 44 percent, but he still only carried three of its four electoral votes because he improved in the wrong places. In the already-blue First, he posted a nearly 10 percentage point gain on Clinton's result. But his improvement in the Second was relatively meager: Biden only clawed back three percentage points, losing it by 7.4 percent instead of 10.5 percent.

If Nebraska's Second District highlighted Democrats' underperformance in the House, Maine's Second District hurt their prospects in the Senate. Down the ballot, Maine saw its most competitive senatorial race in decades. In one of the biggest surprises of the night, Republican Senator Susan Collins held on against Democratic state House Speaker Sara Gideon—Collins even claimed a 51 percent majority statewide. Collins was competitive in the First District, coming within five percentage points of Gideon there, but the senator also carried the Second District by a Nixonian 23 percentage point spread.

NEW ENGLAND: A BANNER REGION FOR BIDEN

Though Biden didn't carry all of Maine's electoral votes statewide, he still performed six percentage points better than Clinton. In fact, throughout New England, Biden's performance was much closer to Obama's than to Clinton's—after Trump made some inroads there in 2016, this represented a notable snap back to Democrats.

Let's go one state west of Maine. Summed up in its "Live Free or Die" motto, New Hampshire has an independent streak. This has shown up in its voting patterns, as it's the most recent New England state to have voted Republican: in 2000, George W. Bush took a 48 percent plurality there, and 16 years later, Trump nearly carried it. In 2020, Biden improved over Clinton in all 10 of the Granite State's counties—his 53 percent to 45 percent margin there topped Obama's 2012 showing. Perhaps not surprisingly, Biden's largest improvements over Clinton came in Rockingham and Hillsborough counties, which both sit along the Massachusetts border and skew wealthier and more educated. It was somewhat ironic that Biden ended up performing so well in the Granite State, considering how his year started out—in its famous "First in the Nation" primary, back in February 2020, he finished a poor fifth place.

Though there was no question that Vermont's three electoral votes would end up on the Democratic side, one notable trend was the lack of write-in votes in 2020, especially compared to 2016. Though Clinton carried the state with 57 percent to Trump's 30 percent in 2016, nearly 6 percent of Vermont voters, some 18,000 in all, wrote in the state's most famous politician, Senator Bernie Sanders.[4] Sanders gave Clinton spirited competition in the primary, but still lost the nomination decisively. The senator ran in the 2020 presidential primary but fared worse in his home state: the 86 percent vote share there he took in 2016 was down to a bare majority in 2020. In a more two-party election, Biden carried the Green Mountain State with 66 percent of the vote, a result that basically matched what Obama took there twice. Unlike Obama, though, Biden didn't sweep all the state's counties: in the northeastern part of the state, rural Essex County flipped to Trump in 2016, and stayed red. Representative Peter Welch was the only statewide Democrat to carry Essex County, and by a narrow 47 percent plurality—so even in safely blue states, some areas are growing more resistant to the Democratic Party.

Still, in other New England states, Biden bounced back to some degree in rural areas compared to Clinton. In 2016, Trump became the first Republican presidential nominee since George H. W. Bush to carry a majority of towns in Connecticut, taking 88 of 169. But Biden gained almost everywhere in the Nutmeg State, and 2020 seemed like a return to form: he carried 115 of its towns, or two-thirds of them (see map 5.1). There were no Clinton-to-Trump towns.

In the southwestern corner of the state, Connecticut's Fourth District contains mostly Clinton-to-Biden towns. Due to its proximity to New York City, the district has attracted many wealthy residents who work in the financial services industry—a fact that has earned the area the nickname as Connecticut's "Gold Coast." The Fourth is now the state's most Democratic district because some of its affluent towns have seen some truly seismic shifts in the Trump era: the only two towns in the district that gave Mitt Romney over 60 percent in 2012, Darien and New Canaan, gave Biden 61 percent and 59 percent, respectively. At the congressional level, Representative Jim Himes,

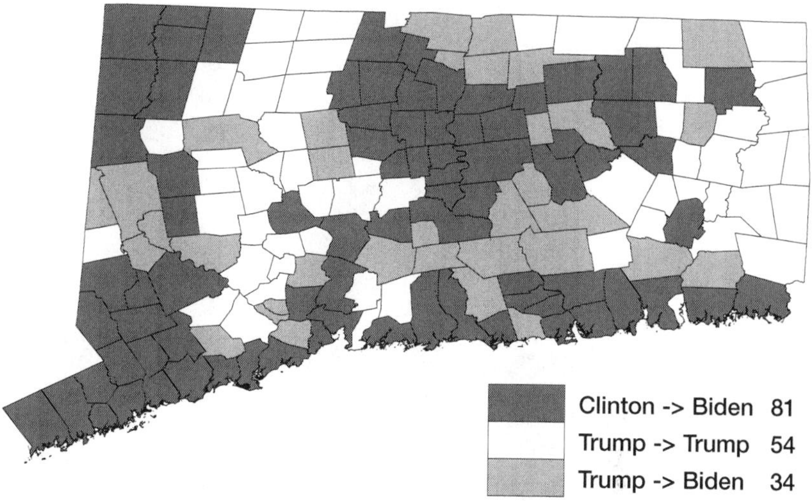

Map 5.1. Town Loyalty in Connecticut, 2016 vs. 2020

who was first elected in 2008, carried both towns in 2020 for the first time in his career.

Biden improved on Clinton's standing in upscale areas of Massachusetts and Rhode Island. In northeastern Massachusetts, Boxford, one of the state's wealthiest towns, was solidly Republican—until the Trump era. Boxford was one of only three towns to vote against the late Senator Ted Kennedy when he was last on the ballot, in 2006. Two years later, it was the sole town that then-Senator John Kerry lost. Though it wouldn't support those two Democratic senatorial powerhouses, Clinton carried Boxford with a 48 percent plurality, and Biden expanded that to a 56 percent majority. Rhode Island's only Romney-to-Clinton town, East Greenwich, is one of the state's top three wealthiest towns. Biden cleared 60 percent of the vote in East Greenwich, up from Clinton's 52 percent.

During the 2020 campaign, the importance of the Hispanic vote was often discussed in the context of contested states in the Sun Belt (more on that later). But again, just because a state is considered safe for either party doesn't mean that prevailing trends don't apply to it. Broadly, Biden lost ground with Hispanics—not coincidentally, in both Massachusetts and Rhode Island, the municipalities that swung most toward Trump are majority Hispanic.[6] Lawrence, Massachusetts, which isn't far from Boxford, is home to large Dominican and Puerto Rican populations. Though Biden still carried Lawrence comfortably, his 73 percent share was down from Clinton's 82

Table 5.1. 2016 to 2020 Change in the 12 Least Religious States

State	*% "Highly Religious"*	*2016 D - R Margin*	*2020 D - R Margin*	*D - R Change*
New Hampshire	33%	0.4%	7.4%	7.0%
Massachusetts	33%	27.2%	33.5%	6.3%
Vermont	34%	26.4%	35.4%	9.0%
Maine	34%	3.0%	9.1%	6.1%
Connecticut	43%	13.6%	20.0%	6.4%
Wisconsin	45%	-0.8%	0.6%	1.4%
Washington	45%	15.7%	19.2%	3.5%
Alaska	45%	−14.7%	−10.1%	4.7%
New York	46%	22.5%	23.1%	0.6%
Hawaii	47%	32.2%	29.5%	−2.7%
Colorado	47%	4.9%	13.5%	8.6%
Oregon	48%	11.0%	16.1%	5.1%

Source: "2014 Religious Landscape Survey," Pew Research Center, https://www.pewresearch.org/fact-tank/2016/02/29/how-religious-is-your-state/?state=alabama.

percent. Biden saw an almost identical drop in Rhode Island's Central Falls, an old mill town which is now two-thirds Hispanic.

One final note on New England: Biden's strength in the region speaks to his gains with secular whites across the country. Table 5.1 considers the top dozen least religious states, according to Pew Research's 2014 Religious Landscape Survey. In nine of the 12, Biden improved by a margin greater than his national 2.4 percentage point gain over Clinton. Aside from the northeast, the Pacific Northwest also stands out.

The five least religious states are all located in New England, and Biden saw mid-single digit gains in each. The sixth New England state, absent from the list, is Rhode Island. As the nation's most Catholic state, it was, appropriately, John F. Kennedy's best state in 1960—Biden, as the second Catholic president, still saw a healthy five percentage point bump over Clinton in the Ocean State.[7]

MOVING BLUE: VIRGINIA AND MINNESOTA

When Barack Obama carried the Center for Politics' home state, in 2008, it marked the first time since 1964 that the Old Dominion voted Democratic in a presidential election. For Obama's elections, Virginia roughly matched the national vote. In 2016, with a Virginian, Senator Tim Kaine, as her running mate, Clinton won the state by just over five percentage points. Four years later, Biden expanded that advantage to slightly over 10 percentage points, becoming the first postwar Democrat to win the state by double-digits. Powered by his strength with college-educated voters, Biden flipped several populous localities. Along the state's "Urban Crescent," he claimed Stafford County, Chesterfield County, James City County, and the city of Virginia Beach—but his gains weren't limited to urban areas.[8] Biden became the first Democratic nominee since Harry Truman to carry the city of Lynchburg, situated east of the Blue Ridge Mountains. The city houses the evangelical Liberty University, which made Lynchburg's result a somewhat symbolic blow to Trump, as religious conservatives were the foundation of his national coalition.

Two of Virginia's Trump-to-Biden localities have an especially high concentration of active-duty military personnel, veterans, and defense contractors: Stafford County sits just south of Marine Corps Base Quantico, while the Virginia Beach area is home to dozens of federal facilities and defense installations. Biden's strength with the military vote in Virginia seemed symptomatic of a larger national story. Colorado saw an acute blue shift in 2020, which was partially from Colorado Springs' El Paso County. South of the Denver metro area, El Paso County is home to two Air Force bases and is among the most populous Republican-leaning counties in the country—Biden still lost it, but he cut Trump's percentage margin in half, from 22 points to 11. Sarpy County, which makes up part of Nebraska's pivotal Second District, saw an almost identical shift. Home to Offutt Air Force Base, Sarpy was the only county in Nebraska where Trump performed more than 10 percentage points worse than 2016.

Back in Virginia, Democratic Senator Mark Warner's recent electoral career has had the trajectory of a roller coaster, but it's run on a path increasingly calibrated by national patterns: initially elected to the Senate by a roughly two-to-one margin in 2008, he was nearly defeated in 2014. In 2020, Virginians returned Warner to the Senate with 56 percent of the vote—a comfortable margin, if one that tracked closely to the presidential result. When Warner first successfully ran for statewide office in Virginia, in the 2001 gubernatorial race, he found uncommon support in Appalachia. As state politics has become more nationalized, Warner has steadily become more of a generic Democrat. In 2014, he carried rural Alleghany County by nine percentage points—by then, it was the only county along the West Virginia border that he won, and no Democrats since then have carried it. While Warner lost Alleghany County in 2020 by nearly 30 percentage points, he flipped another county along the West Virginia border: Loudoun. With an exploding population in Northern Virginia, this suburban county has been ground zero for Democratic gains in the state. In low-turnout 2014, Warner lost the county by 458 votes out of 92,698 cast. Six years later, with more than double the turnout, he won it by 24 percentage points. These types of trades—Loudoun County for Alleghany County—are why Republicans have struggled to win statewide office for the past decade.

In Minnesota, the parties have made a similar trade that works out in favor of Democrats. Minnesota has voted for every Democratic presidential nominee since 1976, the longest streak of any state in the nation, though one that's partially attributable to the presence of native son Walter Mondale on the 1984 ticket. Perhaps intrigued by the idea of potentially breaking that streak, Trump made several visits to the state in 2020. Immediately after 2016, there were some signs that Minnesota's Democratic loyalty was ebbing. To wit, Hillary Clinton's 1.5 percentage point margin there was less than her 2 percentage point popular vote edge, making 2016 the first time since 1952 that the state voted right of the nation.

The focal point of the Trump campaign's efforts in the state seemed to be in the northeastern part of the state. Known as the Iron Range, the area is north of Duluth, a port city on Lake Superior, and is home to rich deposits of iron ore.[9] With a vibrant labor presence, the area had been firmly in the Democratic camp since the advent of Franklin Roosevelt's New Deal. But the national Democratic Party's shift toward environmentalism, and its perceived hostility to mining that went with that, has helped push the region rightward. The Iron Range sits in the state's Eighth District. In the anti-Obama 2010 midterm, its voters ousted the late Representative Jim Oberstar, a Watergate Baby who still holds the record as the longest-serving congressman in the state's history. While it was a shock to political observers at the time, Oberstar's loss was something of a canary in the iron mine. When Obama was on the ballot, Minnesota's Eighth voted close to the statewide result, but Trump carried it by 15 percentage points in 2016, and it stayed about the same in 2020.

Still, there's evidence that the Trump campaign's emphasis on the Iron Range yielded only minor returns. Let's consider the most populous county in the Eighth District, St. Louis. Since 2000, the city of Duluth has cast just over four in 10 of the county's votes, while the rest of the county—where iron is mined —makes up the balance. As table 5.2 shows, Biden actually gained 10 percentage points in Duluth over Clinton, and his margins were actually better than Obama's. While Trump still carried the remainder of the county by 1.6 percent, that was just a slight uptick from his 2016 showing.

Though Biden couldn't match Obama's margins in St. Louis County, we don't need to travel far to see signs of his strength. In Cook County, which occupies the northeastern tip of the state, Biden added 12 percentage points to Clinton's 2016 margin, winning it by 34 points instead of 22, which represented his greatest county-level improvement in the state. With a prime location on

Table 5.2. St. Louis County, MN, Breakdown

	Duluth			Rest of County			St. Louis County, MN		
Year	DEM	GOP	D - R	DEM	GOP	D - R	DEM	GOP	D - R
2000	60.8%	31.3%	**29.5%**	59.0%	34.2%	**24.9%**	59.8%	33.0%	**26.8%**
2004	67.3%	31.5%	**35.8%**	63.6%	35.2%	**28.4%**	65.2%	33.5%	**31.7%**
2008	68.5%	29.4%	**39.2%**	62.4%	35.1%	**27.3%**	65.1%	32.6%	**32.5%**
2012	67.4%	29.7%	**37.7%**	60.5%	37.0%	**23.5%**	63.5%	33.9%	**29.6%**
2016	59.6%	30.5%	**29.1%**	45.2%	46.7%	**−1.5%**	51.4%	39.7%	**11.7%**
2020	68.4%	29.0%	**39.4%**	48.1%	49.8%	**−1.6%**	56.6%	41.0%	**15.6%**

Source: Dave Leip's Atlas of U.S. Presidential Elections
https://uselectionatlas.org/.

Lake Superior, Cook County contains several state parks and 80 percent of its economy is based on tourism.[10] Trump's poor handling of the COVID-19 pandemic, and the loss of tourism revenue associated with it, likely hurt his standing there. From an electoral perspective, this dynamic also opened doors for Biden in states that were more competitive. Specifically, Biden flipped Door County, Wisconsin—situated on a peninsula that sticks out into Lake Michigan, the county bills itself as the "Cape Cod of the Midwest." Across the lake, Biden made significant gains along Michigan's "Cherry Coast," in the northwestern part of the state (the area is named for its main agricultural product).[11] Each summer, Traverse City, known as the "Cherry Capital of the World," hosts the annual National Cherry Festival—this major tourist draw was canceled in 2020, as its organizers cited health concerns.[12]

Though Cook County fit neatly into a larger pattern that benefitted Democrats, it only cast a relative handful of votes. Much of Biden's improvement over Clinton in Minnesota was driven by his gains in the populous Twin Cities metro area. During the Democratic presidential primary season, Senator Amy Klobuchar, a veritable electoral titan in the state, pointed to her strong electoral track record in the state. Specifically, in her 2018 reelection bid, she cleared 60 percent overall and carried all eight of the state's congressional districts. But in Minnesota's largest county, Minneapolis' Hennepin, Biden came close to matching Klobuchar's share—he finished with just over 70 percent there, only marginally short of her 73 percent from 2018. While Minneapolis itself has become more Democratic over the last decade, Biden's gains in its higher-income suburbs padded his margin in Hennepin County. The Gopher State's Third District, which is largely based in those suburbs, would have, in its current form, given George H. W. Bush a 13 percentage point margin in the 1988 election—likely the late Republican's best district on the current map.[13] A little more than three decades later, the Third District is now a comfortably Democratic constituency (see map 5.2).

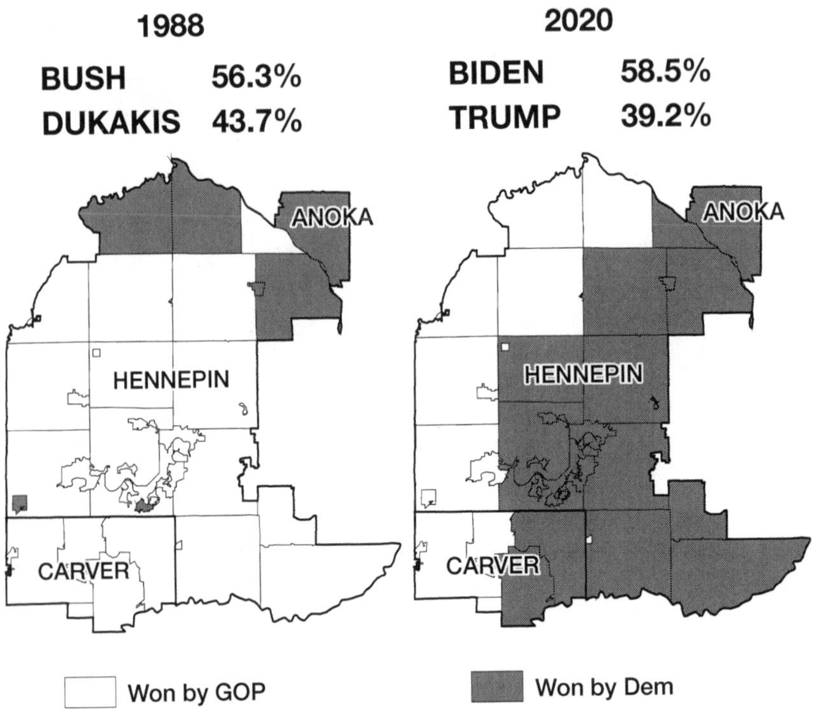

Map 5.2. Minnesota's Third Congressional District, 1988 vs. 2020

Biden's nearly 326,650 raw vote margin in Hennepin County was greater than his 233,012 statewide edge over Trump. In 2016, the county also provided Clinton the votes for her much narrower win. While Republicans have gained in the rural parts of Greater Minnesota, the firewall that Democrats have built in the Twin Cities metro acts a formidable barrier to the GOP's statewide prospects.

MOVING RED: IOWA AND OHIO

One state south of Minnesota, Iowa has drifted to the rightward edge of the presidential playing field. Of the states that supported Obama twice but flipped to Trump, Iowa saw the sharpest shift from 2012 to 2016, moving 15 percentage points more GOP between the years. Clinton carried just six of the state's 99 counties—her counties were either home to urban centers or major colleges. The 2020 election was very much a continuation of 2016 in the Hawkeye State, as Biden carried the same six counties, and Trump held the state with 53 percent to Biden's 45 percent.

Trump carried all four of Iowa's congressional districts, but Biden came closest in the Third District, which he lost by just 567 votes—nestled in the southwestern corner of the state, it contains the state capital of Des Moines and runs west to the Omaha suburbs. A county to watch here in the future is Dallas County, west of Des Moines' Polk County. The fastest-growing county in the state, Biden cut the 12 percentage point deficit that Obama sported there in 2012 to a slight loss. As its politics seem to be increasingly influenced by the growing Des Moines suburbs, Dallas County will almost certainly support the next Democratic nominee who wins Iowa. Still, the trends elsewhere in the state make such a Democratic victory seem like a dicey prospect.

While swapping blue-collar whites for college-educated suburbanites has helped Democrats secure states like Virginia and Minnesota, it simply hasn't been a beneficial trade for them in Iowa. When Obama carried the state twice, he ran best on the eastern half of the state, where farms and factories are ingrained in the landscape—he carried the Third District, the most suburban seat in the state, but by margins smaller than what he received statewide. The First District, which takes up the northeastern quadrant of the state, was always Obama's best district: it gave him 58 percent in 2008 and only a slightly smaller 56 percent in 2012. The First District is located in a geographic zone known as the Driftless Area (during the most recent ice age, its topography was untouched by glacial drift), which extends to southern Minnesota, western Wisconsin, and northwestern Illinois.[14] In the 2000 and 2004 presidential elections, the Driftless Area was a rare rural swath where Democratic nominees carried counties that were almost monolithically white. Obama swept most of the counties in the area, with 60 percent or more of the vote in many of them, and his numbers largely held in 2012. Enter Trump. In 2016, he limited Clinton to a few, relatively urban counties in the Driftless Area, and Iowa's First District was a great microcosm of the region. After Obama carried 17 of its 20 counties in 2012, Clinton was limited to the district's two most populous counties, Linn and Black Hawk. Despite its elasticity in recent presidential elections, the Driftless Area lived up to its name in 2020: electorally, it didn't drift much. As the 2000 edition of the *Almanac of American Politics* pointed out, Phil Alden Robinson's 1989 cinematic masterpiece *Field of Dreams* is set in Iowa's current First District; for decades, baseball fans and entrepreneurs have been paraphrasing, "*If you build it, they will come.*" But the lofty thinking summed up in this line doesn't fully represent the region's demographic picture. Outside of a few urban beachheads, eastern Iowa skews older, has lower levels of four-year college attainment, and is losing population—electorally, these are all ingredients for future reddening.

Ohio's trajectory in presidential races has tracked closely with Iowa's: It gave Obama majorities twice, flipped to Trump in 2016, then barely budged in 2020. Trump's 53 percent to 45 percent margin in Ohio was unchanged from his 51 percent to 43 percent spread in 2016, though unlike Iowa, the Buckeye State saw a few counties change hands. Lorain County, just west of Cleveland's Cuyahoga, was the closest county in the state in 2016, going to Clinton by 131 votes out of 140,562 cast. Trump flipped Lorain County by 3,853 votes in 2020. While Biden improved in the eastern part of the county, closer to Cleveland, Trump made double-digit gains in the precincts that make up the city of Lorain.[15] One potential explanation was the city is home to a major U.S. Steel Corporation plant—in May 2020, the plant announced it was laying off staff and idling production.[16] It's easy to see how Trump's protectionist rhetoric on trade may have resonated there. Lorain is also about a quarter Hispanic—given trends elsewhere, this may have also been a factor in Trump's improved showing in the city.

Trump was the first Republican nominee since Richard Nixon, in 1972, to carry Mahoning County, where Youngstown is located. This economically ailing area has been hit hard by deindustrialization. In some ways, Trump was a candidate reminiscent of the area's bombastic former representative, the late Jim Traficant. Though a Democrat, Traficant, who served from 1985 to 2002, was known as a fierce opponent of free trade and for his hawkish immigration stances—politically, it played well in the working-class area.[17] Still, Democrats' struggles in the Mahoning Valley seem to extend past Trump and will likely persist. In 2018, running a well-known candidate, Democrats lost state Senate District 33, which is made up of Mahoning County and its neighbor to the south, Columbiana—though Democratic U.S. Senator Sherrod Brown, known for his own populist tendencies, carried District 33 in his race, he couldn't match Obama's performance there six years earlier. More broadly, in the state House, Ohio Republicans gained four seats in 2020, all of which are located near the Youngtown metro area. Representative Tim Ryan, who started his career in Congress working for Traficant, holds the state's Thirteenth District, which runs from Youngstown to Akron. Ryan's district, which gave Obama 63 percent of the vote in 2012, lurched right of the national vote in 2020, while Ryan himself had the closest race of his career.[18]

The third Ohio county that changed hands between 2016 and 2020 was actually in Biden's favor—in the southwest, Biden flipped Dayton's Montgomery County. For Democrats, carrying Montgomery is a necessary, but not sufficient, ingredient to winning statewide. Though Dayton is the county's most populous city, the suburb of Centerville stood out. More than half (54 percent) of Centerville's residents over 25 years old have a bachelor's degree or higher, a figure nearly double Ohio's statewide 27 percent. Though Trump carried it, his margin was cut from 17 percentage points to 8.

North of the state capital Columbus, Biden was the best-performing Democratic presidential nominee in Delaware County in decades. While Trump held it by 6.8 percentage points, 2020 marked the first year since 1924 that Delaware County was less Republican than the statewide result. This rapidly growing county takes in many affluent neighborhoods and was the political base of former Republican Governor John Kasich during his decades in office. As a presidential candidate in 2016, Kasich tried to strike a postpartisan and compassionate tone—so naturally, he butted heads with his party's then-ascendant nominee. After years of criticizing Trump, he cut a video for the 2020 Democratic National Convention where he endorsed Biden. It's hard to know how many voters Kasich's endorsement moved, but it's probably safe to say his video served as something of a green light to moderate Republicans that Biden was an acceptable choice. By the same token, Kasich's endorsement may have been something of a double-edged sword, as he was never an especially popular figure in parts of Appalachian Ohio. In 2012, Obama lost Pike County, in Appalachia, by just one vote—Clinton lost it by 37 percent four years later, and Biden did 12 percentage points worse than that, his biggest drop in the state from 2016.

DEMOCRATIC DISAPPOINTMENTS: FLORIDA, NORTH CAROLINA, TEXAS

Though the region is increasingly being pushed to the forefront of the electoral playing field, it's clear that Democrats have a bit more work to do in the Sun Belt, at least in a critical trio of states. After making serious attempts at Florida's electoral votes and gubernatorial contests every two years, Democrats have frequently come up short there. In 2008, with a formidable ground game and sky-high Black enthusiasm, Obama became the first Democratic candidate since 1976 to carry North Carolina—in the three presidential elections since then, the state has remained tantalizingly out of reach for his party. Finally, though Democrats made substantial gains there in the 2018 midterms, Trump won Texas by a larger-than expected margin. All three of these states stayed in the GOP column, in part, because of Trump's gains with minority voters.

Early on election night, a promising sign for Trump was Miami-Dade County. Within 20 minutes of Florida's 7 p.m. poll closing time, the county posted its early and absentee vote totals, which made up the vast majority of its returns: Biden was only carrying the state's most populous county with 54 percent of the vote, down considerably from the 63 percent to 34 percent spread that Clinton beat Trump by four years earlier.[19] Miami-Dade's swing alone was enough to keep Florida red—indeed, Florida ended up being one of just six states were Trump improved his margin from 2016.

In 2016, Clinton benefited from Trump's unique unpopularity with Cuban voters, and Democrats since then have struggled to replicate her margin in the Miami area. In 2018, despite flipping four large, Trump-won counties, then-Senator Bill Nelson lost his seat to now-Senator Rick Scott—Nelson ran eight percentage points behind Clinton in Miami-Dade County. During the 2018 midterms, Republicans attacked the Democratic Party as sympathetic to socialism, and ratcheted up that messaging in 2020—this may have prompted Cubans, a bloc that remembers Fidel Castro's communist regime, to give Trump another look. While Biden's 617,864 vote total in Miami-Dade County was only a modest decline from Clinton's 624,146, Trump astonishingly found nearly 200,000 more voters his second time around, going from 333,999 in 2016 to 532,833 in 2020. One Clinton-to-Trump voter was now-Representative Carlos Gimenez, who ousted first-term Democrat Debbie Mucarsel-Powell in the Twenty-sixth District. Next door, the Twenty-seventh District swung 16 percentage points in Trump's direction—though Biden narrowly held the district, the regional riptide that Trump generated up the ballot helped Republicans take reelection away from then-Representative Donna Shalala.[20]

Biden's weakness with Hispanics in Florida wasn't limited to Miami's Cubans. Thinking back to 2018, in addition to mitigating Nelson's margin in the Miami area, Scott reached out to Puerto Ricans.[21] Precinct-level returns suggest that Scott's playbook may have been instructive to Sunshine State Republicans in 2020. In central Florida, Biden saw some slippage in Orlando's Orange County, though he still carried it easily. In many of the county's Hispanic-majority precincts—it's home to a large Puerto Rican community—Biden saw double-digit percentage drops compared to Clinton's 2016 showing.[22] As an aside, in Orange County, the precinct that includes Walt Disney World became more Democratic—so the pro-Biden trend in tourism-dependent areas that we saw in the Midwest seemed to show up in the Sun Belt, too. In fact, California also contains a racially diverse Orange County that houses a Disney theme park. In the city of Anaheim, Biden improved in Disneyland's precinct. It must be a small world, after all.

Though polling averages suggested that North Carolina was primed to flip back into the Democratic column, Biden fell just over one percentage point short. Some of the most pro-Trump shifts in the state were in the Sandhills region, a collection of southeastern counties near the South Carolina border. Though largely rural, several counties there have high minority populations. At the center of the region is Robeson County—home to the Lumbee Indian tribe, it's the state's only plurality-Native American county, by racial composition. Southeastern North Carolina is historically one of the most Democratic regions of the state, and the Lumbee were no exception. But Trump carried the Lumbee vote in 2016, and did even better with them in 2020. Fifteen precincts there are majority Native American by registration: They collectively supported Obama by 20 points in 2012 but gave Trump two-thirds of their vote in 2020.

Though the state of North Carolina recognizes the Lumbee, the federal government does not, so they don't have access to benefits and funding that other tribes across the nation do. Shortly before the election, Trump held a rally in nearby Fayetteville where he pledged federal recognition to the Lumbee—Biden promised the same thing, to be fair, though the word of the incumbent president seemed to matter more.[23] It's tempting to chalk up Trump's strength with the Lumbee solely to his support for tribal recognition, but that ignores some other factors. In May 2012, North Carolina voters passed Amendment 1, which is now moot, that effectively banned gay marriage in the state. In most Lumbee precincts, Amendment 1 received more than 90 percent support. In presidential years, North Carolinians elect a slate of 10 statewide officers, known as the Council of State (these are offices such as governor, attorney general, treasurer, etc.). Even as Trump carried Robeson County in 2016, most Democratic statewide candidates won it that year, too. In 2020, Robeson voters preferred Republicans for every state office, an indication that presidential patterns are solidifying down the ballot.

In rural North Carolina, the March 2020 presidential primary would serve as a leading indicator for the fall. In the Democratic primary, 1.6 percent of voters chose the "No Preference" option on the ballot, instead of supporting an actual candidate. With 15 candidates on the primary ballot, Democrats certainly didn't have a shortage of options, so could these voters just not make up their minds? It seems more likely that "No Preference" turned into a protest vote, as it polled best in the Sandhills and in the northeast—these areas are culturally conservative but have a lengthy history with the Democratic Party. In North Carolina's semi-closed primary system, registered Democrats who've grown disenchanted with the party can't vote in Republican primaries, so the result is often protest voting on the Democratic side. On map 5.3, almost all the counties where Trump improved in for the general election had a high protest vote in the Democratic primary. Robeson County, in the darkest shade of gray, takes this to the extreme: It gave "No Preference" its highest share of any county, and it was the only county where Trump added more than 10 percentage points to his 2016 margin.

North Carolina Democrats have undoubtedly made enormous strides in the state's metro areas: Biden cleared 60 percent of the vote in both the state's most populous counties, Raleigh's Wake and Charlotte's Mecklenburg—no

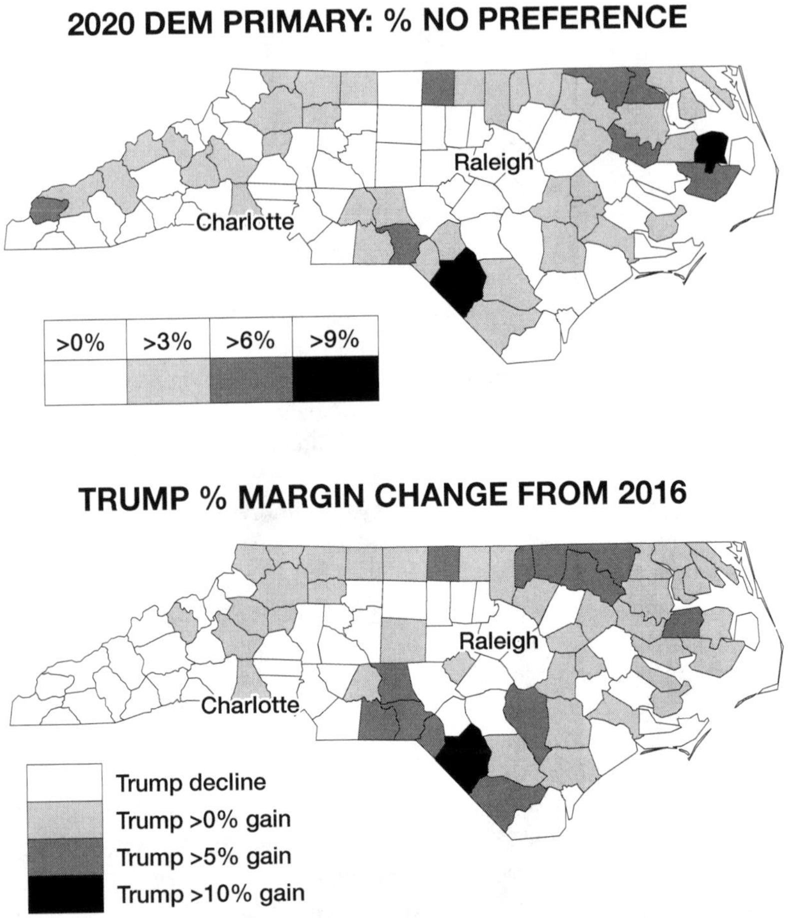

Map 5.3. North Carolina % No Preference in March 2020 Democratic Primary and Trump % Margin Change from 2016

other national Democrat has accomplished that in the postwar era. But losses in smaller counties across the state, like in the Sandhills, added up. As the state Democratic Party becomes more urban, it will also have to limit the bleeding in those rural areas.

Finally, a quick word on Texas. Overall, in terms of fundamental partisan coalitions, 2020 was not the type of realigning election that 2016 was. In other words, compared to 2016, where it was common to see counties across the country swing double-digits to one party or another, there were few seismic regional-level shifts in 2020. One exception was south Texas. Starr County, which is almost entirely Hispanic, saw the largest swing in the country: Biden held it 52 percent to 47 percent, but that was a 55 percentage point drop from the 79 percent to 19 percent margin Clinton posted in 2016. Next door, Trump became the first Republican since 1920 to carry the demographically similar Zapata County. In fact, across south Texas, Trump carried five counties that voted against Ronald Reagan in his 1980 and 1984 landslides: in addition to Zapata, he took Frio, Jim Wells, Kenedy, and La Salle counties.

Why such a drastic change? Republicans seemed to out-organize Democrats there. With the COVID-19 pandemic, Democrats halted door-to-door campaigning while the Republicans didn't—in an area where quality broadband is sometimes hard to come by, in-person campaigning seemed to matter.[24] The oil and gas industry is a major employer in the region, so as with the Iron Range in Minnesota, the Democratic Party's environmentalism likely took an electoral toll.[25] Both Starr and Zapata counties gave Democratic Representative Henry Cuellar, a popular figure in the area, large majorities, though he's sported more robust margins in his past contested elections (he was unopposed in 2018). If the inroads Trump made in the Rio Grande Valley hold, or deepen, in 2024, a blue Texas could be further off in the future than some think—even if Democrats continue to gain in the suburbs.

Donald Trump won the presidency in 2016 and beat expectations in 2020 because of his ability to turn out infrequent voters. Going forward, the political future of south Texas—and, the Sun Belt overall—may depend on if other Republican nominees will inspire that same type of turnout. In terms of raw votes, Starr County was similar to Miami-Dade, except on a smaller scale: while Biden's 9,123 vote total in the county was down slightly from Clinton's 9,289, Trump nearly quadrupled his tally from 2016, going from 2,224 to 8,247. Will those voters come out for other Republicans?

THE END OF THE ROAD—FOR NOW

Throughout this chapter, we've driven by about 20 states, linking groups of them together through common political trends. While our sampling is by no means exhaustive, it illustrates that, often, states have fascinating electoral movements churning under the hood. Sometimes these shifts aren't perceived as consequential: from the perspective of raw Electoral College math, Biden's gains with suburban and military voters pushed Virginia from blue to bluer, but he still won the same number of electoral votes from the state that Clinton and Obama did. But thinking longer term, 2020's results will likely inform the political parties' strategies. In Ohio, state Democrats have almost certainly noticed the blue movement in places like Delaware County, and will try to capitalize on that in future statewide races. By the same token, Texas Republicans, who have seen their once-safe state become more competitive as suburbanites have left the party, may find themselves trying to keep the state red by expanding on their recent gains with Hispanic voters—something few observers would have predicted when Trump became the face of the national party.

The example of Texas also shows that voting behavior among certain demographics or regions can be volatile and unpredictable. Looking to 2022, the political surprises we encounter then will probably shape our post-election travel itinerary.

NOTES

1. J. Miles Coleman, "The Electoral College: Maine and Nebraska's Crucial Battleground Votes," *Sabato's Crystal Ball*, January 9, 2020, https://centerforpolitics.org/crystalball/articles/the-electoral-college-maine-and-nebraskas-crucial-battleground-votes/

2. Jake Lahut, "The Demographic That Won Election: Higher-Earning College-Educated White People Near Major Cities," *Business Insider*, December 11, 2020, https://www.businessinsider.com/higher-earning-college-educated-white-voters-biden-election-2020-12.

3. Kyle Kondik and J. Miles Coleman, "Notes on the State of the 2020 Election," *Sabato's Crystal Ball*. November 12, 2020, https://centerforpolitics.org/crystalball/articles/notes-on-the-state-of-the-2020-election/.

4. April McCullum, "Bernie Sanders Wins 18,000 VT Votes," *Burlington Free Press*, November 16, 2016, https://www.burlingtonfreepress.com/story/news/politics/2016/11/15/bernie-sanders-wins-18000-vt-votes/93897044/.

5. Tweet from J. Miles Coleman, March 5, 2020, https://twitter.com/JMilesColeman/status/1235613339889197056?s=20.

6. Nicholas Riccardi and Adriana Gomez Licon, "Confounding Democrats, Trump Makes Inroads with Latinos," *Associated Press*, November 6, 2020, https://apnews.com/article/election-2020-joe-biden-donald-trump-race-and-ethnicity-virus-outbreak-27fe2a1e8dd84d2dadae893ceb824c39.

7. Ted Nesi, "RI Remains Most Catholic State in the Country," WPRI 12, September 6, 2017, https://www.wpri.com/news/eyewitness-news-investigates/ri-remains-most-catholic-state-in-the-country/.

8. Geoffrey Skelley, "The New Dominion: Virginia's Ever-Changing Electoral Map," *Sabato's Crystal Ball*, July 13, 2017, https://centerforpolitics.org/crystalball/articles/the-new-dominion-virginias-ever-changing-electoral-map/.

9. Katie Galioto, "Trump Claims Credit for Jobs, Touts Mining, Pipelines, at Rally In Duluth, Minnesota," *Star Tribune,* October 1, 2020, https://www.startribune.com/trump-is-back-in-minnesota-to-raise-money-and-rally-supporters/572591282/.

10. Dan Kraker, "Cook County to second-home owners: Stay Away, for Now," *MPR News*, March 25, 2020, https://www.mprnews.org/story/2020/03/24/cook-county-to-secondhome-owners-stay-away-for-now.

11. Tweet from Jackson, January 18, 2020, https://twitter.com/im_sorry_wtf/status/1351295184340860929?s=20.

12. Briana Noble and Charles E. Ramirez, "Traverse City's annual Cherry Fest canceled this year due to COVID-19," *Detroit News*, April 16, 2020, https://www.detroitnews.com/story/news/local/michigan/2020/04/16/traverse-citys-annual-cherry-fest-canceled-year-due-covid-19/5144215002/.

13. Tweet from J. Miles Coleman, September 14, 2020, https://twitter.com/JMilesColeman/status/1305539435753287680?s=20.

14. J. Miles Coleman, "Wisconsin: Decisive Again in 2020," *Sabato's Crystal Ball*, November 19, 2020, https://centerforpolitics.org/crystalball/articles/wisconsin-decisive-again-in-2020/.

15. Tweet from Matty Garen, January 1, 2021, https://twitter.com/MattyGaren/status/1345174332419559430?s=20.

16. Dave O'Brien, "U.S. Steel to Idle Lorain Tubular Plant Lay Off 250 Workers by May 24," *Chronicle-Telegram,* March 23, 2020, https://chroniclet.com/news/207586/us-steel-to-idle-lorain-tubular-plant-lay-off-250-workers-by-may-24/.

17. M.L. Schultze, "Is Donald Trump Channeling Jim Traficant?" WKSU, November 1, 2016, https://www.wksu.org/government-politics/2016-11-01/is-donald-trump-channeling-jim-traficant.

18. Tweet from J. Miles Coleman, November 28, 2020, https://twitter.com/JMilesColeman/status/1332787130783961092?s=20.

19. Tweet from Matthew Isbell, November 3, 2020, https://twitter.com/mcimaps/status/1323781464836755464?s=20.

20. Matthew Isbell, "How Florida's Congressional Districts Voted in the 2020 Presidential Election," MCI Maps, January 21, 2021, https://mcimaps.com/how-floridas-congressional-districts-voted-in-the-2020-presidential-election/.

21. Christopher Heath, "Puerto Ricans Helped Decide Florida's Election — Just Not the Way Most Thought It Would," *WFTV9*, November 21, 2018, https://www.wftv.com/news/local/puerto-ricans-helped-decide-florida-s-election-just-not-the-way-most-thought-it-would/876698084/.

22. Tweet from Matthew Isbell, December 12, 2020, https://twitter.com/mcimaps/status/1337881320513540099?s=20.

23. Paul Woolverton, "President Trump Backs Recognition Bill for the Lumbee Tribe of North Carolina," *Asheville Citizen-Times*, October 21, 2020, https://www.citizen-times.com/story/news/2020/10/21/president-trump-supports-federal-recognition-lumbee-tribe-cherokee/3720700001/.

24. Arya Sundaram, "Local Organizers Explain the Republican Surge in South Texas," *Texas Observer*, November 13, 2020, https://www.texasobserver.org/local-organizers-on-why-democrats-lost-ground-with-latino-voters-in-south-texas/.

25. Mitchell Ferman, "Donald Trump Made Inroads in South Texas this Year. These Voters Explain Why," *Texas Tribune*, November 13, 2020, https://www.texastribune.org/2020/11/13/south-texas-voters-donald-trump/.

6

The House

A Blue Wave Reduced to a Blue Trickle

Kyle Kondik

In what was probably the most surprising overall outcome in the 2020 election, Republicans came close to re-taking the U.S. House of Representatives majority two years after the 2018 "Blue Wave" restored the Democrats to power in the House after an eight-year absence. Republicans won just 200 seats in the 2018 election, but captured what at the time of this writing appeared to be 213 in 2020, coming within five seats of winning the majority (the uncertainty is because there were a couple of races whose outcomes were at least a bit uncertain even in early February, as explained below).

Most major election handicappers, including myself, thought the Democrats would be able to add to their majority in 2020. Instead, they nearly lost it, but scraped together enough seats to build, along with Democratic control of the White House and Senate, a tenuous governing "trifecta" in Washington at the beginning of Joe Biden's presidency.

With the usual midterm burden of holding the White House now passed to Democrats, and with a reapportionment and redistricting cycle looming in 2021-2022 where Republicans held more advantages than Democrats, the 2020 results put the Republicans well within range of being able to recapture the House majority in 2022, although nothing is guaranteed.

WHY DEMOCRATS SEEMED TO HOLD AN EDGE: REDISTRICTING, RETIREMENTS, AND PRIMARIES

Democrats were overextended in the House heading into the 2020 presidential contest. Following the 2018 election, the Democrats held 31 districts carried by Donald Trump in the 2016 election, while Republicans held only three

Hillary Clinton-won districts. All three of those Clinton-seat Republicans held marginal seats where she did not exceed 50 percent of the vote.

Democrats were also pushing the limits of what was plausible even in very Democratic California, where the party had picked up seven new seats in 2018, creating a lopsided 46-7 advantage in that state. While the Democrats did this without having to win a single district carried by Trump—an indicator of just how Democratic California had become—they captured several seats in southern California that had flipped from voting for Mitt Romney in 2012 to Clinton in 2016 but were otherwise historically Republican. The 2020 election would test how Democratic those districts—and others across the country, most notably in traditionally Republicans suburban areas—had truly become not just at the presidential level, but in down-ballot races as well.

Democrats nonetheless appeared well-positioned to hold and even expand their majority throughout the election cycle. Part of the reason for that belief among analysts was a new set of House maps in Republican-gerrymandered North Carolina, which made the Republicans' task of retaking the House a little bit harder.

State courts in North Carolina, led by a Democratic-controlled state Supreme Court, ordered the state's legislative and congressional districts redrawn because they were gerrymandered to favor Republicans. This would lead to the third congressional map in North Carolina in the decade: State Republicans had redrawn the map once before, in advance of the 2016 election, to address a racial gerrymandering ruling. Republicans were able to preserve a 10-3 edge in the delegation on that new map in 2016 and 2018, albeit not without a strange set of circumstances that bled into the 2019 calendar year.

In the 2018 cycle, Republican Representative Robert Pittenger of North Carolina's Ninth Congressional District lost a primary to Mark Harris, a former pastor who had nearly beaten Pittenger in a 2016 primary. Harris faced Democratic veteran Dan McCready in the general election in a GOP-leaning district that covers part of the Charlotte suburbs while sprawling east along the South Carolina border. On Election Night 2018, it appeared that Harris won by almost 900 votes, but there was a catch: The state refused to certify the results because of credible accusations of fraud involving absentee ballots. Harris declined to run again, and Republican state Senator Dan Bishop took his place as the GOP nominee against McCready. Bishop won by two points in the election rerun conducted in September 2019, closing the books on the 2018 election (this ended up being the 200th House seat Republicans won in the 2018 election, technically speaking).

But after the state court ruling in early 2020, Republicans grudgingly drew a new map that effectively gave the Democrats two new seats: one in the Raleigh area and another centered on Greensboro/Winston-Salem. Hillary Clinton carried both of the newly-drawn seats by roughly 20 points in 2016, and Democrats easily won both in the 2020 election as the Republican incumbents who held the prior versions of those seats, George Holding and Mark Walker, retired.[1]

Retirements, more broadly, also seemed to benefit Democrats. Of the 41 Democratic seats rated as competitive in the final *Sabato's Crystal Ball* House ratings, 40 were being defended by incumbents. Meanwhile, of the 48 Republican-held seats listed, 14 did not feature an incumbent running for reelection.[2] The list of vulnerable Republican-held open seats was led by one of the three Clinton-won districts Republicans successfully defended in 2018: GOP Representative Will Hurd of the frequently competitive and geographically huge San Antonio-to-El Paso Texas Twenty-third District retired, giving Democrats a prime target in a majority-Hispanic district they had narrowly lost in 2018.

Republican incumbents also retired in a number of traditionally Republican suburban districts with higher-than-average levels of four-year college attainment, such as Georgia's Seventh District in greater Atlanta, Indiana's Fifth in the Indianapolis suburbs, Texas' Twenty-second in the Houston area, and Texas' Twenty-fourth in the Dallas-Ft. Worth Metroplex. Trump had carried all of these districts in 2016, but by reduced margins from what Republicans usually got. In other words, these districts represented the potential for Democrats to cut even deeper into the suburbs after the strides they had made in 2018.

On the Democratic side, the only truly vulnerable open seat was Iowa's Second, an Obama-to-Trump white, working-class district in southeast Iowa.

The primary season also seemed to open up potential new Republican vulnerabilities. In western Colorado (Colorado's Third) and Central Virginia (Virginia's Fifth), hard-right candidates won the nominations over Republican incumbent Representatives Scott Tipton and Denver Riggleman, respectively, in districts Trump had carried by about a dozen points apiece, adding new defensive responsibilities for Republicans.

However, Republicans arguably benefited from some of their other primary losers: Representatives Ross Spano of Florida's Fifteenth, Steve King of Iowa's Fourth, and Steve Watkins of Kansas' Second all had various liabilities but were replaced by less problematic nominees who all held these seats in the fall. Three Democratic primary losers, Representatives Dan Lipinski of Illinois' Third, Lacy Clay of Missouri's First, and Eliot Engel of New York's Sixteenth, lost to more liberal challengers in safe Democratic seats (Lipinski was one of the least liberal members of the Democratic caucus, and one of the few who did not support abortion).

All told, redistricting, retirements, and the primary season *seemed* to benefit Democrats more than Republicans. But that is not how the results ultimately unfolded.

A HIGHLY NATIONALIZED ELECTION

The presidential election loomed large over the House elections—to a degree, as we will see, unseen in a century or more.

Early in 2020, Trump seemed decently positioned for a second term—probably not a favorite, but not a huge underdog either. Perceptions of his handling of the economy were better[3] than his overall underwater approval rating, and he survived an impeachment fight. On almost entirely party line votes, the House voted to impeach and the Senate to acquit Trump of charges of abuse of power and obstruction of Congress related to a seeming attempt to obtain what amounted to opposition research on Biden, who at the time was not yet the Democratic presidential nominee.

The impeachment fight ended up costing the Democrats a member: Democratic Representative Jeff Van Drew of New Jersey's Second District, one of the party's Trump-district members who had just been elected in 2018, switched parties over impeachment. He may have lost a Democratic primary had he not crossed over.

Democrats lost an additional seat when they couldn't defend a vacancy in California's Twenty-fifth district, a Romney-to-Clinton Southern California seat flipped by Democrat Katie Hill in 2018. Hill resigned from the House in late 2019 after explicit photos of her were leaked online and as she faced allegations of an inappropriate relationship with a staff member. Republican veteran Mike Garcia won the seat by an impressive 10 points in a May special election, although analysts believed he would face a tougher race in the fall with presidential-level turnout.[4]

The national focus shifted, though, as a once-in-a-century pandemic, COVID-19, introduced a new, overarching issue to the election. The disease contributed to hundreds of thousands of deaths by Election Day, and the public generally gave the president poor marks for his handling of the disease.

Throughout the summer and fall, the political environment seemed as though it would be fairly similar to 2018, an environment enough to sustain the Democrats' new House majority and then some. According to *FiveThirtyEight*'s weighted average, Democrats led in the House generic ballot polling by a little over 7 points on Election Day, not that much different from the 8.5-point lead the party enjoyed before the 2018 election. Biden led Trump by about 8.5 points in *FiveThirtyEight*'s national polling average as well.[5]

But for the second straight presidential election cycle, polls seemed to underestimate Trump, who still lost to Biden, but only by about 4.5 points nationally. And were it not for a combined roughly 43,000-vote Biden plurality in Arizona, Georgia, and Wisconsin, Biden's 306-232 Electoral College win over Trump would've been a 269-269 tie. That tie would have been resolved by the newly-elected House of Representatives in January 2021, where Trump likely would have won because of the way ties are broken (all 50 states get a single vote, and Republicans won a majority of the House delegations despite not winning a majority of seats).[6]

While Biden's popular vote victory ended up being the second-largest since 2000, with only Barack Obama's 2008 victory larger, Democrats often lagged behind Biden in House races, and the combined Democratic vs. Republican House vote in all races only gave the Democrats a roughly three-point edge, or a point and a half smaller than Biden's national edge. Instead of the Democrats padding their majority, Republicans netted 13 seats, cutting the Democrats to just a 222-213 edge after the dust cleared from a vote-counting process extended by the greater prevalence of mail-in voting prompted by concerns over the pandemic.

Overall, the results seemed to reinforce some preexisting trends. The number of crossover districts—those that backed one party for president and the other for House—numbered just 17, the lowest in the post-World War II era (markedly smaller than even the 26 in 2012, the previous postwar record). While records from the early twentieth century are incomplete, the percentage of crossover districts probably was at its lowest level since the late 1800s or early 1900s, another era defined by strong party loyalty and limited ticket-splitting.

After Democrats elected 31 members from Trump-won districts in 2018, they elected only seven in 2020. A combination of factors led to the massive decline.

First of all, Van Drew's party switch reduced the group's ranks by one even before the election, and Van Drew won a competitive reelection as Trump once again carried his South Jersey district. In the actual election, almost half (14) of the 30 Trump-won districts flipped to voting for Biden. The Democrats who held these districts all won reelection, although several had close calls, such as Representatives Tom O'Halleran of Arizona's First, Lauren Underwood of Illinois' Fourteenth District, and Abigail Spanberger of Virginia's Seventh.

Of the remaining 16, Republicans defeated eight incumbents. This included long-serving Representative Collin Peterson of Minnesota's Seventh District, the Agriculture Committee chairman who could not survive another 30-point Trump victory in his rural western Minnesota district, especially as Republicans rallied to a challenger, former Lieutenant Governor Michelle Fischbach, who was more credible and better-funded than many of Peterson's past challengers.

Overall, Minnesota was illustrative of the partisan sorting of House results. In 2016, four of its eight districts had voted for different parties for House and for president. In 2020, all eight districts voted the same way: Republicans picked up three outstate districts that voted twice for Trump over the course of 2018 and 2020, while Democrats in 2018 flipped two more suburban-focused seats in the Greater Twin Cities area that voted against Trump either once (the Second District, in 2020) or twice (the Third District) and then held these districts in 2020.

Republicans also knocked off Representatives Abby Finkenauer of Iowa's First, Xochitl Torres Small of New Mexico's Second, Max Rose of New York's Eleventh, Kendra Horn of Oklahoma's Fifth, Joe Cunningham of South Carolina's First, and Ben McAdams of Utah's Fourth, all first-time 2018 winners who couldn't generate enough crossover support to win again as Trump carried their districts once more. Another first-termer, Representative Anthony Brindisi of New York's Twenty-second District, was trailing as of early February in a long-delayed and error-filled vote count.[7] Republicans also flipped the one vulnerable open Democratic seat, the Trump-won Iowa Second, though only by an incredibly tiny six-vote margin. The Democratic candidate asked the U.S. House of Representatives to intervene in the contest; that challenge was unresolved as of this writing, although Mariannette Miller-Meeks, the Republican candidate, was seated by the House. So there were still some questions about these two races months after the election, but they are both counted here as Republican victories.

A few more seasoned Trump-district members, like Representatives Cheri Bustos of Illinois' Seventeenth, Matt Cartwright of Pennsylvania's Eighth, and Ron Kind of Wisconsin's Third, held on, but by reduced margins than what they were used to. Bustos' modest four-point victory was especially notable, as she served as chairwoman of the Democrats' House campaign arm, the Democratic Congressional Campaign Committee.

To a significant extent, the Democratic Trump 2016 seats sorted themselves out—the lion's share either flipped to Biden and retained their Democratic House incumbents, or stuck with Trump and elected Republican House members. Of the remaining Trump-district Democrats, several only backed Trump by a point or less, as was the case in districts retained by first-term Representatives Cindy Axne of Iowa's Third, Elissa Slotkin of Michigan's Eighth, and Andy Kim of New Jersey's Third. Representative Jared Golden of Maine's Second won relatively easily even as Trump once again carried the single electoral vote in Maine's Second District for the second-straight time. Maine and Nebraska are the only two states that award some of their electoral votes by congressional district as opposed to the other states, which are winner-take-all at the statewide level.

The list of Republican victors in Biden-won congressional districts also includes a split electoral vote/House outcome, as Representative Don Bacon of Nebraska's Second won even as Biden carried the electoral vote in his district. Additionally, the only two Republican incumbents running for reelection in 2020 who held 2016 Clinton seats also both won easily: Representatives John Katko of New York's Twenty-fourth and Brian Fitzpatrick of Pennsylvania's First. They won despite Biden performing better in their districts than Clinton had four years prior.

Republicans also held all but one of their vulnerable open seats—setting aside the two redistricting-inflicted casualties in North Carolina—losing just Georgia's Seventh in the Atlanta suburbs, a rapidly diversifying and highly educated district that flipped from Trump 2016 to Biden 2020.

Democrats struck out everywhere else, including the open Texas' Twenty-fourth, which Biden carried but Republicans held in a close contest. Democrats had hopes that their candidates could win several seats in Texas and across the suburban industrial north on the strength of Biden's performance, but while Biden improved on Clinton in a lot of these districts (Indiana's Fifth, Missouri's Second, Ohio's First, Pennsylvania's Tenth, Texas' Twenty-first, and Texas' Twenty-second), he did not carry any of them, and Republican House incumbents/candidates ran ahead of Trump in all of these districts anyway. Just like in 2016, Republicans in suburban districts may have benefited from ticket-splitters who may not have liked Trump but had not become Democrats down the ballot and/or anticipated a Biden victory but did not want to fully empower Democrats in Congress. Political scientist Robert Erikson has found that presidential election-cycle voters will sometimes strategically split their tickets as a way to put a check on the person they expect to win the presidential election.[8]

Republicans enjoyed a bounceback in some California districts, narrowly holding the Twenty-fifth District—the seat won by Republican Mike Garcia in a lower-turnout special election—and clawing back three of the other seats they had lost in 2018, California's Twenty-first (in the Central Valley), as well as the Thirty-ninth and Forty-eighth districts in Orange County. Biden still won these diverse districts, but Republican candidates won each at the House level by tiny margins. Democrats still won a 42-11 edge in the California House delegation, eight seats better than the 34-19 advantage the party held at the start of the decade, but less lopsided than the 46-7 advantage Democrats won in 2018.

Contributing to the Republican resurgence in California and elsewhere was that Trump ran better with Hispanic voters across the country than he had four years prior, which likely aided Republicans in some of the California seats, which are diverse (Trump also likely did better with Asian-American voters, and two of the California winners, Young Kim in the Thirty-ninth and Michelle Steel in the Forty-eighth, are of Asian ancestry).[9]

Pre-election polling picked up on Trump's better numbers with Hispanics, but the size of his improvement didn't become clear until election night when diverse, heavily-Hispanic Miami-Dade County reported its results: Clinton's 29-point victory there fell to just seven for Biden, a shocking drop that ran markedly counter to Biden's overall improvement on Clinton nationally and in the lion's share of states. This turnabout contributed to Republicans retaking two South Florida districts they had lost in 2018, the Twenty-sixth and Twenty-seventh districts, as Trump ran roughly 20 points better in both than he had four years prior. One of the Democratic losers was Representative Donna Shalala of the Twenty-seventh District, a former secretary of the Department of Health and Human Services in the Clinton administration, who later served as president of the University of Miami. Shalala, though, was old for a first-time House member (77 when elected in 2018), and she had other liabilities (she did not speak Spanish in a heavily Hispanic district, for instance). She lost reelection even as Biden retained her district, albeit by a significantly reduced margin (Clinton won it by 20 points while Biden won it by only three).

Another major sign of Democratic weakness among Hispanics came in South Texas. Texas' Twenty-third District, the open, Clinton-won swing seat that seemed like a slam dunk pickup for Democrats, both flipped to Trump and stuck with Republicans at the House level. In the end, no seats in Texas changed party hands, a major disappointment for Democrats, who had hoped to flip several seats there.

In the weeks that followed the election, and as results became finalized, other signs of Democratic erosion among Hispanics emerged across the nation from places ranging from Massachusetts to Arizona, as compiled by CNN analyst Harry Enten. Why Trump did better with Hispanics was an open question in the aftermath of the election, although, as Enten noted, Trump may have just benefited from incumbency—he was the first Republican incumbent president on the ballot since George W. Bush in 2004, who also turned in a relatively strong performance with Hispanic voters.[10] *New York Times* columnist Jamelle Bouie also pointed to the possibility that a round of stimulus checks sent to many Americans to help the economy in the midst of pandemic-related shutdowns helped Trump do better than expected. While Bouie noted that political shifts can have many explanations, to some extent the Republicans' "strong performance can be explained simply by the fact that it was the party in power when the government put a lot of money into the hands of a lot of people who didn't have it before."[11]

Following the election, Biden pointed to Democratic messaging problems, particularly related to an inability to properly respond to Republican attacks that Democrats wanted to "defund the police," a rallying cry adopted by some on the left in response to racial inequities in policing, a major focus of the campaign following the death of a Minneapolis Black man, George Floyd, at the hands of local police.[12] Democrats may have also been hurt by the fact that traditionally Republican voters who did not like Trump could vote against him in 2020 and split their tickets in favor of Republican House candidates—in 2018, the only way for voters to hurt Trump was to vote against his party's candidates down the ballot.

Overall, though, Democrats did maintain control of the chamber, and they did so without much of a margin in the aggregate national House vote: They won about 51 percent of the votes cast for the House, and converted that into about 51 percent of the total seats in the chamber. Democrats in 2020 won a share of seats commensurate with their share of the national House vote for the second straight election. This was after Republicans won a greater share of House seats than their share of the national vote might have indicated in 2012, 2014, and 2016, when Republicans won control of the House in each election.[13]

The unwinding of Republican-drawn House maps, as ordered by state and federal courts over the course of the decade, may have been crucial to the Democrats holding the House. As noted above, Democrats netted an extra two seats out of North Carolina because of new House maps. In 2018, a court-ordered remap in Pennsylvania helped Democrats net four seats that year, and while it is possible that Democrats might have netted those four seats without the remap, the Democrats may not have held those seats under 2020's less rosy political circumstances. In 2016, court-ordered redistricting created a new Democratic district in Virginia, and helped Democrats net two seats in Florida. So if no maps had changed throughout the decade, Republicans might have won the half-dozen or so extra seats they needed in 2020 to flip the House.

PUTTING 2020's HOUSE RESULTS IN HISTORICAL CONTEXT

This was an unusual election in the sense that the winning White House party lost ground in the House, although that was not unprecedented. Four years earlier, Republicans lost ground in the House and the Senate while

Trump was winning. Democrats also lost seats in 1992 when Bill Clinton beat George H.W. Bush, the last time a challenger had defeated an incumbent president. But redistricting and reapportionment helped Republicans in 1992, which was a national redistricting year; in 2020, the only changed maps, those in North Carolina, helped Democrats.

Perhaps a better historical precedent for 2020's House elections is one of the most famous presidential election cycles, 1960. That year, John F. Kennedy defeated Richard M. Nixon in a highly competitive presidential election while Democrats lost 20 net seats in the House. Two years earlier, in 1958, Democrats had enjoyed one of their best years ever, netting 48 seats in the midst of a bad economy during President Dwight D. Eisenhower's second midterm. Democrats elected a big 282-seat majority that year, but they were unable to maintain it in the more competitive environment of 1960, which "seemed to mark the return to the GOP fold of traditionally Republican congressional districts, which had gone Democratic in 1958 as a temporary protest against GOP policies."[14]

Six decades later, this same description could apply to some of the turf that Republicans clawed back from Democrats following a disastrous midterm election two years earlier—both in districts Trump carried in places like Oklahoma City, Staten Island, and Charleston, but also in usually Republican districts in South Florida and Southern California (even if Biden was carrying many of these districts at the presidential level).

But in a testament to the Democrats' House strength in the middle of the last century, the party could sustain a 20-seat loss but still hold 262 seats. Meanwhile, a 13-seat loss in 2020 brought Democrats to the brink of losing their majority.

THE ROAD AHEAD

Losing U.S. House seats was not the only down-ballot disappointment for Democrats in 2020: They also struck out on their state legislative targets, which had consequences for the post-2020 census redistricting process. Democrats hoped to gain a seat at the table in redistricting in GOP-run states such as Georgia, North Carolina, and Texas, but Republicans held their state legislative majorities in all three states.[15] This is explored in much more depth in Mary Frances McGowan's chapter in this book. All told, Republicans retained the power to draw many more districts than Democrats, but close to half of all seats were located in states where there was either a nonpartisan redistricting process or one where both parties had some say.[16] The decennial redistricting process was also poised to get off to a slow start because the U.S. Census Bureau delayed the release of the population figures used to apportion House seats to the states.[17]

Writing in the aftermath of the 2020 election, analyst Sean Trende found that Republicans could net the number of seats they need to win the majority in 2022 essentially just through "modest redistricting, combined with the demands of reapportionment," without even taking into account the possibility of aggressive gerrymandering or the national environment.[18]

Beyond redistricting, Democrats also now have to defend their slim House majority while holding the White House in a midterm year. There have been 40 midterm elections since the Civil War, and the president's party has lost ground in the House in 37 of those elections. The average loss is about 33 seats. The average seat loss since World War II is somewhat smaller, 27, but regardless, Democrats can only afford very minor seat losses to hold onto the House.

It's too early to know at this point what the political environment will look like in November 2022, and whether Democrats can thwart the usual midterm trend, which Republicans themselves were able to do in the 2002 midterm when they successfully defended their own slim majority in George W. Bush's first midterm. But history as well as redistricting realities put the Republicans in a good position to win back the House majority in 2022. If they do, it would be yet another instance of the House changing hands in a midterm as opposed to a presidential election. The House has changed party control 11 times since 1900, but only twice (1948 and 1952) did that shift happen in a presidential year. The other nine instances, including the modern House party changes in 1994, 2006, 2010, and 2018, happened in midterm years.

Republicans came surprisingly close to flipping the House even while losing the presidential race in 2020, leaving them well-positioned to force yet another midterm House party change.

NOTES

1. Greg Giroux, "New N.C. Redistricting Boosts Democrats in 2020 Elections," *Bloomberg*, December 17, 2020, https://about.bgov.com/news/new-nc-redistricting-boosts-democrats-in-2020-elections/.

2. Larry J. Sabato, Kyle Kondik, and J. Miles Coleman, "Final Ratings for the 2020 Election," *Sabato's Crystal Ball*, November 2, 2020, https://centerforpolitics.org/crystalball/articles/21320/.

3. "President Trump Job Approval – Economy," *RealClearPolitics*, https://www.realclearpolitics.com/epolls/other/president_trump_job_approval_economy-6182.html.

4. Kate Irby, "Republican Flips California Congressional Seat. What Does That Mean for November?" *Sacramento Bee*, May 13, 2020, https://www.sacbee.com/news/politics-government/capitol-alert/article242708631.html.

5. For *FiveThirtyEight* Trump vs. Biden national poll average: "Who's Ahead in the National Polls?" *FiveThirtyEight*, January 20, 2021, https://projects.fivethirtyeight.com/polls/president-general/national; For *FiveThirtyEight* 2020 House generic ballot average: "Are Democrats or Republicans Winning the Race for Congress?" *FiveThirtyEight*, November 2, 2020, https://projects.fivethirtyeight.com/congress-generic-ballot-polls; For *FiveThirtyEight* 2018 House generic ballot average: "Did Democrats or Republicans Win the Generic Ballot?" *FiveThirtyEight*, November 6, 2018, https://projects.fivethirtyeight.com/congress-generic-ballot-polls/2018.

6. Kyle Kondik, "The Dreaded 26-269 Scenario: An Update," *Sabato's Crystal Ball*, September 16, 2020, https://centerforpolitics.org/crystalball/articles/the-dreaded-269-269-scenario-an-update.

7. Patrick Lohmann, "Tenney nears victory after judge rules against key Brindisi ballots in NY 22nd race," Syracuse.com, January 29, 2021, https://www.syracuse.com/politics/cny/2021/01/tenney-nears-victory-after-judge-rules-against-key-brindisi-ballots-in-ny-22nd-race.html.

8. Robert S. Erikson, "Congressional Elections in Presidential Years: Presidential Coattails and Strategic Voting," *Legislative Studies Quarterly* 41, no. 3 (August 2016), 551-574.

9. Tweet from Patrick Ruffini, December 15, 2020, https://twitter.com/PatrickRuffini/status/1338865479423651840?s=20.

10. Harry Enten, "Trump Made Big In-Roads in Hispanic Areas Across the Nation," CNN, December 12, 2020, https://www.cnn.com/2020/12/12/politics/trump-hispanic-vote/index.html.

11. Jamelle Bouie, "A Simple Theory of Why Trump Did Well," *New York Times*, November 18, 2020, https://www.nytimes.com/2020/11/18/opinion/trump-election-stimulus.html.

12. Mike Memoli, "In Leaked Recording, Biden Says GOP Used 'Defund the Police' to "Beat the Living Hell" Out of Democrats," NBC News, December 10, 2020, https://www.nbcnews.com/politics/2020-election/leaked-recording-biden-says-gop-used-defund-police-beat-living-n1250757.

13. Theodore S. Arrington, "The Seats/Votes Relationship in the U.S. House 1972-2018," *Sabato's Crystal Ball*, January 31, 2019, http://crystalball.centerforpolitics.org/crystalball/articles/the-seats-votes-relationship-in-the-u-s-house-1972-2018/.

14. Congressional Quarterly, *Congressional Elections 1946-1996* (Washington, D.C.: Congressional Quarterly, 1998), 17-18.

15. Mary Frances McGowan and Leah Askarinam, "Hotline's State Legislative Power Rankings: Democrats Hope to Avenge 2010 Losses," *National Journal*, October 20, 2020, https://www.nationaljournal.com/s/710770/hotlines-state-legislative-power-rankings-democrats-hope-to-avenge-2010-losses.

16. Reid Wilson, "States Plot Next Moves on Redistricting," *The Hill*, December 2, 2020, https://thehill.com/homenews/campaign/528284-states-plot-next-moves-on-redistricting

17. Mike Schneider, "Census Data for Congressional Seats Still Months Away," *Associated Press*, January 27, 2021, https://apnews.com/article/donald-trump-joe-biden-coronavirus-pandemic-census-2020-5ada2303a7b918c029c7dcdd8860ce98.

18. Sean Trende, "Part 2: What Redrawn House Maps Could Mean in 2023," *RealClearPolitics*, November 13, 2020, https://www.realclearpolitics.com/articles/2020/11/13/part_2_what_redrawn_house_maps_could_mean_in_2023_144651.html.

7

The Senate

How Democrats Found the Most Difficult Path to a Majority

Madelaine Pisani

After failing to pick up a Senate majority in 2018's blue wave, Democrats hoped 2020 would be a prime opportunity to overtake Republicans' three-seat advantage. They did, but they took no shortcuts in getting there. Republicans were mostly on defense in 2020, but benefited from the advantages of incumbency and straight-ticket voting trends. Republicans managed to net only one loss on Election Day, but the party's cohesion fell apart after President Donald Trump lost the presidential election in November. As the GOP fractured, Democrats in Georgia—led in large part by Black activists and community leaders—flipped two Republican-held seats to win the slimmest majority possible, with each party controlling 50 seats but Democrats holding the edge because of the tie-breaking vote of Vice President Kamala Harris, who prior to her election was a senator from California. Overall, Democrats netted a gain of three Senate seats in the 2020 election cycle.

In 2018, Republicans gained two Senate seats, holding the majority with 53 seats. Republicans were defending nine states that year while Democrats were on defense in 26 states. That dynamic reversed in 2020, and Republicans had 23 seats to protect, while Democrats only had 12. Republicans were on defense in some of the most competitive and expensive races in the country, such as North Carolina, Maine, and Arizona, while making late defensive plays in states that should have been automatic layups like Kansas, South Carolina, and even Alaska.

Onlookers could predict that Alabama would be an easy pickup from Republicans, while a Republican loss in Colorado would likely cancel it out. Democrats needed to find three other states to flip from red to blue to hit 50 seats. The party's top targets were Arizona, Maine, North Carolina, and Iowa—all states held by Republican incumbents seeking reelection. In fact, the *only* relatively competitive open-seat Senate race held by Republicans in 2020 was Kansas, which Republican Roger Marshall ended up holding by a little more than 10 points. Unseating an incumbent is a difficult task under normal circumstances, but unseating an incumbent from the same party as the presidential candidate who carried the state is even harder.

Democratic Senate leader Chuck Schumer's most strategic path to a Senate majority, which did not initially include Georgia, did not end up matching Joe Biden's path to victory. Biden defeated Trump by winning states like Arizona, Michigan, Pennsylvania, and Wisconsin. Only one of those states, Arizona, offered Senate Democrats an opportunity to pick up a seat on Biden's coattails—the Georgia victories only came later, in January runoffs, after Biden narrowly carried the state in November. Meanwhile, North Carolina and Iowa—states that were top prospects in delivering a Senate majority for Democrats—were must-win states for the Trump campaign. In Maine, despite Biden carrying the state by nine points, Republican Senator Susan Collins was the only Senate candidate to find success through split-ticket voting.

Historic trends show it has become increasingly difficult to win a Senate seat from the opposing party of the presidential candidate who carries the state (see figure 7.1).[1] There has been a marked decline in split-ticket voting since the 1980s, but 2016 and 2020 were particularly notable years because in 2016, no state chose Senate and presidential candidates from opposing parties and only

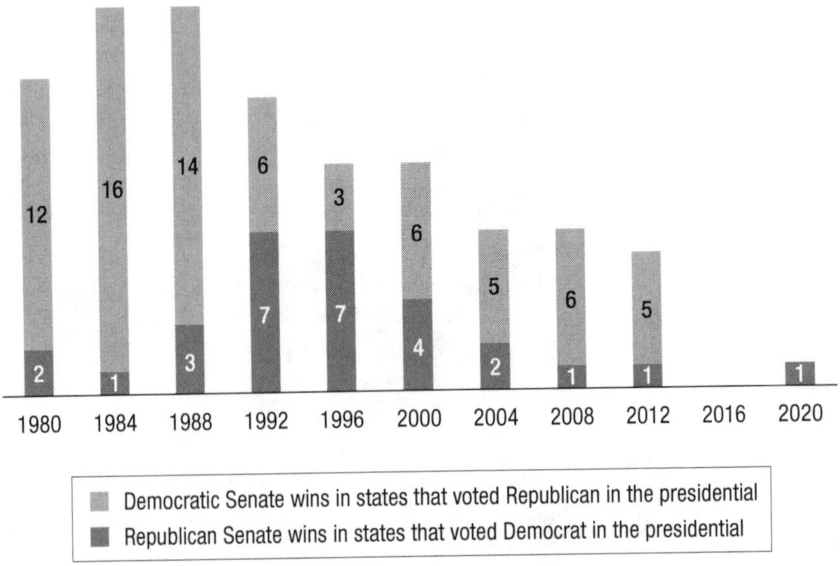

Figure 7.1. Split Outcomes in Presidential/Senate Races
Sources: Pew Research Center, *Sabato's Crystal Ball.*

one Senate race bucked the presidential outcome in 2020 (Collins in Maine).[2] Incumbency and partisan voting behavior were two strong factors working in favor of Senate Republicans and against Democrats' initial idea of how they could reach a Senate majority. According to a Pew Research Center study conducted ahead of the 2020 election, only 11 percent of registered voters nationwide had a plan to vote for Senate candidates and presidential candidates of opposing parties. Meanwhile, 80 percent planned to vote straight-ticket.[3]

In 2020, Republicans were defending two seats in Hillary Clinton-won states—Colorado and Maine—both of which Biden carried as well. Democrats were defending two seats in Trump 2016 states, Alabama and Michigan. Michigan went for Biden in 2020, and Democrats held the Senate seat, but lost Alabama, which remained safely in Trump's column. Democrats flipped one of the Senate seats in Clinton states, with Maine holding out thanks in large part to Collins' fortitude as a seasoned incumbent. Despite Democratic ambitions of pulling upsets in states like Iowa, North Carolina, and even Montana, 2020 reinforced the power of partisan voting trends.

After 2018, only 10 states had split Senate delegations, which was down from 14 split delegations in the previous cycle. With Democratic losses in Alabama and Republican losses in Arizona and Colorado, that number dropped to seven split delegations after 2020—the fifth election cycle in a row during which the number of split delegations has declined.[4] It's also the lowest number of split party delegations in the history of direct Senate elections.[5] Seven may overstate the number of split delegations because it includes Vermont, where there is one Democratic senator, Patrick Leahy, and one independent who nonetheless caucuses with Democrats—Bernie Sanders.

2020 LANDSCAPE: FOR THE LOVE OF MONEY

Despite Republicans' incumbency advantage in key battleground states, Senate Democrats had momentum on their side in the final months of 2020 campaigning. Democratic candidates were raising record amounts of money through ActBlue, the party's digital fund-raising apparatus, which was more advanced than its Republican counterpart, WinRed.[6] In the final financial quarter campaign filing before the election, Democrats outraised Republicans in nearly every competitive Senate race. Democrats in Alabama, Alaska, Arizona, Colorado, Georgia, Iowa, Kansas, Kentucky, Maine, Michigan, Minnesota, Mississippi, Montana, North Carolina, South Carolina, and Texas all raised more than their Republican counterparts, setting in-state records in several cases. The only outlier was New Mexico, an open Democratic seat, where Republican Mark Ronchetti kept pace with his Democratic opponent,

Ben Ray Lujàn, in the final quarter. Both candidates raised roughly $1.8 million in Q3. Democrats were not particularly concerned with funneling money toward Lujàn, as he had shown himself to be an effective fund-raiser early in his race and won the election by six points. Meanwhile, South Carolina Democrat Jaime Harrison set the all-time record for money raised by a Senate candidate in a single general election quarter, bringing in $57.9 million.[7] Overall, Harrison's total fund-raising was a whopping $133 million, but Georgia's Jon Ossoff topped the entire 2020 pack by raising $140 million. Harrison's total made him the second-largest overall fund-raiser of 2020 and Rev. Raphael Warnock, who raised $125 million for Georgia's special Senate election, was the third-largest fundraiser of the cycle according to campaign finance reports covering contributions through December 3,[8] though it should be noted Ossoff and Warnock's races went into overtime. In sum, Democrats got seven wins, including four flips, out of those 18 competitive races mentioned above. Despite lags in fundraising toward the end, Republicans still managed 11 wins, including one flip.

In most of these cases, challengers outraised incumbents. Normally incumbents are the ones with the cash advantage, as they have at least six years in office to develop relationships with donors so long as they are regularly elected. However, Democratic challengers invested in connecting with small-dollar donors through ActBlue, allowing them to capitalize on viral moments and news events. The biggest example of this was the money raised in the wake of Supreme Court Justice Ruth Bader Ginsburg's death.

Ginsburg passed away on September 18, and the *Washington Post* reported that in the following 24 hours, seven times as many people donated to Democrats in competitive Senate races than did the day before.[9] Donors also spread the wealth. The day before Ginsburg's death just 3 percent of donors gave to six or more candidates, but the day after, 40 percent of donors gave to six or more candidates.[10] Republicans did not see such large spikes in donations.

Democrats who had been overlooked by donors in more long-shot states, like Alaska and Mississippi, suddenly saw an influx of cash. When money started flowing in Alaska, national Republican groups had to come in with reinforcements, drawing attention and resources away from the matchups that would ultimately decide the majority. Al Gross, an orthopedic surgeon who hoped to unseat GOP Senator Dan Sullivan as an independent in Alaska, raised nearly $3 million the day after Ginsburg died.[11] In reflecting on his race, which Sullivan won by double digits, Gross said Ginsburg's death "really put this race on the national spotlight." Republican outside groups came in to close the gap in spending that Gross ran up in September. Senate Leadership Fund, a Super PAC aligned with Senate Majority Leader Mitch McConnell, dropped $1.6 million in advertising on Sullivan's behalf in the days following Ginsburg's death. At that point, spending on ads benefiting Gross had doubled the ad spending for Sullivan.[12]

Republicans spent the final months of the election playing whack-a-mole across the country as Democrats threatened incumbents that normally would not need outside help holding their seat. In addition to Alaska, Republicans in Kansas complained national groups were not doing enough to protect the open Senate seat. National groups had already boosted then-Representative Roger Marshall to help him through a contentious and expensive GOP primary. But GOP operatives were worried because Marshall's opponent, Barbara Bollier, a state senator, had raised $20 million in total by the third quarter of 2020 while Marshall had raised only $5 million. Republicans in Kansas told the *Washington Post* they were concerned national Republicans were overlooking their state, despite tight polling, because they were stretched thin with so many candidates getting outraised.[13]

In South Carolina, Democrats were using the surplus of cash to fund ads on behalf of a conservative third party candidate to pull Republican votes from Senator Lindsey Graham. The Lincoln Project, a group of former Republican operatives, took particular glee in targeting their former ally with an ad comparing him to a parasite.[14] Republicans also had to contend with Montana Governor Steve Bullock, who had a record of winning statewide on the ballot with Trump, and Theresa Greenfield in Iowa, who didn't have as much political experience as Senator Joni Ernst, but was a disciplined retail politician who performed well in the polls. In October, McConnell told the *Washington Post* that Republicans had anticipated "spirited races in Montana, Colorado, Arizona, Iowa, North Carolina and Maine," but that Democrats had also "been able to make it competitive in Kansas, Georgia, South Carolina and Alaska." That led the majority leader to view Republicans' chances of keeping control of the Senate as "a 50-50 proposition."[15] Though he was referring to odds, McConnell's 50-50 assessment was remarkably prescient considering that's the margin by which Democrats won the majority.

NORTH CAROLINA: TRUTH HURTS

If Democrats were going to get voters to split tickets in their favor, the most likely place for that to result in a win would have been North Carolina, where they didn't need as many Trump voters to back a Democrat as they did in, say, Montana. Senator Thom Tillis, the Republican incumbent, had only been in office for one term and solidified his alignment with Trump after a rocky start. When Trump first took office, Tillis worked with Democrats on immigration and even initially opposed Trump's emergency order to build a border wall. However, to avoid a conservative primary challenger, Tillis emphasized his allegiance to Trump and frequently defended him, especially against the first impeachment proceeding.[16] His fealty paid off, and Tillis dissuaded any serious primary challenges.

Meanwhile, Democrats nominated former state Senator Cal Cunningham, an Iraq War veteran who initially ran for lieutenant governor, but announced his switch to the Senate race in the summer of 2019. It became clear within days that Cunningham had consolidated support from national Democrats.[17] His main challenger throughout the primary was state Senator Erica Smith, whose lack of fund-raising made it difficult for her to truly threaten Cunningham. However, Republicans attempted to boost her campaign with their own spending, propping up Smith as the true progressive in the race. By the time Cunningham won the primary, groups linked to the Democratic Senatorial Campaign Committee and VoteVets, an outside group that supports Democrats, had already spent $13 million on positive biographical ads.[18] Cunningham rode his positive image comfortably through most of the general election as Tillis struggled with fund-raising and polling. Throughout the month of September, every poll recorded in *FiveThirtyEight*'s poll tracker showed Cunningham ahead by a point or more.[19] However, the race encountered a major shift during the first week of October.

On September 26, Tillis was in Washington attending a ceremony to celebrate the nomination of Supreme Court Justice Amy Coney Barrett, an event that preceded a coronavirus outbreak within the White House and among Trump's allies. The following Thursday, Tillis and Cunningham met for their final debate. Cunningham went into the debate on a high, as he was among the first Democratic Senate campaigns to announce a jaw-dropping Q3 fund-raising number. Cunningham's campaign announced raising $28.3 million, setting the record for a North Carolina Senate candidate's single-quarter fundraising. The following day, Tillis announced he had tested positive for COVID-19 and would halt all in-person campaign events. At that point, Cunningham seemed to be in an ideal position. He was leading most polls, flush with cash, and had run a campaign devoid of scandal—up to that point. In a shocking move the same night Tillis announced he had coronavirus, Cunningham's campaign confirmed the authenticity of extramarital texts between him and a public relations professional named Arlene Guzman Todd. The texts were first published by the conservative site NationalFile.com. Cunningham stated in a release, "I have hurt my family, disappointed my friends, and am deeply sorry. The first step in repairing those relationships is taking complete responsibility, which I do." Guzman Todd confirmed the affair as well and claimed they had been together in July as the campaign was heating up.[20] The scandal overshadowed much of the race dynamic as Cunningham dodged the press and Tillis took every opportunity to elevate the story.

Things were looking bleak for North Carolina Republicans until news of Cunningham's affair broke. From his home, Tillis made the rounds on local media, taking advantage of the opportunity to chip away at Cunningham's appeal as a veteran and family man. By the following week, Tillis and SLF had blanketed the airwaves with attack ads, noting that Cunningham's affair was with a woman "married to a combat veteran" and that "the Army Reserve is investigating ... Cunningham." These ads were more biting and less generic than the previous attack ads against Cunningham that linked him to national Democrats like Chuck Schumer and criticized him as a "socialist." Republicans went all-in on this new line of attack, with SLF dropping a quick $4 million on ads about the affair.[21] A large part of Cunningham's strategy before the scandal was focusing on fund-raising and avoiding unforced errors. Tillis spent the final days campaigning with a slew of high-profile GOP surrogates. Meanwhile, Cunningham skipped several in-person October campaign events, even ones hosted by Kamala Harris and Jill Biden.[22] It is unlikely that some cringeworthy texting would turn off voters who had already made up their minds, but Senate Democrats needed their candidates overperforming the top of the ticket in battlegrounds like North Carolina, not quietly riding Biden's coattails hoping to avoid the glare of the spotlight. Ultimately Tillis won the Senate race with 49 percent to Cunningham's 47 percent. Trump beat Biden in North Carolina, 50 percent to 49 percent.

MAINE: GO YOUR OWN WAY

While Republicans across the map tied their fortunes to Trump, Senator Susan Collins accomplished what no other Senate Republican could: win in a state Biden carried. Collins faced more fervor from her opponents in her 2020 election bid than perhaps any other race in her 24-year career in the Senate due to the backlash over Supreme Court Justice Brett Kavanaugh's confirmation in 2018. Before Democrats came close to settling on a challenger for Collins, money started flowing in for the eventual candidate, a sum that reached $4 million.[23] Ultimately, though, that was a drop in the bucket compared to the money spent on the race by both parties.

Senate campaign ads blanketed the airwaves in Maine for months leading up to the election, leading many to wonder who could possibly remain undecided in a state so oversaturated with political messaging. Collins was regularly outpaced in fund-raising by state House Speaker Sara Gideon, her Democratic opponent, though outside groups did everything possible to close the gap on the airwaves. Collins banked on her skill at grassroots campaigning to make the difference in the final weeks, while Gideon leaned much more toward virtual campaign events by comparison. Since the Kavanaugh vote, most of the conversation in Maine was about the credibility of Collins as a Republican who appeals to independents. But when the issue of the Supreme Court came up again, just weeks before her election, Collins carved a niche where she seemed to placate both constituencies—if not among pundits, at least among Mainers. Collins opposed Trump's speedy action to confirm a new justice and was the only Republican to vote against Coney Barrett's confirmation, though she praised the judge's credentials and insisted her opposition was solely due to the manner of confirmation.[24] That, coupled with independent-minded Mainers' frustration with out-of-state cash seeking to influence the race, as well as Collins' commitment to retail politicking was likely the recipe to overcome some of the odds stacked against her.

Democrats had to make the case that Collins did not deserve a return ticket to the Senate and that Gideon was an appealing replacement. Gideon had a strong record in the legislature and drove home her alignment with Joe Biden, highlighting the fact that having her in Congress would increase Biden's ability to act on his legislative agenda. In the third quarter of 2020, Gideon raised $39.4 million while Collins only brought in $8.3 million.[25] Republicans sought to characterize Gideon as a "risky" Biden rubber stamp funded by out-of-state liberals, while Democrats linked Collins to Trump and McConnell and characterized her as a corrupt politician. Despite polls predicting otherwise, Collins did not even fall under the 50 percent threshold that would have triggered the state's ranked-choice voting system. Some Republicans were concerned Trump loyalist Max Linn would syphon votes from conservatives, but Linn likely disqualified himself in the minds of many voters with one of the most bizarre debate performances of 2020. Linn started out one debate with a show of cutting up masks worn in the midst of the COVID-19 public health crisis in protest of "government overreach," and went on to call both Collins and Gideon "weak women." When he realized how misogynistic he sounded, he tried and failed to backtrack, but he had cemented his status as a sideshow candidate.[26] With conservatives and a good chunk of moderates consolidated behind her, Collins clinched the race with 51 percent of the vote to Gideon's 42 percent.

PICKUPS: BREAK IT TO ME GENTLY

If only three Senate seats were going to flip parties on November 3, most onlookers would be able to predict that those would be Alabama, Arizona, and Colorado. However, there were moments during each race that it looked like the incumbent might have a path to holding on.

Democrats largely considered Alabama a lost cause, but a volatile primary for the Republican nomination did add a level of uncertainty to the equation. Trump enthusiastically backed Tommy Tuberville, who coached Auburn University's football program from 1999 to 2008. Tuberville was running against former U.S. Attorney General Jeff Sessions. Sessions, who left the Senate after a 20-year tenure to serve in the Trump administration, resigned in 2018 after their relationship went sour. Sessions walked a difficult line, often praising Trump and touting their history of cooperation, while Trump hurled insults at his former ally. In the final stretch of the primary, Trump said appointing Sessions was his biggest regret.[27] Democrats hoped that if Sessions did emerge from the primary, he would be wounded enough that Senator Doug Jones could find a lane to reelection. Jones ended up losing to Tuberville by 20 points.

In Colorado, Senator Cory Gardner was not in as much trouble as Jones, but it was still a tall order to elect a Republican in a blue state when Trump tolerated very little daylight between himself and legislators who needed his endorsement. Gardner was up against John Hickenlooper, a former two-term governor who touted his record as the state's former top executive on the trail. Gardner hoped to weaken that message by portraying Hickenlooper as "corrupt" and emphasizing an ethics violation that was found against Hickenlooper over the summer, resulting in a fine.[28] Toward the end of the campaign cycle, it became clear Gardner was on a sinking ship, and national groups started redirecting money to other states, which was particularly stinging to Gardner, who chaired the National Republican Senatorial Committee two years prior. Senator Martha McSally, who had been appointed to fill the seat John McCain once held, also met a stinging end to her campaign.

McSally, who lost to Senator Kyrsten Sinema in 2018, has the unique distinction of overseeing Republicans' forfeiture of both of Arizona's Senate seats over the span of two years. Monmouth University Polling Director Patrick Murray noted McSally's tenure marked "the first time in 68 years the GOP hasn't held at least one" of the two seats.[29] McSally has a compelling biography as the first female fighter pilot to fly in combat for the Air Force. However, her opponent, Mark Kelly, had his own powerhouse résumé including piloting a space shuttle for NASA after serving as naval aviator in the Gulf War. Despite McSally being one of the best fund-raisers among Republican candidates in 2020, Kelly consistently outpaced her, raising $100 million overall to McSally's $74 million.[30] Arizona was a slugfest throughout, and McSally also had to deal with a short-tempered Trump rushing her off campaign stages toward the end of the race.[31]

GEORGIA: THE FINAL COUNTDOWN

As the results of the November 3 election solidified, Georgians braced themselves for a deluge of political messaging because the national fight for the Senate majority had descended on the Peach State. Georgia hosted two Senate races in 2020, one special election for the seat vacated by retiring Republican Senator Johnny Isakson and another regular election for the seat held by Republican Senator David Perdue, who was first elected in 2014. The Perdue seat was initially considered a solid Republican seat with other races more likely to attract Democrats as pickup opportunities. Meanwhile, the special election race was somewhat of an unknown quantity, but comparatively offered an easier target without a true incumbency advantage.

Governor Brian Kemp, a Trump endorsee, appointed wealthy finance executive Kelly Loeffler to Isakson's seat in January 2020. Kemp chose Loeffler over Trump's preferred choice of Doug Collins, a congressman who was one of Trump's top defenders in the House during the impeachment hearings. Kemp's decision to opt for Loeffler marked early tensions brewing between the president and governor that would compound to epic proportions by the end of 2020. Democrats would have loved for Stacey Abrams to run for either seat, having proven her status as one of Georgia's most successful Democrats in her narrow election loss to Kemp in 2018. Abrams declined to run for the Senate, likely biding her time for a 2022 rematch with Kemp, but threw her full support behind Raphael Warnock, the senior pastor at Ebenezer Baptist Church where Dr. Martin Luther King Jr. preached, to get the nod from the DSCC in the special election.[32]

Of the Democrats vying for the regular election nomination, Jon Ossoff, who built a name for himself during a 2017 special election House race, was the favorite to secure the nomination.[33] Ossoff emerged from the primary unscathed, with enough votes to avoid a potentially expensive runoff for the nomination. Ossoff and Perdue then launched into a general election slugfest in which Perdue painted the 33-year-old Ossoff as an inexperienced liberal with vague ties to China, while Ossoff slammed Perdue as a corrupt politician whose investment portfolio benefited from a pandemic he downplayed.[34] Perdue led in the general election, but did not break 50 percent, which sent the regular election to a January runoff.

While Perdue and Ossoff duked it out in the regular election, Warnock laid the groundwork for a late-surge strategy because the special election was almost certainly going to go to a runoff. In the 20-candidate special election field, Warnock had consolidated Democratic support, thanks in part to the backing from Abrams and national Democrats. Meanwhile, Collins and Loeffler were in a heated competition to win over Georgia's conservative base vote. When Loeffler emerged bruised, but victorious, she met a rested Warnock who anticipated her attack ads with ones joking about puppies and Christmas tree lights. Warnock largely left the attack ads against Loeffler to outside groups.

In the runoffs, the two sets of candidates each essentially ran as a ticket. However, Warnock bore the brunt of GOP attacks as records of his sermons offered content for operatives to pick apart.[35] While Democrats were unified, Republicans were growing increasingly fractured throughout the runoff period. Trump grew agitated and more focused on claims of election fraud than helping senators win elections in a state that snubbed him. Overall, nearly $500 million in advertising was spent on these two races, a sum that shattered Senate spending records in other states.[36] Hundreds of millions of those dollars came from Republican donors, but Trump torched their efforts by making claims that cast doubt on Georgia's voting system and slamming Kemp, whom he considered a traitor for defending Georgia's presidential vote count. When Trump held two rallies in Georgia, the bulk of his speeches were devoted to airing grievances about the election outcome. Shortly before the runoff elections, a recording of a coercive call between Trump and Georgia Secretary of State Brad Raffensperger, a Republican, emerged.[37] On the call, Trump acknowledged that he was likely depressing turnout among Republicans, and threatened Raffensperger by saying, "Because of what you've done to the president, a lot of people aren't going out to vote, and a lot of Republicans are going to vote negative because they hate what you did to the president. Okay? They hate it. And they're going to vote. And you would be respected, really respected, if this can be straightened out before the election."

When the results came in, Warnock and Ossoff had won close but clear victories, and both outperformed Biden across most of the state. Unlike many Democratic campaigns earlier in the year, Warnock and Ossoff invested heavily in socially distanced, in-person campaigning, backed by a robust grassroots field operation. Black voters turned out for the Democrats, not just in the cities and suburbs, but in Georgia's rural "black belt" region as well.[38] Warnock won his race by two points while Ossoff won his by a little more than one point.[39] Georgia made history by electing its first Black senator and its first Jewish senator, securing the majority for Democrats in the process.

2022 PREVIEW: HERE I GO AGAIN

There are 34 Senate seats up for election in 2022 and, for a second cycle in a row, Republicans will be overexposed. Republicans hold seats in 20 states up for election next cycle, including at least two open seats in arguably the most competitive states on the map: North Carolina and Pennsylvania. Democrats have 14 seats to defend. Two of those seats are held by Democrats who will have just taken over after winning special election races: Raphael Warnock and Mark Kelly. Both newcomers will have just two years in the majority to set their legislative records. Democrats will be defending Kelly and Warnock, as well as Republican pick up attempts in Nevada and New Hampshire. Popular Republican New Hampshire Governor Chris Sununu has not ruled out challenging Senator Maggie Hassan in 2022.[40]

In addition to the open seats in North Carolina and Pennsylvania, a state Biden carried in 2020, Republicans also have to defend Senator Ron Johnson's seat in Wisconsin. Wisconsin and Pennsylvania are the only states Biden won where Republicans will defend Senate seats. Johnson, a staunch ally of Trump's, would be in a vulnerable position if he runs for reelection, but the seat could be even more at-risk without the advantage of incumbency. Iowa Senator Chuck Grassley, at 87 years old, could be a contender for retirement as well. Florida Senator Rick Scott, the incoming NRSC chair, expressed optimism in early 2021 that both incumbents would run again in 2022.[41]

A major question for Senate Republicans in 2022 will be how they balance the fractures within the party driven by Trump. In the wake of the January 6 attack on the Capitol by Trump supporters, the Republican Senate caucus was split on how to handle Trump's false claims that the election had been rigged and stolen from him. Some GOP senators like Ted Cruz and Josh Hawley gave credibility to his conspiracy by opposing the certification of votes in Arizona and Pennsylvania.

Meanwhile, minutes before violent Trump supporters invaded the Capitol, McConnell offered a grave warning to his colleagues from the Senate floor. "We cannot simply declare ourselves a national board of elections on steroids," he said. "Voters, courts and the states have all spoken. If we overrule them, it would damage our republic forever. . . . I will not pretend such a vote would be a harmless protest gesture while relying on others to do the right thing. I will vote to respect the people's decision and defend our system of government as we know it."[42]

NOTES

1. Gary C. Jacobson, "Extreme Referendum: Donald Trump and the 2018 Midterm Elections," *Political Science Quarterly* 134, no. 1 (2019), 28.

2. Drew DeSilver, "Most Senate elections reflect states' presidential votes," News in the Numbers, Pew Research Center, September 1, 2020, https://www.pewresearch.org/fact-tank/2020/09/01/most-senate-elections-reflect-states-presidential-votes/.

3. "Large Shares of Voters Plan To Vote a Straight Party Ticket for President, Senate and House," U.S. Politics & Policy, Pew Research Center, October 21, 2020, https://www.pewresearch.org/politics/2020/10/21/large-shares-of-voters-plan-to-vote-a-straight-party-ticket-for-president-senate-and-house/.

4. Larry J. Sabato and Kyle Kondik, eds. *The Blue Wave: The 2018 Midterms and What They Mean for the 2020 Elections* (Lanham, MD: Rowman & Littlefield, 2019).

5. Eric Ostermeier, "117th Congress Will Have Fewest Split US Senate Delegations in History," Smart Politics, University of Minnesota, November 29, 2020, https://smartpolitics.lib.umn.edu/2020/11/29/117th-congress-will-have-fewest-split-us-senate-delegations-in-history/.

6. Madelaine Pisani, "GOP Senate Candidates Confront a Reckoning Digital Fundraising," *National Journal*, July 23, 2020, https://www.nationaljournal.com/s/708630/gop-senate-candidates-confront-a-reckoning-on-digital-fundraising.

7. Madelaine Pisani, "Hotline's Q3 Senate Fundraising Chart: Democrats sweep competitive races," *National Journal*, October 16, 2020, https://www.nationaljournal.com/s/710680/hotlines-q3-senate-fundraising-chart-democrats-sweep-competitive-races.

8. "Raising: by the Numbers," Federal Election Commission, https://www.fec.gov/data/raising-bythenumbers/?office=S.

9. Alyssa Fowers, "Ginsburg Death Set Off Month-Long Donor Rush for Senate Democratic Candidates," *Washington Post*, October 23, 2020, https://www.washingtonpost.com/politics/2020/10/22/senate-democrats-rbg-donor-enthusiasm/?arc404=true.

10. Ibid.

11. Shane Goldmacher, Jeremy W. Peters, "How Ginsburg's Death Has Reshaped the Money Race for Senate Democrats," *New York Times*, September 21, 2020, https://www.nytimes.com/2020/09/21/us/politics/ginsburg-senate-donations.html.

12. Ben Kamisar, "Senate GOP group jumping into Alaska Senate race with $1.6 million in ads," NBC News, September 18, 2020, https://www.nbcnews.com/politics/meet-the-press/blog/meet-press-blog-latest-news-analysis-data-driving-political-discussion-n988541/ncrd1240383#blogHeader.

13. Annie Gowen, "'Not a Fair Fight': In Kansas, GOP Frustrated as Money Rolls in for Democrat and Senate Race Tightens," *Washington Post*, October 21, 2020, https://www.washingtonpost.com/politics/senate-trump-kansas-republicans/2020/10/21/bfecd048-1286-11eb-ad6f-36c93e6e94fb_story.html.

14. Leah Askarinam, Madelaine Pisani, "For the Lincoln Project, Defeating Lindsey Graham is Personal," *National Journal*, September 9, 2020, https://www.nationaljournal.com/s/709644/for-the-lincoln-project-defeating-lindsey-graham-is-personal.

15. Paul Kane, "McConnell Says Barrett Nomination Helped Some Vulnerable GOP Incumbents, Gives Even Odds on Holding the Senate," *Washington Post*, October 27, 2020, https://www.washingtonpost.com/politics/senate-republicans-mcconnell-trump/2020/10/27/f668b9e6-1873-11eb-befb-8864259bd2d8_story.html.

16. Burgess Everett, "Trump's New Best Friend in North Carolina," *Politico*, November 18, 2019, https://www.politico.com/news/2019/11/18/trump-thom-tillis-north-carolina-071091.

17. Brian Murphy, Jim Morrill, "One Tillis Challenger Emerges as the Favorite of Democratic Leaders and Donors," *Raleigh News & Observer*, July 8, 2019, https://www.newsobserver.com/news/politics-government/article232404482.html.

18. Brian Murphy, "Cunningham and Tillis Win, Setting Up NC as a Battleground for Control of Senate," *Raleigh News & Observer*, March 3, 2020, https://www.newsobserver.com/news/politics-government/election/article240813671.html.

19. "Latest Polls," *FiveThirtyEight*, https://projects.fivethirtyeight.com/polls/senate/north-carolina/.

20. Brian Slodysko and Gary D. Robertson, "Democrat's Personal Scandal Roils N. Carolina Senate Race," *Associated Press*, October 6, 2020, https://apnews.com/article/election-2020-virus-outbreak-senate-elections-north-carolina-thom-tillis-de011b865bb05df79a4d15a995ffe843.

21. Madelaine Pisani, "Republicans Bet the House on Cunningham's Affair," *National Journal*, October 8, 2020, https://www.nationaljournal.com/s/710465?unlock=KV1OUMGTC91DHXE9.

22. James Arkin, "Tillis Scrambles, Cunningham Lies Low in Closing Days of N.C. Senate Race," *Politico*, November 1, 2020, https://www.politico.com/news/2020/11/01/tillis-cunningham-north-carolina-senate-race-final-days-433783.

23. Kate Ackley, "Kavanaugh-fueled Bounty Awaits Challenger to Sen. Susan Collins," *Roll Call*, July 2, 2020, https://www.rollcall.com/2020/07/02/kavanaugh-fueled-bounty-awaits-challenger-to-sen-susan-collins/.

24. Madelaine Pisani, "Susan Collins Casts Sole GOP 'No' Vote as Barrett Is Confirmed," *National Journal,* October 27, 2020, https://www.nationaljournal.com/s/710956/susan-collins-casts-sole-gop-no-vote-as-barrett-is-confirmed?.

25. Jessica Piper, "Sara Gideon Raises Eye-popping $39.4m in 3 Months, Widens Money Lead On Susan Collins," *Bangor Daily News*, October 16, 2020, https://bangordailynews.com/2020/10/16/politics/sara-gideon-raises-eye-popping-39-4m-in-last-3-months-widens-money-lead-on-susan-collins/.

26. Tweet from Madelaine Pisani, September 28, 2020, https://twitter.com/MadelainePisani/status/1310725020214333441?s=20.

27. William Thornton, "Trump: My Biggest Regret Is Jeff Sessions," AL.com, June 23, 2020, https://www.al.com/news/2019/06/trump-my-biggest-regret-is-jeff-sessions.html.

28. Jon Murray, "John Hickenlooper's Ethics Violations Raise Question in Senate Race: Will Voters Care?" *Denver Post*, June 14, 2020, https://www.denverpost.com/2020/06/14/john-hickenlooper-ethics-violations-senate-primary-election/.

29. Tweet from Patrick Murray, November 6, 2020, https://twitter.com/PollsterPatrick/status/1324750218730983424?s=20.

30. "Raising: by the numbers," Federal Election Commission, https://www.fec.gov/data/raising-bythenumbers/?office=S.

31. Vaughn Hillyard and Dareh Gregorian, "'Quick, Quick, Quick': Trump Rushes McSally at Rally as She Fights to Hold Her Senate Seat," *NBC News*, October 28, 2020, https://www.nbcnews.com/politics/2020-election/quick-quick-quick-trump-rushes-mcsally-rally-she-fights-hold-n1245203.

32. Jim Galloway, "Why Stacey Abrams Isn't Running for the U.S. Senate," *Atlanta Journal-Constitution*, October 7, 2019, https://www.ajc.com/blog/politics/why-stacey-abrams-isn-running-for-the-senate/d2Z9mpoRKKXvz0VbmvOZ7J/.

33. Perry Bacon Jr., "Warnock and Ossoff Are Testing a New Strategy For Democrats in the South," *FiveThirtyEight*, December 14, 2020, https://fivethirtyeight.com/features/georgia-democrats-may-have-found-their-own-southern-strategy-a-black-centric-campaign/.

34. Daniel Dale, "Fact Check: Breaking Down Attack Ads in the Perdue Vs. Ossoff Georgia Senate Race," CNN, December 10, 2020, https://www.cnn.com/2020/12/10/politics/fact-check-perdue-ossoff-ads-georgia-senate-runoff/index.html.

35. Astead W. Herndon, "Raphael Warnock's Win Is One for the History Books," *New York Times*, January 5, 2021, https://www.nytimes.com/2021/01/05/us/politics/raphael-warnock-georgia-senate.html.

36. Sarah Fischer, "Nearly $500 Million Spent on Ads for Georgia Senate Races," *Axios*, January 5, 2021, https://www.axios.com/georgia-runoffs-senate-fundraising-0142c22e-5732-4a19-bee7-2906c2543ae4.html.

37. Amy Gardner, "'I just want to find 11,780 votes': In Extraordinary Hour-Long Call, Trump Pressures Georgia Secretary of State to Recalculate the Vote in his Favor," *Washington Post*, January 3, 2021, https://www.washingtonpost.com/politics/trump-raffensperger-call-georgia-vote/2021/01/03/d45acb92-4dc4-11eb-bda4-615aaefd0555_story.html.

38. Greg Bluestein, "With Ossoff Victory, Democrats Cement Georgia as Swing State," *Atlanta Journal-Constitution*, January 6, 2021, https://www.ajc.com/politics/no-doubt-about-it-democratic-runoff-wins-cement-georgia-as-swing-state/DVHG-6M7YRFHEBMITYBUHGKMFOI/.

39. "Georgia Senate Runoff Election Results," *New York Times*, https://www.nytimes.com/interactive/2021/01/05/us/elections/results-georgia-runoffs.html.

40. Zach Cohen, "What a Quiet 2020 Means for New Hampshire—in 2022," *National Journal*, November 2, 2020, https://tribunecontentagency.com/article/what-a-quiet-2020-means-for-new-hampshire-in-2022/.

41. Paul Steinhauser, "Scott says Democratic 'Overreach' Will Help Win Back Senate in 2022," Fox News, January 11, 2020, https://www.foxnews.com/politics/rick-scott-republicans-win-back-senate-2022.

42. Clare Foran and Ali Zaslav, "McConnell Warns Overruling Voters 'Would Damage Our Forever,'" CNN, January 6, 2021, https://www.cnn.com/2021/01/06/politics/mcconnell-trump-electoral-college/index.html.

8

Governors and State Legislatures

Republicans Retain Strength as Redistricting Looms

Mary Frances McGowan

When our collective reality was turned on its head during the coronavirus pandemic, the quiet presence that state governments played in the majority of Americans' lives suddenly became singular authorities on how best to navigate uncertain times, catapulting otherwise overlooked races into prominence. The guidance emanating from the White House was often contradictory or misleading,[1] and governors who weren't otherwise used to the spotlight were suddenly thrust into it.

Even with the unique variables this year brought to campaigns, a true shift in power wasn't anticipated at the gubernatorial level. For sitting governors running for reelection, it gave them a formidable advantage on top of their already comfortable footing,[2] as they were able to lead on the top-of-mind issue, pandemic relief, in a way that their challengers couldn't compete with. This only solidified incumbents' confidence entering the cycle, and further, the confidence Republicans had in maintaining their six incumbent governors compared to Democrats' three.[3]

The complexities of campaigning during a global health crisis only exacerbated the challenges of those seeking to topple incumbents. Even in more predictable circumstances, the path to victory for challengers this cycle was difficult, as they faced a field of popular governors who held an advantage in name recognition, resources, and political infrastructures. Challengers also found themselves unable to compete in earnest with the media omnipresence of COVID-19 press conferences, and in the early days of the pandemic, participate in traditional fund-raising and campaign events during statewide lockdowns. As safety restrictions loosened, a fundamental strategic difference appeared between Republican and Democratic candidates. Republicans got back to hitting the campaign trail and were able to make crucial connections, fund-raise in-person, and build coalitions in their party. Some even held large, crowded indoor events while ignoring the safety regulations that, in some cases, they encouraged from their own gubernatorial pulpit.[4] For some, this even meant contracting the coronavirus, as was the case with Governor Mike Parson of Missouri, who was forced to quarantine in the final stretch of his campaign against Democratic state Auditor Nicole Galloway.[5]

Democrats, meanwhile, stuck to the script written by the Biden campaign and national Democratic Party, holding largely virtual events and investing in digital media.[6] When candidates did make public appearances, events were generally small, distanced, and masked. While their strategy earned them praise from their existing base of support and national Democrats, it still made it difficult to raise their profile by retail politicking in the way many needed.

Despite early questions about whether incumbent governors' pandemic response—good, bad, or otherwise—would impact their ability to get reelected, not a single sitting governor was unseated. As uncertainty dominated federal races, it seems as if voters at the state level stuck to what they knew.[7] Incumbents' resounding success was also much higher than the historic average. As table 8.1 shows, at least 75 percent of incumbent governors in 26 of the 38 election cycles since 1946 have succeeded in their bids for reelection.

The dynamics taking place at the state legislative level were packed with more pressure than contests for the governor's mansion, as the chance to draw congressional and state legislative maps following the 2020 census was on the line in a handful of battleground states. After losing the White House in 2008, Republicans quietly poured scads of resources into state legislative races in the hopes to take majorities in chambers across the country in order to have a hand in the redistricting process. The strategy paid off, and in 2010, Republicans netted control of 20 chambers, substantially handicapping Democrats' ability to draw legislative maps that would determine political power for the next decade.[8] Table 8.2 shows the partisan balance of state legislatures over the last decade.

This year, Democrats had the opportunity to avenge their losses from 10 years prior. Before the 2020 election, Democrats controlled 39 legislative chambers out of 98 total chambers, excluding Nebraska, which is unicameral. In 2020, Democrats focused on expanding their influence in 19 chambers in 13 states, with 10 chambers as top targets: the Arizona House, Arizona Senate, Iowa House, Michigan House, Minnesota Senate, North Carolina House, North Carolina Senate, Pennsylvania House, Pennsylvania Senate, and lastly, the Texas House.[9] Republicans, meanwhile, focused on defending these chambers.

Democrats knew the task of flipping chambers would not be easy. The Republican State Leadership Committee entered the cycle with a comparatively

Table 8.1. Post-World War II Election Performance by Incumbent Governors

Year	*Incumbent Running Again*	*Lost Primary*	*Lost General*	*Won*	*Incumbent Success Rate*	*General Election Rate*
1946	20	3	3	14	70.0%	82.4%
1948	24	4	8	12	50.0%	60.0%
1950	20	1	4	15	75.0%	78.9%
1952	21	2	3	16	76.2%	84.2%
1954	19	3	4	12	63.2%	75.0%
1956	20	2	4*	15	75.0%	78.9%
1958	20	0	9	11	55.0%	55.0%
1960	14	0	6	8	57.1%	57.1%
1962	28	2	11	15	53.6%	57.7%
1964	15	1	2	12	80.0%	85.7%
1966	24	2	7	15	62.5%	68.2%
1968	14	0	4	10	71.4%	71.4%
1970	25	1	7	17	68.0%	70.8%
1972	11	2	2	7	63.6%	77.8%
1974	21	0	5	16	76.2%	76.2%
1976	8	1	2	5	62.5%	71.4%
1978	23	2	5	16	69.6%	76.2%
1980	11	1	3	7	63.6%	70.0%
1982	25	1	5	19	76.0%	79.2%
1984	6	0	2	4	66.7%	66.7%
1986	18	1	2	15	83.3%	88.2%
1988	9	0	1	8	88.9%	88.9%
1990	23	0	6	17	73.9%	73.9%
1992	4	0	0	4	100.0%	100.0%
1994	23	2	4	17	73.9%	81.0%
1996	7	0	0	7	100.0%	100.0%
1998	25	0	2	23	92.0%	92.0%
2000	6	0	1	5	83.3%	83.3%
2002	16	0	4	12	75.0%	75.0%
2004	7	1	2	4	57.1%	66.7%
2006	27	1	1	25	92.6%	96.2%
2008	8	0	0	8	100.0%	100.0%
2010	14	1	2	11	78.6%	84.6%
2012	6	0	0	6	100.0%	100.0%
2014	29	1	3	25	86.2%	89.3%
2016	5	0	1	4	80.0%	80.0%
2018	20	1	3	16	80.0%	84.2%
2020	9	0	0	9	100.0%	100.0%
Total	625	36	128	462	75.8%	79.6%

Note: *In 1956, Utah Republican Governor J. Bracken Lee lost renomination in the GOP primary, but then ran as an Independent in the general election, which he also lost.

Sources: CQ Guide to U.S. Elections, vol. ii, 6th ed., 1558; *Crystal Ball* Research.

Table 8.2. Partisan Control of State Legislatures 2010-2020

Election	*Democratic*	*Republican*	*Other*
Before 2010	60	37	2
2010	38	59	2
2011	35	60	4
2012	41	56	2
2013	41	56	2
2014	30	68	1
2015	30	68	1
2016	31	68	0
2017	32	67	0
2018	37	61	1
2019	39	59	1
2020	37	61	1

Source: "State Legislative Elections, 2020," *Ballotpedia*, December 4, 2020, https://ballotpedia.org/State_legislative_elections,_2020.

gargantuan financial war chest and were aided in many cases by maps they drew themselves after the 2010 GOP wave. Just like at the gubernatorial level, Democratic state legislative candidates attempting to topple Republican incumbents, often with little to no name recognition, ran their campaigns virtually, making crucial in-person connections impossible. When all was said and done, not a single chamber flipped in the Democrats' favor; in fact, they lost two chambers, both in New Hampshire.[10] In a year when the party slogan was "Flip Everything," it was an almost poetic defeat. According to the National Conference of State Legislatures, Republicans now hold trifectas—unified control of the governorship and both legislative chambers—in 23 states, compared to Democrats' 15. Republicans also control the governorship and hold state legislative majorities in both chambers in Alaska, but Republicans have been unable to elect a speaker in the state House in recent years. If they are able to—the battle for control was unresolved as of this writing—Alaska would be the 24th Republican trifecta. Eleven states have divided governments. Heading into 2021 redistricting, Republicans hold over half— nearly 55 percent—of all legislative seats.

2020 GUBERNATORIAL ELECTION RESULTS: THE INCUMBENTS

Of the total 11 gubernatorial races, nine of them featured a sitting governor seeking re-election: Delaware, Indiana, Missouri, New Hampshire, North Carolina, North Dakota, Vermont, Washington, and West Virginia.

According to the University of Virginia Center for Politics' *Crystal Ball* pre-election ratings, none of the states were expected to change hands.[11] The remaining two races included open seats in Utah and Montana. The results of the gubernatorial contests are detailed below.

Republicans successfully defended six incumbent governors—Governors Eric Holcomb of Indiana, Chris Sununu of New Hampshire, Phil Scott of Vermont, Doug Burgum of North Dakota, Mike Parson of Missouri, and Jim Justice of West Virginia.

In Indiana, Governor Eric Holcomb faced few obstacles in his reelection contest against Democratic former state Health Commissioner Woody Myers.[12] Throughout the general election, Holcomb held a comfortable lead in public polling and maintained an immense fundraising gap.[13] In their third quarter finances filed on October 15, Holcomb reported raising $1.8 million and had $6 million on hand. Myers, meanwhile, had raised $464,000 with $80,000 on hand heading into the last stretch of the campaign. This gap allowed Holcomb to dominate television and digital advertising. But even without his sizable resources, Holcomb entered his re-election bid with all the classic advantages of a popular incumbent governor—his long history in state politics earned him connections across party lines and high statewide approval ratings from Hoosiers. Holcomb ultimately outperformed President Trump, who carried Indiana by 16 points, and won his reelection by a 24-point margin.[14]

A similar dynamic played out in New Hampshire, where Republicans successfully defended Governor Chris Sununu's seat.[15] While Sununu easily cleared his primary, the Democratic contest was more competitive. State Senator Dan Feltes won the primary against Executive Councilor Andru Volinsky,[16] a progressive backed by Bernie Sanders.[17] In the Democratic primary, 4,276 Democratic voters wrote in Sununu on the ballot, a metric Republicans pointed to in order to prove his popularity across party lines.[18] Republicans were cautious to take anything for granted considering the state's history as a battleground, but were confident throughout the cycle that Sununu had a clear advantage. He enjoyed stronger financial resources, a favorable reception to his pandemic response,[19] and the influence of a political family dynasty. Because of Sununu's perceived strength on state-level issues, Democrats were forced to widen their messaging scope, and focused their attacks on tethering the governor to the president, driving home the message that a vote for the governor was a vote for Donald Trump, who trailed Joe Biden in the polls and also narrowly lost the state in 2016 (and ultimately again in 2020). Ultimately, Biden's success[20] in the state did not translate into weakness for Sununu, who ended up carrying counties that Biden did as well—this included Concord, which Biden carried by 32 points and Sununu by five points, and

Exeter, which Biden carried by 34 points and Sununu carried by eight points. Sununu ultimately ended up carrying the state 65 percent to 33 percent even as Biden won statewide by seven points.[21]

In Vermont, Republican Governor Phil Scott was reelected by the widest margin in state history, defeating his opponent, Democratic Lieutenant Governor David Zuckerman, by 41 points. Put more plainly, of the state's 251 towns, Zuckerman carried only 4.[22] While Scott was among the most popular governors before the pandemic, his response to it only strengthened his footing.[23] Despite Zuckerman's support from Vermont heavyweight Senator Bernie Sanders, Scott's popularity overwhelmed any possibility of toppling him.

In July, the *Crystal Ball* newsletter changed its ratings for the Missouri governor's race from "Likely Republican" to "Leans Republican," spurring late questions about the competitive nature of the race.[24] Republican Governor Mike Parson's comparative vulnerability was a reflection of the fact that his built-in advantage as an incumbent wasn't bolstered by his pandemic response in the way that it had lifted other sitting governors. In fact, according to a survey by the COVID-19 Consortium for Understanding the Public's Policy Preferences Across States at Harvard's Kennedy School, Northeastern University, and Rutgers University,[25] Parson's net approval of his pandemic response declined from 60 percent in late April to 39 percent in late August. Parson's opponent, Democratic state Auditor Nicole Galloway, capitalized on this, centering much of her messaging on criticizing Parson's response—namely, his refusal to implement a statewide mask mandate (which his allies called "draconian"),[26] ignoring social-distancing guidelines on the campaign trail, and reopening schools[27] amid climbing case numbers. Those criticisms were only sharpened in late October, when Parson and his wife, Teresa, contracted COVID-19 and returned to the campaign trail 10 days later.[28] Parson and Galloway were also competitive in their fund-raising: third quarter finance reports released in mid-October showed that Parson had $1.7 million cash on hand, compared to Galloway's $1.6 million. But while his pandemic response didn't all-but ensure his reelection, it also didn't make much of a dent in public polling,[29] and Parson continued to lead every public poll released. Ultimately, Parson carried the state by 17 points, performing a little bit better than Trump.[30]

In the Mountain State, Republican Governor Jim Justice unsurprisingly held on to his post as chief executive of West Virginia, defeating his opponent, Democratic Kanawha County Commissioner Ben Salango. Justice's unilateral allocation of CARES Act funding fractured state-level Republicans and drew ire from Democrats.[31] But despite his often-polarizing response to the pandemic, Justice comfortably led in public polling throughout the cycle and carried the state by 34 points.[32] Republicans also defended the governorship in North Dakota, where Governor Doug Burgum defeated Democratic veterinarian Shelley Lenz by 43 points.[33]

Democrats successfully defended incumbent Governors John Carney of Delaware, Jay Inslee of Washington, and Roy Cooper of North Carolina. While Carney and Inslee did not face competitive races, the race in the Tar Heel State deserves a closer examination.

The governor's race in North Carolina was once thought to be one of the most competitive gubernatorial elections in the 2020 cycle, less because of any questions surrounding Democratic Governor Roy Cooper's general popularity but due to the state's history of razor-thin races.[34] In 2016, for example, Cooper defeated then-Governor Pat McCrory by less than a point. But Cooper's strength was only solidified through the pandemic. Cooper already eclipsed his opponent, Republican Lieutenant Governor Dan Forest in both fund-raising and name recognition, but his media omnipresence with daily COVID-19 updates and a popular pandemic response, in addition to Forest's inability to fund-raise during shutdowns or become a more authoritative voice on the global health crisis than the state's chief executive, made it nearly impossible for him to catch up. Although neither camp was willing to get comfortable throughout the tight race, Cooper's lead in public polling during the cycle proved to be a reliable indicator of what was to come. Cooper defeated Forest by four points—while tighter than some other contests this cycle, the result provided a striking contrast nonetheless to 2016.[35] Cooper won even as Republicans won the state's other two marquee contests, for Senate and president.

The results detailed above confirm the dynamic since March—although every race was defined by issues particular to the state, the driving force was the unique advantage incumbent governors had in addressing the issue that was on top in the minds for all Americans: the coronavirus pandemic.

OPEN RACES

In addition to the nine contests featuring incumbent governors, the 2020 gubernatorial map featured two open seats.

In Montana, term limits prevented Democratic Governor Steve Bullock from running again (Bullock would go on to lose a Senate race). The *Crystal Ball* newsletter rated Montana as the cycle's only gubernatorial Toss-up before shifting it to Leans Republican before the election. The race featured a contest between Democratic Lieutenant Governor Mike Cooney and Republican Representative Greg Gianforte.[36] Unlike some races, where national politics maintained an inescapable presence, the race in Montana centered almost entirely on drawing distinctions between the two candidates and focusing on state-level issues.[37] For Cooney, that meant touting his partnership with popular outgoing Governor Steve Bullock, including their administration's efforts to protect public lands, address the coronavirus pandemic, and plans to protect the Affordable Care Act and expand Medicaid in the state. Gianforte's messaging, meanwhile, focused on highlighting contrasts between himself and his opponent. While he wasn't shy about his relationship with Trump, his message also wasn't reliant on it. On the first day of the general election, the Gianforte campaign released a statewide television ad labeling Cooney a "career politician and a government bureaucrat," a familiar cry in Republican talking points.[38] In the end, Gianforte defeated Cooney by 13 points, breaking the Democrats' 16-year streak of control over the governor's mansion. He was aided by his comparatively stronger name recognition from being on the gubernatorial ballot in 2016 and Cooney's underperformance in counties where Bullock dominated four years prior. This includes Glacier, which Bullock carried by 48 points and Cooney carried by 35 points; and Lewis and Clark, which Bullock carried by 23 points and Cooney carried by two points. Cooney also lost three counties that Bullock carried in 2016: Lake near the Flathead Native American reservation; Cascade, which includes Great Falls; and Hill, which lies along the northern border with Canada.[39]

In deep red Utah, the action was limited to the Republican primary for the open seat that became available thanks to Republican Governor Gary Herbert not seeking another term. The contest featured Beehive State Republican heavyweights Lieutenant Governor Spencer Cox, former state House Speaker Greg Hughes, former Governor Jon Huntsman, and former GOP state chairman Thomas Wright. Because candidates knew that the winner of the contest was all but assured the governor's mansion, the stakes were high, and candidates spent and raised millions of dollars over the course of the contest.[40] As it became apparent that the race was tightening to a battle between Cox and Huntsman, a political scandal emerged—Herbert tried to cut a deal with Wright by encouraging him to drop out of the primary in exchange for his full support in running for Senate against Republican Senator Mike Lee, a rumor he later admitted to.[41] While Cox ended up the victor of the primary,[42] Huntsman flirted with the possibility of running as a write-in candidate for some time before finally giving in.[43] Cox went on to handily defeat his Democratic opponent, law professor Chris Peterson, by a margin of 32 points.[44]

STATE LEGISLATIVE ELECTIONS RESULTS

The amount riding on state legislative elections in 2020 cannot be overstated. In 2010, Democrats lost control of 20 state legislative chambers, which limited their influence in drawing congressional and state legislative maps. In the 2020 cycle, they hoped to pull off the same sort of upset, and sunk millions of dollars into over a dozen states in order to expand their influence. But ultimately, not a single targeted chamber went in their favor. The election results of each competitive legislative chamber are detailed below.

On top of defending all the chambers targeted by Democrats, Republicans gained a trifecta in New Hampshire by flipping the state House and state Senate. According to the National Conference of State Legislatures, chambers in New Hampshire are very prone to changing political hands, as evidenced by the fact that the body has changed majorities in the last six out of eight elections. The state House especially is prone to party change, due in part to minuscule districts with an average of 3,400 constituents.[45]

In the state Senate, power shifted from a 14-10 Democratic majority to a 14-10 Republican majority. Democrats held a 230-157 majority in the state House heading into the election.[46] All 400 seats were up for grabs, including 13 vacant seats, due to three deaths and 10 resignations. Republicans ultimately netted 56 seats, making the power dynamic a 211-186 Republican majority. The absolute shift in power in New Hampshire was unexpected for both parties.[47] The Republican State Legislative Committee credited their winning on Sununu's overwhelming popularity, saying his political coattails were "long and strong." They said their success there can be tracked by following the counties carried by Biden previously detailed in this chapter, including Concord and Nashua. Democrats agreed that Biden's coattails in the state were comparatively short.

In Arizona, Democrats targeted both chambers of the state's legislature, following the path of Senator Kyrsten Sinema's victory in 2018.[48] Democrats needed to flip two state Senate seats and three state House seats to take the chambers. It is important to note that in the Grand Canyon State, the legislative districts are different from most other states in that each one is represented by one state senator and two state House members. This cycle, the Democratic State Legislative Committee concentrated their efforts in suburban legislative districts near Flagstaff, as well as the greater Phoenix area. Despite the victories of now-Democratic Senator Mark Kelly and Joe Biden in the state and record spending of millions of dollars from candidates and outside groups in both parties, Democrats netted just one state senate seat in the 28th District, where Democratic teacher Christine Marsh bested Republican state Senator Kate Brophy McGee.[49] Ultimately, Republicans maintained their trifecta in the state that they have held since 2009. Republicans now hold a 31-29 advantage in the House and 16-14 majority in the state Senate. Although Democrats will not have the ability to check Governor Doug Ducey's power like they had hoped, the state's redistricting will not be impacted because the state draws congressional and state legislative lines through an independent commission.

Biden's coattails did not extend far enough to pull Democratic state legislative candidates across the finish line in Georgia, where the party hoped to make inroads in the state House.[50] In 2018, Democrats made their largest gains in two decades in the state legislature by picking up 11 seats in the House and two in the Senate. This year, they hoped to keep that momentum going by targeting 25 more Republican-held House seats (eight of which were particularly vulnerable) in suburbs and exurbs trending toward the Democrats.[51] This included seats in Cobb, Gwinnett, and Fulton counties in the Greater Atlanta area, in addition to Athens, a college town.[52] While taking back the Georgia House was an unlikely outcome for Democrats, who needed to gain 16 seats to flip the chamber, Republicans feared they were vulnerable in the state following their losses two years prior, a razor-thin gubernatorial race featuring Stacey Abrams and now-Governor Brian Kemp, and an increasingly fractured state party. Heading into 2020, Republicans held a 105-75 advantage in the House. Despite casting a wide net, Democrats only netted one seat in the House and now face a 103-76 deficit, which includes one vacancy. With Republicans holding their trifecta, they will be able to control drawing congressional and state legislative maps for the next decade.

In Iowa, Democrats targeted the state House after gaining five seats in 2018, hoping to continue their advances against a handful of vulnerable Republican incumbents in suburban districts. But they had their work cut out for them, because in addition to playing offense, they would have to defend a series of rural Democratic districts that Republicans were targeting. This dynamic provided Republicans with more paths to preserve their 53-47 majority than it gave Democrats to topple it. After all was said and done, Republicans gained six seats, bringing the balance of power to 59-41. The tough night for Democrats in Iowa won't have the same kind of grave consequences it will in other states—while the legislature is responsible for adopting and approving maps, the actual task of drawing the lines is done by a nonpartisan legislative staff. A simple majority of the legislature is required to adopt the maps, which Republicans will easily be able to manage.

In Michigan, Democrats hoped to continue the momentum they started in 2018, when the party took back the governor's mansion, broke a supermajority in the state Senate, and netted five seats in the state House.[53] Democrats needed to net five more this year to take the chamber, and saw their path rooted through the Detroit suburbs where Governor Gretchen Whitmer shined in her 2018 victory. But they also faced unique challenges in their quest to retake the state House, because a handful of their incumbents were vulnerable, meaning they needed to likely flip more than four to have a true shift in power, an ambitious task in a swing state. While Biden was able to take back the state after Trump carried it in 2016, his successes didn't translate down ballot, and Democrats ended up only picking up one vacant seat. The power dynamic won't impact Democrats' ability to take part in the redistricting process after the state installed an independent commission in 2018, but the party also lost their opportunity to provide Whitmer with a legislative ally in the state to help her accomplish her policy goals.

The Minnesota Senate was among the most competitive chambers this cycle, in part because it hadn't been on the ballot since President Trump's election (except for a single special election), and the 2018 "blue wave" effects that had crashed down in other states hadn't had the chance to play out there yet. The Democratic Farmer-Labor Party only needed to net two seats to take the state Senate and create a trifecta in the state. Democrats saw their path rooted in 10 Republican-held districts concentrated largely in the Twin Cities suburbs that Governor Tim Walz carried in 2018. Before the election, Republicans also agreed that the chamber was their most vulnerable. Republicans entered the cycle with a 34-32 majority with one vacancy. The results in Minnesota are a bit complicated—while the Democratic Farmer-Labor Party gained one seat, the Republican advantage stayed the same after two DFL members left the caucus to become independents. Democrats chalked up their losses to ticket-splitting voters. In the state, 1,716,578 voters cast ballots for Biden, compared to 1,596,658 who voted for Democrats at the state level. That's a difference of roughly 119,000 voters—which is impactful in races that are often won by razor-thin margins. The surprising loss for Democrats in Minnesota will have far-reaching consequences because the state legislature is responsible for drawing congressional and state legislative lines and is split between the two parties.

Both chambers in North Carolina were targeted by Democrats, who were emboldened to make inroads after a federal court threw out their old, Republican-drawn maps during mid-cycle redistricting, which made the playing field a bit less daunting for Democrats.[54] Democrats needed to take five seats in the Senate and six in the House in order to flip the chambers and were confident they could at least run up the numbers because of strong candidate recruitment and the popularity of Governor Cooper. Republicans started the cycle with a 65-55 majority in the House and ended it by gaining four, bringing the balance of power to 69-51. In the state Senate, Republicans had a 29-21 advantage entering the cycle. After the election, Democrats gained one seat, bringing their deficit to 28-22. Democrats' inability to flip either chamber will take away their ability to play a role in the redistricting process this year, because the state legislature draws congressional and state-level lines, and the governor has no veto power over the maps. However, Democrats currently control the state Supreme Court, four to three. Should they take issue with any portion of the eventual legislative maps, Democrats can petition the court to review them.

In 2018, Democrats in Pennsylvania netted 11 seats in the state House, and they hoped to continue their gains in 2020 by targeting vulnerable seats in the Philadelphia suburbs. While netting the necessary nine seats to flip the chamber in 2020 was going to be a heavy lift, they found five targeted Republican districts outside of Philadelphia that Clinton carried and a handful outside of Harrisburg that were particularly promising.[55] Candidly, Republicans thought that having native son Joe Biden at the top of the ticket could possibly translate to overwhelming turnout and consequently long, liberal coattails, and while they were skeptical that the chamber could change hands, they were prepared to face a very slim majority at the end of the cycle. But as was common in the 2020 election at the state level, very little changed, and Democrats' hopes were dashed. Democrats ended up losing three seats, bringing their deficit to 113-90. The results mean that Republicans in the state legislature will have control over drawing congressional lines, although Democratic Governor Tom Wolf has veto power. However, an independent commission is in charge of drawing state legislative maps.

While the presidential race and Senate contests in Texas may have received attention, Democrats also hoped to turn the state House blue. Their enthusiasm was evidenced by millions of dollars from outside groups like Forward Majority, DLCC, and Michael Bloomberg's Everytown for Gun Safety. Democrats needed to grab nine seats to flip the chamber, and saw their path rooted in Republican seats that Beto O'Rourke carried in his 2018 Senate race, mainly in suburban Houston and Dallas.[56] They were motivated not only by redistricting, but to break the Republican trifecta in the state. However, Democrats failed to make up any ground in the Texas House, which will allow Republican state legislators to control drawing both congressional and state legislative maps.[57]

The results of elections across state legislatures this cycle isn't merely surprising because of the millions of dollars invested in vain or expectations falling short, but also because it is an outlier by historical standards. According to the National Conference of State Legislatures (NCSL), tracking changes of political power at the state legislative level should be done in two-year cycles, in order to account for states that hold odd-year elections. In 2019, Democrats took back both chambers of the Virginia General Assembly. This year, Republicans flipped both chambers of the New Hampshire state legislature, meaning four chambers flipped this cycle. According to the NCSL data going back to 1900, an average of 12 chambers have flipped per two-year cycle.

Democrats and political experts have offered a series of explanations as to why the political power in the states was barely altered this cycle. At the state legislative level, Democrats didn't get the Election Night they were hoping for. While Biden's short coattails were partially at fault, Democrats also said ticket-splitters and roll-off voters were partially to blame—meaning that there was a significant number of voters who backed Biden, regardless of their party, but either supported Republicans down-ballot, or left their state legislative selection blank.[58]

LOOKING AHEAD AT 2021-2022

The outcome of state legislative elections puts Republicans in a good position for redistricting once again. Ahead of redistricting this year, 14 states use independent or bipartisan political commissions, meaning state legislatures do not play a part in the process. In three states, there is a hybrid redistricting process, where a state legislature works in tandem with a commission. In the remaining 33 states, the legislature draws state and congressional lines. Of those, 20 are held by Republicans; 11 are held by Democrats; one, Minnesota, is split; and Nebraska is a nonpartisan unicameral legislature.[59]

While governors' races were a bit sleepy this cycle, there is much to look forward to over the next two years. The lion's share of states, 38 of 50, will hold gubernatorial elections in 2021 and 2022, and while it may have been too early to study the impacts of governors' pandemic responses this year, voters will have had plenty of time to formulate their stances on their leadership styles.

In 2021, New Jersey and Virginia will elect new governors. In the Garden State, incumbent Democratic Governor Phil Murphy will defend his seat, with a handful of Republican challengers already throwing their hat into the ring. If Murphy were to defend his seat, he would be the first Democrat to win a second term since Brendan Byrne in 1977.[60]

In Virginia, Democrats will be defending their seat in an open contest because Governor Ralph Northam is term limited (Virginia, alone among the states, does not allow governors to run for consecutive terms). At the time of publication, the Democratic primary includes a number of prominent candidates—former Governor Terry McAuliffe as well as several other state-level Democrats. Who Democratic voters choose will be a fascinating case study in the sort of party Democrats will be in years to come. The Republican contest will also measure the type of party they plan to be going forward, and the gubernatorial race is, in many ways, Republicans' final gasp in their attempt at being a functioning state party in a deeply blue state. As it stands, the race features two candidates from opposing sides of conservative thought—former state House Speaker Kirk Cox, a traditional Republican, and state Senator Amanda Chase, a Trumpian Republican who was present at a Washington rally that preceded the insurrection at the U.S. Capitol.

Virginia will also be tasked with defending their ground in both chambers of their state legislature, and in 2022, 88 out of the 99 state legislative chambers nationwide will hold elections. Although the outcomes will not result in either party's ability to draw district lines, political action bubbling in the states will be imperative to monitor over the next two years. Before the United States Capitol fell prey to a fatal domestic terrorist attack, violent protests occurred in state capitals. State lawmakers, including governors, secretaries of state, and attorney generals, were on the receiving end of armed protests outside their residences. Michigan Governor Whitmer was even the target of a kidnapping attempt. Beyond the action taken by citizens, the insurrection was attended by at least 13 state lawmakers.

Supreme Court Associate Justice Louis Brandeis once called state governments "laboratories of democracy." As the *Associated Press* eloquently wrote following the insurrection, they have unfortunately also become "training grounds for violent dissent."[61]

NOTES

1. Cameron Peters, "A Detailed Timeline of All the Ways Trump Failed to Respond to the Coronavirus," *Vox*, June 8, 2020, https://www.vox.com/2020/6/8/21242003/trump-failed-coronavirus-response.

2. Alan Greenblatt, "COVID-19 Gives Governors' Re-Election Hopes a Boost," *Governing*, October 13, 2020, https://www.governing.com/now/COVID-19-Gives-Governors-Re-election-Hopes-a-Boost.html.

3. "Governors Races Overview," *Stateside*, https://www.stateside.com/election/2020-gubernatorial-elections.

4. Jack Suntrup, "Mixed Messages: Despite State Guidance, Parson Goes Maskless, Calls Coverings 'Dang Masks,'" *St. Louis Post-Dispatch*, July 14, 2020, https://www.stltoday.com/news/local/govt-and-politics/mixed-messages-despite-state-guidance-parson-goes-maskless-calls-coverings-dang-masks/article_b4023aa1-e4a3-522a-bbdf-280902abdd73.html.

5. David A. Lieb and Jim Salter, "Missouri Governor, Opponent of Mandatory Masks, Has COVID-19," *Associated Press*, September 23, 2020, https://apnews.com/article/virus-outbreak-archive-michael-brown-ec3963a041c3061abba62493aa0bb2be.

6. Mini Racker, "Facing the New Normal, Student Organizers Give 2020 the Old College Try," *National Journal*, September 27, 2020, https://www.nationaljournal.com/s/710125/facing-the-new-normal-student-organizers-give-2020-the-old-college-try.

7. Mary Frances McGowan, "Consistency Defines Governor Races—except in Montana," *National Journal*, November 4, 2020, https://www.nationaljournal.com/s/711143/consistency-defines-governors-racesexcept-in-montana.

8. "State Legislative Elections, 2020," *Ballotpedia*, December 4, 2020, https://ballotpedia.org/State_legislative_elections,_2020.

9. Mary Frances McGowan, "Hotline's State-Legislative Power Rankings: Democrats Hope to Avenge 2010 Losses," *National Journal*, October 20, 2020, https://www.nationaljournal.com/s/710770/hotlines-state-legislative-power-rankings-democrats-hope-to-avenge-2010-losses.

10. Annie Ropeik, "New Hampshire's Was Only State Legislature That Changed Parties In 2020 Election," *New Hampshire Public Radio*, November 12, 2020, https://www.nhpr.org/post/new-hampshire-s-was-only-state-legislature-changed-parties-2020-election#stream/0.

11. Larry J. Sabato, Kyle Kondik, and J. Miles Coleman, "Final Ratings for the 2020 Election," *Sabato's Crystal Ball*, November 2, 2020, https://centerforpolitics.org/crystalball/articles/21320/.

12. Mary Frances McGowan, "Democrats Are Taking on Missouri's Governor. Why Not Indiana's, Too?" *National Journal*, April 21, 2020, https://www.nationaljournal.com/s/706232/democrats-are-taking-on-missouris-governor-why-not-indianas-too.

13. Chris Sikich, "Holcomb Has Vast Fundraising Lead over Myers, Rainwater," *Indianapolis Star*, October 15, 2020, https://www.indystar.com/story/news/politics/2020/10/15/indiana-elections-holcomb-has-vast-fundraising-lead-over-his-opponents/3665438001/.

14. "Indiana Governor Election Results," *Associated Press,* January 5, 2021, https://www.nytimes.com/interactive/2020/11/03/us/elections/results-indiana.html?action=click&module=ELEX_results&pgtype=Interactive®ion=RaceSubNav.

15. Mary Frances McGowan, "Republicans Hope Sununu's Family Ties Trump His Political Affiliation," *National Journal*, September 17, 2020, https://www.nationaljournal.com/s/709810/republicans-hope-sununus-family-ties-trump-his-political-affiliation.

16. "New Hampshire Governor Primary Election Results," *New York Times*, September 10, 2020, https://www.nytimes.com/interactive/2020/09/08/us/elections/results-new-hampshire-governor-primary-election.html.

17. Paul Cuno-Booth, "Bernie Sanders Endorses Volinsky for Governor," *Keene Sentinel*, January 30, 2020, https://www.sentinelsource.com/news/local/bernie-sanders-endorses-volinsky-for-governor/article_5665f89d-60c2-54d4-b13d-fac14d3423fe.html.

18. Kevin Landrigan, "Dem Write-Ins for Sununu, Vote-Skippers Ominous for Feltes," *New Hampshire Union Leader*, September 12, 2020, https://www.unionleader.com/news/politics/statehouse_dome/dem-write-ins-for-sununu-vote-skippers-ominous-for-feltes/article_77c234c5-ea29-510c-b6a1-0ef176747589.html.

19. Ethan DeWitt, "Sununu's Popular Handling of Pandemic Proves Too Much for Feltes to Overcome," *Concord Monitor*, November 3, 2020, https://www.concordmonitor.com/Gov-Chris-Sununu-Dan-Feltes-New-Hampshire-gubernatorial-race-results-37113474.

20. "Democrat Joe Biden Wins New Hampshire," PBS NewsHour, November 3, 2020, https://www.pbs.org/newshour/politics/biden-wins-new-hampshire.

21. "New Hampshire Election Results," *New York Times*, January 11, 2021, https://www.nytimes.com/interactive/2020/11/03/us/elections/results-new-hampshire.html.

22. Don Turner, "Don Turner: Three Key Takeaways from the Vermont Election Results," *Vermont Digger*, November 17, 2020, https://vtdigger.org/2020/11/17/don-turner-three-key-takeaways-from-the-vermont-election-results/.

23. Xander Landen, "In Profile: Gov. Phil Scott Touts 'Steady Hand' but Keeps Veto Pen at the Ready," *Vermont Digger*, October 9, 2020, https://vtdigger.org/2020/10/09/gov-phil-scott-touts-steady-hand-but-keeps-veto-pen-at-the-ready/.

24. "2020 Rating Changes," *Sabato's Crystal Ball*, https://centerforpolitics.org/crystalball/2020-rating-changes/.

25. David Lazer et al., "The State of the Nation: A 50-State COVID-19 Survey," vol. 19 (The COVID-19 Consortium for Understanding the Public's Policy Preferences Across States).

26. Mary Frances McGowan, "Show-Me State Showdown Turns on Parson Diagnosis," *National Journal*, October 8, 2020, https://www.nationaljournal.com/s/710457/show-me-state-showdown-turns-on-parson-diagnosis

27. Jasmyn Willis, "Parson: Schools Reopening as COVID-19 Cases Rising, Medicaid Expansion," KRCG, August 5, 2020, https://krcgtv.com/news/local/parson-holds-press-conference-at-300-pm-08-05-2020.

28. Jaclyn Peiser, "Missouri's Governor Has Refused to Mandate Masks. Now He's Tested Positive for the Coronavirus," *Washington Post*, September 24, 2020, https://www.washingtonpost.com/nation/2020/09/24/parson-missouri-governor-covid-positive/.

29. "Missouri Governor Polls," *FiveThirtyEight*, January 8, 2021, https://projects.fivethirtyeight.com/polls/governor/missouri/.

30. "Missouri Governor Election Results," *New York Times*, December 10, 2020, https://www.nytimes.com/interactive/2020/11/03/us/elections/results-missouri.html.

31. Mary Frances McGowan and Erin Durkin, "COVID-19 Funds Drive a Wedge in West Virginia," *National Journal*, July 30, 2020, https://www.nationaljournal.com/s/708820/covid-19-funds-drive-a-wedge-in-west-virginia.

32. "West Virginia Election Results," *New York Times*, January 10, 2021, https://www.nytimes.com/interactive/2020/11/03/us/elections/results-west-virginia.html.

33. "North Dakota Governor Election Results," *New York Times*, November 24, 2021, https://www.nytimes.com/interactive/2020/11/03/us/elections/results-north-dakota-governor.html.

34. Mary Frances McGowan, "N.C. Republicans Express Concern about Forest's Gubernatorial Prospects," *National Journal,* May 14, 2020, https://www.nationaljournal.com/s/706807/in-state-republicans-express-concern-about-forests-gubernatorial-prospects.

35. Brian Gordon, "NC Election Results: Roy Cooper Wins NC Governor's Race," *Citizen Times*, November 3, 2020, https://www.citizen-times.com/story/news/2020/11/03/roy-cooper-nc-governor-race-over-dan-forest-2020-election/6155462002/.

36. Mary Frances McGowan and Madelaine Pisani, "Montana's Top Candidates Implement Lone-Ranger Strategy," *National Journal*, October 27, 2020, https://www.nationaljournal.com/s/709518/montanas-top-candidates-implement-lone-ranger-strategy?

37. "Governor Candidate Cooney Lays out Public Lands Agenda," *Helena Independent Record*, July 19, 2020, https://helenair.com/news/state-and-regional/govt-and-politics/governor-candidate-cooney-lays-out-public-lands-agenda/article_8c4a82e5-bc38-56ef-9964-f03e87de8912.html.

38. Mike Dennison, "Stark Contrasts Separate Cooney, Gianforte in Montana's Race for Governor," *Missoula Current*, June 30, 2020, https://missoulacurrent.com/government/2020/06/cooney-gianforte-governor-2/.

39. "Montana Governor Election Results," *New York Times*, December 5, 2020, https://www.nytimes.com/interactive/2020/11/03/us/elections/results-montana-governor.html.

40. "Republican Candidates for Governor Spent Nearly $4 Million on Advertising Ahead of the Primary," *Utah Policy*, August 12, 2020, https://utahpolicy.com/index.php/features/today-at-utah-policy/24603-republican-candidates-for-governor-spent-nearly-4-million-on-advertising-ahead-of-the-primary.

41. Thomas Burr, "Sen. Mike Lee Criticizes Gov. Gary Herbert, Lt. Gov. Spencer Cox over Reported Election Antics," *The Salt Lake Tribune*, June 17, 2020, https://www.sltrib.com/news/politics/2020/06/17/sen-mike-lee-criticizes/.

42. "Republican Candidates for Governor Spent Nearly $4 Million on Advertising Ahead of the Primary," *Utah Policy*, August 12, 2020, https://utahpolicy.com/index.php/features/today-at-utah-policy/24603-republican-candidates-for-governor-spent-nearly-4-million-on-advertising-ahead-of-the-primary.

43. Bryan Schott, "Huntsman Says No to Write-in Campaign, but His Supporters Hope to Change His Mind," *Utah Policy*, July 13, 2020, https://utahpolicy.com/index.php/features/today-at-utah-policy/24340-huntsman-says-no-to-write-in-campaign-but-his-supporters-hope-to-change-his-mind.

44. "Utah Governor Election Results," *New York Times*, January 11, 2020, https://www.nytimes.com/interactive/2020/11/03/us/elections/results-utah-governor.html.

45. Annie Ropeik, "New Hampshire's Was Only State Legislature That Changed Parties in 2020 Election," *New Hampshire Public Radio*, November 12, 2020, https://www.nhpr.org/post/new-hampshire-s-was-only-state-legislature-changed-parties-2020-election#stream/0.

46. "NH State Senate Flips to GOP, House Balance Still Unknown," *US News*, https://www.usnews.com/news/best-states/new-hampshire/articles/2020-11-04/still-unknown-which-party-controls-nh-state-legislature.

47. Mary Frances McGowan, "Hotline's State-Legislative Power Rankings: Democrats Hope to Avenge 2010 Losses," *National Journal*, October 20, 2020, https://www.nationaljournal.com/s/710770/hotlines-state-legislative-power-rankings-democrats-hope-to-avenge-2010-losses.

48. Dylan Wells, "Arizona's Other Senate Race: Republicans Defend Their Majority," *National Journal*, June 10, 2020, https://www.nationaljournal.com/s/707445/arizonas-other-senate-race-republicans-defend-their-majority.

49. Kevin Mahnken, "Democrats Fall Short of Majority in Arizona Legislature," *The 74 Million*, November 12, 2020, https://www.the74million.org/democrats-fall-short-of-majority-in-arizona-legislature/.

50. Beau Evans, "Georgia Republicans Fend Off Democrat's Push to Flip the State House," Georgia Public Radio, November 5, 2020, https://www.gpb.org/news/2020/11/05/georgia-republicans-fend-off-democrats-push-flip-the-state-house.

51. Mary Frances McGowan, "Republicans' Vulnerabilities in Georgia Stretch down to the State House," *National Journal*, June 9, 2020, https://www.nationaljournal.com/s/707370/republicans-vulnerabilities-in-georgia-stretch-down-to-the-state-house.

52. "Georgia GOP Fears Changing Demographics Could End Party's Long Dominance," *New Hampshire Public Radio*, June 7, 2020, https://www.nhpr.org/post/georgia-gop-fears-changing-demographics-could-end-partys-long-dominance#stream/0.

53. Mary Frances McGowan, "Democrats Hope to Provide an Ally to 'That Woman from Michigan,'" *National Journal*, July 15, 2020, https://www.nationaljournal.com/s/708387/democrats-hope-to-provide-an-ally-to-that-woman-from-michigan.

54. Mary Frances McGowan, "North Carolina's Other Senate Race," *National Journal*, April 8, 2020, https://www.nationaljournal.com/s/705927/the-other-north-carolina-senate-race.

55. Alex Clearfield, "Democrats Need 'Perfect Storm' to Capture Pennsylvania State Senate," *National Journal*, March 18, 2020, https://www.nationaljournal.com/s/705485/democrats-need-perfect-storm-to-capture-pennsylvania-state-senate.

56. Erin Covey, "Democrats Count on Trickle-up Economics to Turn Texas Blue," *National Journal*, September 2, 2020, https://www.nationaljournal.com/s/709549/democrats-count-on-trickle-up-economics-to-turn-texas-blue.

57. Erin Covey, "Democrats Messed with Texas and Got the Horns," *National Journal*, December 16, 2020, https://www.nationaljournal.com/s/711666/democrats-messed-with-texass-bull-and-got-the-horns?

58. Mary Frances McGowan, "Millions of Dollars Later, the Makeup of State Legislatures Remains Nearly Identical," *National Journal*, November 29, 2020, https://www.nationaljournal.com/s/711428/millions-of-dollars-later-the-makeup-of-state-legislatures-remains-nearly-identical.

59. Tim Henderson, "A Nationwide Primer on Redistricting," Stateline, January 31, 2021, https://www.marylandmatters.org/2021/01/31/a-nationwide-primer-on-redistricting/

60. Steven Shepard and Sabrina Rodriguez, "Three-Quarters of States Will Elect Governors in the Next 2 Years. Here's a Field Guide," *Politico* December 6, 2020,

https://www.politico.com/news/2020/12/16/governors-guide-election-2021-2022-445430.

61. Rebecca Boone, "Armed Statehouse Protests Set Tone for US Capitol Insurgents," *Associated Press,* January 7, 2021, https://apnews.com/article/election-2020-coronavirus-pandemic-oregon-elections-idaho-688fc8894f44992487bb6ee45e9abd77.

9

Parties, Presidents, and the Black Electorate's Gender Gap

Theodore R. Johnson

One year before President Joe Biden's inauguration, his bid for the Democratic Party's nomination was faltering. National polling showed his campaign losing steam while Vermont Senator Bernie Sanders, former New York City Mayor Michael Bloomberg, and South Bend, Indiana, mayor Pete Buttigieg all seemed to be gaining traction.[1] The Democratic primary's changing state of play in January 2020 resembled the uncertainty in the nation's politics: the United States Senate's trial to consider removing impeached President Donald Trump from office was underway, the foreign policy community was on edge after a surprise United States airstrike killed a senior Iranian military commander in Iraq, and Americans began hearing about the novel coronavirus that would soon grind the nation to a halt. Amidst all the volatility, however, one thing remained remarkably stable: Biden's substantial and resilient lead with Black voters.[2] Thanks to this steady support, his campaign recovered from its early struggles, and the former vice president soon won the party's nomination—his historic 2020 presidential run rescued from the footnotes of history by the pragmatism of the Black electorate.

When the dust settled following a contentious, hyperpartisan, and norm-trashing election season, Biden won the White House with a tally of 306 in the Electoral College and by more than 7 million popular votes. The election, though, was closer than those numbers suggest; his victory essentially came down to just 43,000 votes across three states: Wisconsin, Georgia, and Arizona.[3] As such, no one group is responsible for Biden's win, but Black voters certainly delivered the nomination and played an outsized role in the general election by voting for him with overwhelming margins. Cities in battleground states with majority or plurality Black populations—Detroit, Milwaukee, Philadelphia, Atlanta—were a primary reason their respective states moved into the win column for Biden after Donald Trump carried them in 2016. In an election with the highest voter turnout in more than a century, exit polling from the *Associated Press*' VoteCast shows that Biden won 90 percent of the Black electorate to Trump's 8 percent.[4] Though Biden's share of this electorate held fairly steady from Hillary Clinton's showing in 2016, the rise in turnout increased the Democratic Party's advantage.[5]

None of this is particularly surprising, but the gender gap was one feature of the Black electorate that had the potential to introduce additional uncertainty into the presidential election. Indeed, peeling off just enough Black men to place Biden's chances of victory at greater risk was part of the Trump campaign's strategy—using symbolic and direct policy appeals to either win more of their votes or dissuade them from voting at all.[6] It was not an accident that at the Republican National Convention, Black men featured prominently in the speaker lineup. Less than two months before the election, Trump unveiled an initiative known as the Platinum Plan, a $500 billion package of policy proposals advertised as providing Black communities with economic empowerment and educational opportunities.[7] The campaign and the Republican National Committee rolled out endorsements and spotlighted pro-Trump comments from Black athletes and rappers like Herschel Walker, 50 Cent, and Lil Wayne. These signals, coupled with Trump's theatrical masculinity and crafted personal narrative portraying him as a self-made man, were designed in part to help improve on the 13 percent of Black men he won in 2016 and the consequential number who sat the election out in battleground states.[8] With Black women remaining the most loyal partisans in the American electorate, Black men were Trump's best chance at hurting the Democratic Party where it was strongest. As such, in the 2020 election, the story of the Black electorate is succinctly captured in the bloc's gender gap.

BLACK MEN AND WOMEN IN THE ELECTORATE

Except for a few presidential cycles in the mid-twentieth century, near-uniform voting behavior has been a feature of the Black electorate since its inception.[9] The gender gap among Black voters has been present for just as long. Initially, this was a function of women being excluded from the right to vote even as formerly enslaved Black men obtained the franchise following ratification of the Fifteenth Amendment in 1870. After the Nineteenth Amendment extended access to the ballot to women in 1920, the oppressive and violent measures of the Jim Crow era continued to deprive Black women and men alike of their constitutional rights. In the early organized civil rights politics, which tended to adhere to patriarchal norms of the day, Black men were placed in leadership roles throughout the movement. But the political and civic engagement of Black women in communities, grassroots efforts, churches, and in the civil rights movement writ large was indispensable to the spate of social and statutory gains for racial equality. This history undergirds the gendered differences in election participation, political ideology and partisanship, and choices on election days found in modern-day Black America.

Though 2020 election data are still being collected, the most rigorous exit polling available suggests that Black voters were the largest racial or ethnic minority bloc, making up 11 percent of the overall electorate. Black men accounted for 4 percent of all voters, and Biden won 87 percent of them to Donald Trump's 12 percent. Black women were 6 percent of the overall electorate, and Biden won them 93-6.[10] Some exit polls show Trump won as much as 12 percent of Black voters, including 19 percent of Black men and 9 percent of Black women.[11] These latter numbers, coupled with polling leading up to the election, led to a flood of declarations that the Trump version of the Republican Party was making significant inroads with Black voters, particularly men.

Stepping back from 2020, however, it was unremarkable that Black women's share of the electorate was 50 percent higher and that Black men were twice as likely to vote for the Republican candidate. In terms of turnout, Black women have consistently outperformed Black men in voter participation rates over the last four decades, with the gender gap ranging from five to 10 points in presidential elections—the largest such gaps among any race or ethnicity in the nation.[12] An examination of presidential elections from 1972 to 2004 reveals that the Black American gender gap in support for Democratic presidential candidates averaged about eight percentage points, which correlates to Black men being anywhere between 50 to 100 percent more likely to vote against the Democrat.[13] As was to be expected in Barack Obama's historic candidacy in 2008, the gender gap closed to 1 percent, with more than 95 percent of Black voters casting ballots for the nation's first Black president. But by Obama's reelection campaign in 2012, the gender gap had returned: Black men were three times more likely to vote for Republican nominee Mitt Romney—a ratio that held for the 2016 election.

In other words, the gender gap observed in 2020 was not a sign that Trump's Republican Party was converting or attracting new Black voters, but simply that the Black electorate was returning to form following the presidency of the first Black American. The 1964 presidential election was the culmination of the parties' racial realignment, when Black Americans supported the Democratic Party en masse. Since then, Black men have been more receptive to the Republican Party's messaging than Black women. Conservatives' emphasis on free market capitalism, individualism, and self-determination meshed more with certain expressions of Black masculinity and its desire for the long-denied personal agency rooted in a "sweat of your brow" politics. Even then, conservatism is defined differently in Black America, which explains why roughly a quarter of Black Americans identify as conservative but less than one in 10 have voted Republican in the last two decades.[14] In this way, it is both notable that Black Republicans returned to the party following the Obama presidency and important to note that this was mostly a reversion to the historical mean.

Perhaps in a typical election year, the return of Black men's relatively small but disproportionate support of the Republican Party would have led to a favorable result for Donald Trump. In addition to the economic policies in the Platinum Plan, the Trump campaign routinely cited passage of the First Step Act of 2018, a federal prison reform law that purported to be particularly helpful to incarcerated Black men. Trump also regularly pointed to the historically low Black unemployment rate as a reason for Black voters to support him and even ran a commercial during the Super Bowl featuring an all-Black cast specifically designed to appeal to Black voters.[15] While the ads and rhetoric rarely called out gender, the campaign was well aware that its outreach had a far better chance of reaching Black men than Black women.

But 2020 was anything but a typical year. Trump's poor handling of the coronavirus pandemic spotlighted racial health disparities and tripled Black unemployment by May 2020, weakening his pitch.[16] And his callous response to the killing of George Floyd by a Minneapolis police officer and hardline position toward protesters—parroting the Jim Crow-era quote, "When the looting starts, the shooting starts"[17]—dimmed the allure of his criminal justice reform message. The summer of racial justice protests and the stay-at-home directives in states across the country contributed to an upswing in civic engagement and interest in the election. And one of the results of exceedingly high-turnout general elections is that Republicans' share of the Black electorate needs to increase substantially to offset Democrats' real number gains in the popular vote. Black outreach focused on marrying policy appeals to perceived areas of interest to Black men was going after low-hanging fruit in a year where much bolder strokes would be necessary.

Election year challenges aside, strategies to narrow or widen the Black electorate's gender gap that rely on policy appeals are unlikely to succeed. Political scientist Tasha Philpot examined the political evaluations of Black women and men on five measures: affirmative action, defense spending, size of the social safety net, sociotropic evaluations of the economy, and feminist issues. Philpot found the gender gap on each measure to be quite minimal, suggesting that there is not much distance at all between Black women and men on the issues.[18] On gendered topics—such as perceptions of Black women in leadership, gender discrimination, feminist activism, and abortion—scholars have noted that both Black women and men maintain high levels of support for Black feminist ideals.[19] Moreover, despite Black men holding sexist political and domestic attitudes comparable to men of other races and ethnicities, political scientists Ana Bracic, Mackenzie Israel-Trummel, and Allyson Shortle found that such views have no statistically significant effect on how Black men vote in presidential elections.[20]

Considering these insights together demonstrates that the Democratic ticket of Joe Biden and Senator Kamala Harris held an enormous advantage in 2020, and the Trump campaign's approach to denting that advantage was insufficient and misguided. What is to be learned from the 2020 election about how electoral strategies from both parties can be devised to leverage the gender gap? More specifically, can Democrats permanently close the gap among the Black electorate as Barack Obama was able to do temporarily in 2008? Can Republicans expand the gap by attracting more Black men or make gains with Black women? To answer these questions, a deeper dive into the electoral behavior of Black men and women is required.

GENDER DIFFERENCES IN BLACK VOTING BEHAVIOR

To gain a better understanding of the relationship between gender and the relative influence various factors have on voting choices, I conducted a factorial survey of Black men and women from October to December 2015, just before the 2016 presidential primaries. Sociologists Peter Rossi and Andy Anderson devised the factorial survey to help identify the fundamental criteria that figure into human judgments of social objects.[21] To accomplish this goal, they made use of vignettes containing a range of social objects that help determine the influences on respondents' decisions. Vignettes are realistic scenarios that incorporate dimensions, which are the independent variables containing a fixed set of values or levels. For example, if a vignette references colors of the flag of the United States of America, the color dimension contains the levels red, white, and blue. In the factorial survey, vignettes contain multiple dimensions and, by independently varying the levels of each dimension, researchers can determine the discrete impact of each dimension and level on the choices made by respondents. This provides valuable insight into the role each social object plays in individual judgments.

Scholars have tested the validity of factorial surveys to approximate actual choices made in the real world and found they "perform remarkably well in capturing the structural effects of attributes that drive voting behavior."[22] To conduct this study, I asked Black voters to read vignettes describing a realistic presidential election scenario and rate the likelihood of supporting a particular candidate based on ten factors. The factorial survey consisted of standardized scenarios that varied across ten dimensions determined in the course of a literature review: national economic well-being, African American unemployment rate, crime rate, health care costs, approach to civil rights assurances, candidates' stance on same-sex marriage, candidates' stance on abortion, incumbency status, candidates' race, and candidates' party (see table 9.1).

Table 9.1. Vignette Dimensions and Levels

Dimensions	*Levels*
Economy	Strong
	Weak
African American economic well-being	More African Americans have jobs
	More African Americans are out of work
Violent crime	Up
	Down
Health care costs	Have gone up
	Have gone down
Civil rights	Supports the Black Lives Matter movement and believes new laws are necessary to ensure African Americans have access to good schools, safe neighborhoods, and the right to vote.
	Believes increasing economic opportunity for African Americans' and encouraging hard work is the best way to address racial inequality and discrimination.
Candidate's view on same-sex marriage	Supports
	Against
Candidate's view on abortion	Right to choose
	Outlawed except in certain circumstances
Incumbency	President
	Member of Congress
Race of candidate	Black
	White
Party of candidate	Democrat
	Republican

Survey respondents were presented with three randomly assigned and distinct vignettes in serial order and prompted to indicate their vote choice. The factorial survey garnered 366 Black respondents who successfully completed each vignette and successive demographic questions. Given that the vignette, and not the respondent, is the unit of analysis in factorial surveys, the study had 1,098 participants: Women constituted 62.6 percent (687) of the survey responses and 37.4 percent (411) were men, comparable to the ratio typically seen in presidential elections.

Given the structure of the vignette, it was possible to determine if Black voters' choices were more the result of a comparison of the candidates or based on a performance assessment of the sitting president. The only factors that had a statistically significant effect on Black voters' support for the presidential challenger were partisan affiliation and the approach to civil rights. As anticipated, the congressional member who was a Democrat was far more likely to receive Black support. Additionally, Black voters were more likely to vote for the congressional member supporting stronger statutory

Please read the scenario below carefully and provide responses to the questions that follow. Be sure to pay close attention as some details will change in each scenario.

You are trying to decide which candidate to vote for in a presidential election. One candidate is currently the president who is seeking re-election, and the challenger is a member of Congress.

Under the current president, the economy is weak but more African Americans have jobs. At the time of election, violent crime is up and healthcare costs have gone up.

The president believes increasing economic opportunity for African Americans and encouraging hard work is the best way to address racial inequality and discrimination.

The member of Congress supports the Black Lives Matter movement and believes new laws are necessary to ensure African Americans have access to good schools, safe neighborhoods, and the right to vote.

Finally the president is against same-sex marriage and believes in a woman's right to choose to have an abortion.

Based on the scenario above...

... how likely is it that you would VOTE FOR THE PRESIDENT, a WHITE REPUBLICAN, to be re-elected?

Very Unlikely	Unlikely	Somewhat Unlikely	Undecided	Somewhat Likely	Likely	Very Likely
○	○	○	○	○	○	○

Figure 9.1. Sample Vignette

civil rights protections and the Black Lives Matter movement when running against an incumbent president who believes economic empowerment is the better approach.

Conversely, when determining whether to support the sitting president, every issue except health care costs had a statistically significant effect on Black voters' choices. In order of salience, this electorate's votes were most impacted by the candidate's party, stance on abortion, civil rights approach, Black unemployment rate, the candidate's race, stance on same-sex marriage, the crime rate, and the overall status of the economy. Their electoral decisions seem to be guided more by assessments of the incumbent president than by the potential of the challenger—that is, Black Americans are aligned to theories of retrospective voting that punishes incumbent officeholders and parties in presidential elections.[23]

To understand the contribution of Black men and women to these outcomes and ascertain if, and to what extent, a gender gap exists in political evaluations and electoral choices, a contrast of gendered subgroups is required. Because of the Black electorate's focus on the sitting president, it serves as a solid basis for determining the differences between Black women and men. Figure 9.2 shows the results of this analysis. There is virtually no gender gap in how Black voters consider the Black unemployment rate, party, and the incumbent's stance on abortion when making electoral decisions—both men and women heavily penalize the incumbent for increasing unemployment,

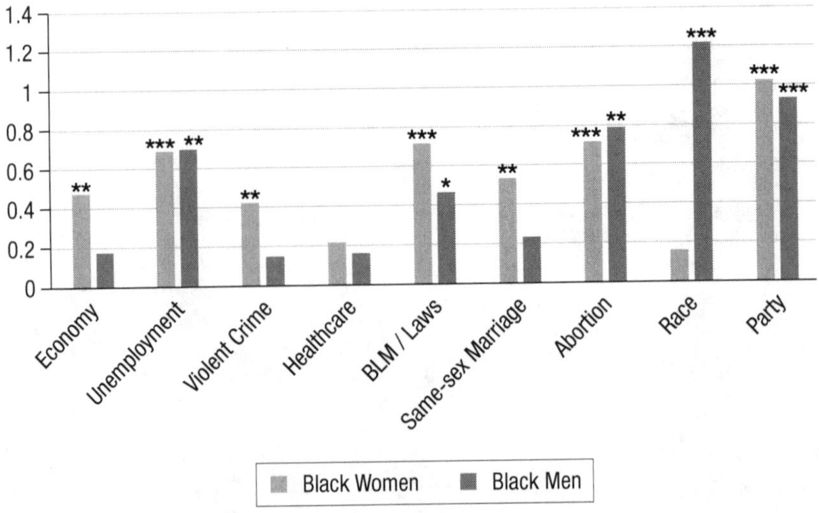

Figure 9.2. Issue Salience in Vote Choice
Note: Stars indicate levels of statistical significance: *p ≤ .1; **p ≤ .05; ***p ≤ .001

being Republican, and opposing a woman's right to choose, each with statistically high significance.

But there are clear gender differences. Black women penalize the sitting president for the status of, or position on, every factor considered except two: the incumbent's race and health care costs—both of which have relatively low influences on whether a Black female voter will support the sitting president. The factors with the largest effects on Black women's vote choice are the incumbent's party, position on abortion, approach to civil rights, and oversight of Black unemployment. Conversely, and somewhat surprisingly, Black men place a particularly high priority on candidates' race in their electoral calculus, even more than party. Black men prefer Black candidates for office much more than white ones, suggesting descriptive representation is of particular importance to them. When taken along with party, it appears Black men place an emphasis on candidate attributes, whereas Black women prioritize socioeconomic condition and policy positions.

Of note, the influence of the abortion issue—the only gendered factor in the vignette—and the preference for pro-choice presidential candidates was approximately the same for men as it was for women. The abortion issue represented an especially tight alignment between Black men and women's electoral behavior among all the assessed factors with sizable effects. This confirms previous scholarship that indicates Black feminist consciousness aligns the concerns of Black men with Black women on those policies perceived to be women's issues when such issues do not pit racial identity against gender identity.[24]

The data suggest areas of gendered subgroup constancy and variation. Black voters, regardless of gender, prioritize a candidate's party and are more likely to vote for a candidate who supports racial justice protests and statutory civil rights protections. Notably, however, Black retrospective voting appears to be slightly gendered—practiced more by Black women than Black men—and centers group well-being instead of self-interest as in traditional conceptions of the theory.

The findings suggest Black women prioritize party, policy, and present conditions, and Black men prioritize party and the attributes—race and experience—of the candidate running for office. Even in the party dimensions where both genders clearly prefer Democratic presidential nominees to Republican candidates, the effect size of party on Black women was slightly larger than it was for Black men. This finding is consistent with previous scholarship on the general differences between men and women that find women tend to be more supportive of Democratic candidates, and it confirms the specific applicability to Black voters.[25]

THE BLACK GENDER GAP IN 2020 AND BEYOND

The findings of this study provide some confirmation of the Black voting behavior observed in the 2020 presidential election. First, the Trump campaign's decision to focus on economic messages accords with the importance Black voters place on the unemployment rate and conservative Black men's willingness to consider economic solutions to racial inequality. Further, though being a Republican puts a candidate at a serious disadvantage, Black men are slightly more open to supporting someone from that party. The study found the gender gap evidenced in previous decades and reconfirmed in 2020 to be fairly predictable. The anomaly, then, was not how well Donald Trump did with Black voters in 2016 and 2020, but how poorly Barack Obama did with Black men in 2012. Given the salience of a candidate's race to Black men, that 11 percent of them voted against Obama in his re-election after just 5 percent voted against him in his initial election is a more noteworthy occurrence.

Second, Joe Biden's decision to select a Black woman, then-Senator Kamala Harris, as his running mate may have tapped into the importance of race to Black men. Political scientists have found that turnout in majority Black congressional districts increases when Black Democrats are on the ticket up and down the ballot; as such, Harris' presence not only may have contributed to the increased turnout among Black voters, it may have also compelled some Black men who would be more open to voting for a Republican to instead support the Biden-Harris ticket.[26] The number of Black Trump supporters the campaign highlighted could not compete with Democrats having a Black elected official on a ticket. There was speculation that Trump was considering replacing Vice President Mike Pence with former U.N. Ambassador Nikki Haley, adding an ethnic minority to his run for re-election. But if Black men were the minority bloc his campaign prized most, then perhaps a Black running mate would have been the better option. Consider the two Black Republicans to run in the same years that Trump was a presidential candidate—Senator Tim Scott of South Carolina in 2016 and Michigan senatorial challenger John James in 2020. According to exit polling, Scott did twice as well with Black voters than Donald Trump in South Carolina, and James did 25 percent better with Black voters than Trump in Michigan.[27] His campaign's policy pitches could not match the descriptive representation found in the Biden-Harris ticket.

And third, because Black women are more likely to prioritize socioeconomic policy in their electoral calculations whereas Black men place an emphasis on a candidate's attributes, Republicans looking to affix policy challenges to Democratic leadership was the wrong message. The Trump campaign attempted to frame Joe Biden and Kamala Harris as the faces of a racially discriminatory criminal justice system, charged Democratic mayors in large cities with causing relatively high Black poverty and unemployment rates, and argued a Biden-Harris administration would raise taxes on the average American. But policy appeals resonate more with Black women, who are especially averse to voting for Republicans and are more likely to agree with Democratic approaches to civil rights and social safety net programming. This holds particularly true in a year that saw racial justice protests, a public health pandemic, and an economy leaving behind workers and small businesses at a time when Black women were the fastest growing group of entrepreneurs.[28] The Trump campaign may have been better served focusing on the candidate himself and leaning into his manufactured narrative as an outsider, hypermasculine businessman being stifled by professional politicians. While he certainly would have still lost the overwhelming majority of Black men, winning one in five, for example, would likely have made the difference in Georgia. Of course, that Trump was a rather bad candidate with enduring high disapproval rates among Black Americans likely prevented even the best outreach strategy from being effective.

What does this all mean for presidential elections? There is nothing occurring in our two-party system of democracy that suggests the Black electorate will vote less uniformly. In fact, as the parties are becoming more racially segregated—with more people of color leaning toward the Democratic Party and white Americans moving into the Republican Party—the near-uniformity will likely further solidify and become more entrenched in the Black electorate's political identity.[29] The early thinking around Republican presidential primaries in 2024 is that Senators Tom Cotton, Ted Cruz, and Rick Scott are likely contenders. And Donald Trump immediately floated running again in 2024, even amid clumsy attempts to overturn the outcome of the 2020 election. But none of these candidates' performances in previous elections suggest they'll be able to attract more Black voters. Republican Governor Larry Hogan of Maryland, who won more than a quarter of Black voters in his 2018 gubernatorial re-election run, is another rumored contender, but translating statewide support to national support in a presidential election is exceptionally difficult.

Another complicating factor is that party polarization appears to be a reaction to political and ideological polarization. That is, the Trump version of the Republican Party moved rightward, courting racially intolerant factions of the far right and practicing an uncompromising absolutism on a range of issues that seems disproportionately focused on communities of color. Meanwhile, the Democratic Party is trending left, fueled in part by Senator Bernie Sanders' strong showing in recent presidential primaries.

Increasingly progressive members have won congressional seats and are making demands of more moderate Democratic leadership. Black voters, however, have not followed suit—the number of Black voters identifying as conservative, moderate, and liberal has held fairly steady for decades, with the plurality of such voters (44 percent) identifying as moderate in 2019. As such, while political identities and the theory of electoral capture—an argument that Black voters are taken for granted by Democrats and ignored by Republicans—make the Black electorate seem rather secure for Democrats, they presume that Black voters' policy preferences are somewhat aligned to the party platform. In other words, in an increasingly progressive Democratic Party, will the nearly three in four Black voters who do not identify as liberal accept the party's new direction?

And one final consideration is, perhaps, the most obvious one: descriptive representation. Though the race of the candidate figures differently into the electoral calculations of Black men and women, descriptive representation has proven to increase Black turnout for Democrats. In addition to Barack Obama's prominent example, when Black Democratic candidates run in mayoral, senatorial, and gubernatorial races, the party's share of the Black vote increases. And this phenomenon is particularly pronounced among Black women, as both experienced candidates and voters.[30] There are dozens of Black congressional members and mayors that provide the Democratic Party with a relatively deep bench from which to draw talent. Elected Republicans, on the other hand, are increasingly homogenous. Of the 212 Republicans in the 117th Congress' House of Representatives, only two are Black, both of whom are freshmen. In the Senate, only one of the 50 Republicans is Black. There are no Black Republican mayors of any sizable locale in the nation, and there's never been a Black Republican governor, less the 35-day stint of P.B.S. Pinchback in Louisiana in 1872-1873 when Black voters were almost entirely Republican. The best hope Republicans have of expanding the Black gender gap in presidential elections is probably running a viable, moderate Black nominee, and they are woefully short on options. An inability to field and elect Black politicians is an insurmountable hurdle for the Republican Party that only a genuine desire for change, an enduring commitment, resources, and time can ameliorate.

President Biden's ability to appeal to Black voters helped him finally win the White House on his third try. And Donald Trump's inability to improve on his share of the Black male electorate is both a commentary on his striking inability to recognize electoral opportunities beyond white working-class voters and on the Republican Party's reliance on rhetoric and symbolic gestures alone for Black outreach. In other words, the Black electorate and the parties' approach to voters within it went exactly as expected, as reliable as always. And the gender gap between Black men and women is representative of the challenges and opportunities that lay ahead for the parties and future presidential candidates.

NOTES

1. "Latest National Presidential Primary Polls," *FiveThirtyEight*, December 8, 2020, https://projects.fivethirtyeight.com/polls/president-primary-d/national/.
2. Scott Clement, Cleve R. Wootson Jr., Dan Balz and Emily Guskin, "Biden Holds Wide Lead among Black Voters in Democratic Presidential Race, Post-Ipsos Poll Finds," *Washington Post*, January 11, 2020, https://www.washingtonpost.com/politics/biden-holds-wide-lead-among-Black-voters-in-democratic-presidential-race-post-ipsos-poll-finds/2020/01/11/76ecff08-3325-11ea-a053-dc6d944ba776_story.html.
3. "Biden Projected to be President-Elect," ABC News, https://abcnews.go.com/Elections/2020-us-presidential-election-results-live-map.
4. "Understanding the 2020 Electorate: AP VoteCast Survey," NPR, November 3, 2020, https://www.npr.org/2020/11/03/929478378/understanding-the-2020-electorate-ap-votecast-survey.
5. "An Examination of the 2016 Electorate, Based on Validated Voters," Pew Research Center, August 9, 2018, https://www.pewresearch.org/politics/2018/08/09/an-examination-of-the-2016-electorate-based-on-validated-voters/.
6. Brandon Tensley, "Trump's Least Racist Claim Falls Flat for Many. Yet His Campaign Still Holds Appeal for Some Black Men," CNN, October 23, 2020, https://www.cnn.com/2020/10/23/politics/trump-least-racist-Black-men/index.html; See also Theodore R. Johnson and Leah Wright Rigueur, "Trump's Message to Black Voters: Vote for Me (But Really Don't Vote.)," *Washington Post*, October 22, 2020, https://www.washingtonpost.com/outlook/trump-Black-voters-outreach-strategy-depress/2020/10/22/ad64f348-13c5-11eb-bc10-40b25382f1be_story.html.
7. Kriston Capps, "What's in Trump's 'Platinum Plan' for Black America?" *Bloomberg*, September 29, 2020, https://www.bloomberg.com/news/articles/2020-09-29/trump-shines-up-a-platinum-plan-for-Black-voters.
8. Sabrina Tavernise, "Many in Milwaukee Neighborhood Didn't Vote — and Don't Regret It," *New York Times*, November 20, 2016, https://www.nytimes.com/2016/11/21/us/many-in-milwaukee-neighborhood-didnt-vote-and-dont-regret-it.html.
9. Theodore R. Johnson, "How the Black Vote Became a Monolith," *New York Times Magazine*, September 16, 2020, https://www.nytimes.com/2020/09/16/magazine/Black-vote.html.
10. "Understanding the 2020 Electorate: AP VoteCast Survey," NPR, November 3, 2020, https://www.npr.org/2020/11/03/929478378/understanding-the-2020-electorate-ap-votecast-survey.
11. See CNN 2020 presidential election exit polls, https://www.cnn.com/election/2020/exit-polls/president/national-results.

12. Ruth Igielnik, "Men and Women in the U.S. Continue to Differ in Voter Turnout Rate, Party Identification," Pew Research Center, August 18, 2020, https://www.pewresearch.org/fact-tank/2020/08/18/men-and-women-in-the-u-s-continue-to-differ-in-voter-turnout-rate-party-identification/.

13. "National Exit Polls Table," *New York Times*, November 5, 2008, https://www.nytimes.com/elections/2008/results/president/national-exit-polls.html.

14. Hannah Gilberstadt and Andrew Daniller, "Liberals Make Up the Largest Share of Democratic Voters, But Their Growth has Slowed in Recent Years," Pew Research Center, January 17, 2020, https://www.pewresearch.org/fact-tank/2020/01/17/liberals-make-up-largest-share-of-democratic-voters/; Lydia Saad, "The U.S. Remained Center-Right, Ideologically, in 2019," Gallup, January 9, 2020, https://news.gallup.com/poll/275792/remained-center-right-ideologically-2019.aspx.

15. Annie Karni and Maggie Haberman, "Trump and Kushner Saw Super Bowl Ad as Way of Making Inroads with Black Voters," *New York Times*, February 4, 2020, https://www.nytimes.com/2020/02/04/us/politics/trump-super-bowl-ad.html.

16. "Civilian Unemployment Rate," U.S. Bureau of Labor Statistics, https://www.bls.gov/charts/employment-situation/civilian-unemployment-rate.htm.

17. Michael Wines, "'Looting' Comment From Trump Dates Back to Racial Unrest of the 1960s," *New York Times*, May 29, 2020, https://www.nytimes.com/2020/05/29/us/looting-starts-shooting-starts.html.

18. Tasha S. Philpot, "Race, Gender, and the 2016 Presidential Election." *PS: Political Science & Politics* 51, no. 4 (2018): 755–61. https://www.cambridge.org/core/journals/ps-political-science-and-politics/article/abs/race-gender-and-the-2016-presidential-election/3F99CCC585F8957B720406344B33F90B.

19. Evelyn M. Simien and Rosalee A. Clawson, "The Intersection of Race and Gender: An Examination of Black Feminist Consciousness, Race Consciousness, and Policy Attitudes," *Social Science Quarterly* 85, no. 3 (2004), 793-810. https://www.jstor.org/stable/42955973

20. Ana Bracic, Mackenzie Israel-Trummel, and Allyson Shortle, "Is Sexism for White People? Gender Stereotypes, Race, and the 2016 Presidential Election," *Political Behavior* 41, no. 2 (2019), 281-307. https://link.springer.com/article/10.1007%2Fs11109-018-9446-8.

21. Peter H. Rossi and Andy B. Anderson, "The Factorial Survey Approach and Introduction," in Peter H. Rossi and Stephen L. Nock (editors), *Measuring Social Judgments: The Factorial Survey Approach* (Beverly Hills: Sage Publications, 1982), 15-67.

22. Jens Hainmueller, Dominik Hangartner, and Teppei Yamamoto, "Validating Vignette and Conjoint Survey Experiments Against Real-World Behavior," *Proceedings of the National Academy of Sciences of the United States of America 112,* no. 8 (2015), 2395-2400.

23. Morris P. Fiorina, *Retrospective Voting in American National Elections* (New Haven: Yale University Press, 1981); Gerald H. Kramer, "Short-Term Fluctuations in U.S. Voting Behavior, 1896–1964," *American Political Science Review*, 65, 131–43.

24. Evelyn M. Simien and Rosalee A. Clawson, "The Intersection of Race and Gender: An Examination of Black Feminist Consciousness, Race Consciousness, and

Policy Attitudes," *Social Science Quarterly* 85, no. 3 (2004), 793-810. https://www.jstor.org/stable/42955973.

25. Andra Gillespie and Nadia E. Brown, "#BlackGirlMagic Demystified: Black Women as Voters, Partisans, and Political Actors," *Phylon* 56 no. 2 (2019), 37-58. https://www.jstor.org/stable/26855823; Evelyn M. Simien, "African American Public Opinion: Past, Present, and Future Research," *Politics, Groups, and Identities* 1 no. 2 (2014), 263-74.

26. For more on this argument, see Theodore R. Johnson, "If Democrats Want to Win, They Need a Black Politician on the Ticket," *Washington Post*, March 20, 2020, https://www.washingtonpost.com/outlook/2020/03/13/if-democrats-want-win-they-need-Black-politician-ticket/.

27. See CNN 2020 presidential election exit polls, https://www.cnn.com/election/2020/exit-polls/president/national-results.

28. Ruth Umoh, "Black Women Were among the Fastest-Growing Entrepreneurs—Then Covid Arrived," *Forbes*, October 26, 2020, https://www.forbes.com/sites/ruthumoh/2020/10/26/Black-women-were-among-the-fastest-growing-entrepreneurs-then-covid-arrived/.

29. See more on this argument in Ismail K. White and Chryl N. Laird, *Steadfast Democrats: How Social Forces Shape Political Behavior* (Princeton: Princeton University Press, 2020).

30. Tasha S. Philpot and Hanes Walton Jr., "One of Our Own: Black Female Candidates and the Voters Who Support Them," *American Journal of Political Science* 51, no. 1 (2007), 49-62. https://www.jstor.org/stable/4122905.

10

Media Coverage of the 2020 Election

Journalists and Influencers in the Misinformation Age

Diana Owen

Media coverage of politics and elections in the digital age extends far beyond the boundaries of legacy newsroom journalism. Platforms and personalities that previously were on the sidelines have become essential campaign media players. Social media platforms have been a factor in elections for more than a decade, but their influence in the 2020 campaign reached new heights. Social media influencers gained prominence in the media ecosystem and became essential to the candidates' communications strategies, while voters relied more heavily on social media to follow the election than ever before. The mainstream media were similarly dependent upon social media as sources for stories and commentary. Journalists have been forced to compete with countless alternative sources that provide news to voters. Reporters working for legacy news organizations have been doing their job with fewer resources for years as business models shifted and revenues diminished. They have diversified their outreach to readers through podcasts, social media posts, and other nontraditional formats.[1]

Misinformation was a big part of the media story of the 2020 election. An unprecedented amount of content was circulated during the campaign that was misleading or simply untrue. Voters had to navigate a convoluted media environment where the distinctions between legitimate news sites, imposters, and social media became muddied. Differentiating between sources employing standard editorial practices and those eschewing them entirely has become increasingly difficult. At the same time, the political polarization dividing the American electorate was reflected in voters' media choices. Audiences were widely fragmented across sources and platforms based on party identification, ideology, and candidate preference. Isolated within these media echo chambers, rampant misinformation coupled with incendiary rhetoric served to escalate tensions and widen rifts between political factions.

NEWS MEDIA COVERAGE

Established trends in the media industry were exacerbated by the COVID-19 pandemic, which affected newspaper and television news organizations in different ways. Newspapers, which had already been struggling to adapt to the digital environment, were hit hard by the pandemic. More than one-fourth of the country's newspapers have been shuttered since 2005, and half of the trained journalists lost their jobs. Between 2018 and 2020, 300 newspapers closed, 6,000 journalists became unemployed, and print newspaper circulation declined by five million. While some national newspaper brands, like the *New York Times*, experienced audience growth in recent years, the industry overall has suffered. During the pandemic, as the election was in full-swing, newspaper advertising revenues plummeted by a median of 42 percent and circulation dropped by 8 percent.[2] Dozens of newspapers and thousands of journalists at legacy and digital news operations were furloughed or laid off.[3] Thus, there were fewer trained print journalists covering the election and providing in-depth, factual stories at a time when news was breaking almost constantly.

Cable TV news channels experienced a surge in the size of their audiences during the Trump administration, which continued throughout the campaign season. CNN, MSNBC, and Fox News have had a small, but steady, growth in revenue over the past decade. As the pandemic forced people to spend more time at home, the audiences for these networks grew substantially. CNN more than doubled its primetime audience. Despite the growth in audience, only Fox News, whose ratings soared during the election, saw an increase in advertising revenues. The decline in advertising on CNN and MSNBC was due to the limitations on professional sports and marketers pulling or delaying ad campaigns.[4] The preponderance of election coverage on cable news featured heated commentary—pro and con—about Trump.

SPOTLIGHT ON TRUMP

Rarely in the country's history have journalists had to cover so many consequential events as they coalesced. Media coverage of the election was both influenced and overshadowed by the COVID-19 pandemic, demonstrations opposing systemic racism against Black citizens, and an economic crisis that caused millions of people to struggle. These interlocking stories scaffolded journalists' coverage of the campaign, especially as they reported on the candidates' positions, actions, and responses.

The media spotlight, as it had throughout his presidency, shined brightly on Donald Trump throughout the campaign, often leaving Joe Biden in the shadows. Trump's outrageous antics, Twitter rants, relentless attacks on friends and foes, and constant ploys to gain press attention worked. With great flourish, he fired officials in his administration for perceived transgressions. He flouted local pandemic regulations and held large campaign rallies without masks and social distancing that became superspreader events. After being admitted to Walter Reed Medical Center for treatment of COVID-19, Trump took a ride in a motorcade, grinning and waving to supporters. News organizations that were highly critical of Trump, such as CNN and MSNBC, amplified his messages even as they disparaged his behavior.

Biden all but disappeared at certain points in the campaign, especially as he followed pandemic safety guidelines and bunkered in the basement of his Delaware home. While incumbents running in presidential elections habitually receive more coverage than their opponents, the bonus that Trump received was supersized. An analysis of candidate coverage in 11 major U.S. newspapers found that for every 10 candidate mentions, seven to eight of them were about Trump and two to three of them were about Biden. This imbalance, which was roughly twice as large as the margin over the last 40 years, was evident across media outlets and endured throughout the campaign. Voters trying to decide about Biden were seriously disadvantaged by the dearth of available information from reliable sources.[5]

Interestingly, Biden won the ratings race when he faced Trump head-to-head during televised town halls held in lieu of the second presidential debate, which was canceled because Trump refused to appear virtually. Biden's appearance on ABC garnered at least 15.1 million viewers compared to Trump's 13.5 million viewers on NBC. The forums were a stark contrast in style and spectacle. Biden, whose town hall was moderated by George Stephanopoulos, addressed issues facing the country in a somber tone. When asked by moderator Savannah Guthrie to denounce QAnon and white supremacy and to clear up concerns about his medical condition following his bout with COVID-19, Trump pushed back, deflected, and evaded the questions. Biden's viewership grew over the course of the event to an estimated 16.7 million as Trump's declined.[6]

ELECTION NEWS AUDIENCES

Voters got their election news from myriad sources ranging from legacy organizations, such as the *Washington Post*, to sites with strong ideological leanings like *Breitbart News* and the *Daily Caller*. Distinct partisan and ideological divides characterized the audiences for specific sources of campaign news. The Pew Research Center found severe partisan divisions in the news sources that Americans trust, which have increased steadily over five years. Republicans trust Fox News far more than any other news source, while Democrats trust a wider range of sources, including CNN, the *New York Times*, and ABC News. Conservative Republicans and liberal Democrats now exist in two divergent news media universes.[7]

Survey data collected by the Civic Education Research Lab at Georgetown University[8] revealed significant differences in the sources Biden and Trump voters relied on regularly for news (see table 10.1). In general, Biden voters (40 percent) were slightly more inclined than Trump's supporters (35 percent) to get campaign news frequently from television, although Trump voters relied marginally more on local news. The conventional wisdom that CNN and MSNBC are preferred by Democrats and more liberal-leaning viewers, and Fox News by Republicans and conservatives, was confirmed. CNN was by far the cable news network preferred by Biden supporters, with

Table 10.1. Biden and Trump Voters' News Sources (% Relied on Source Frequently)

Media Source	*Biden*	*Trump*
Television News	40%	35%
Local TV News	25%	29%
CNN	44%	25%
MSNBC	28%	18%
Fox News	21%	28%
Print Newspapers	21%	17%
Online News	53%	44%
Local Newspapers	22%	21%
Print Magazines	14%	11%
New York Times	36%	17%
Washington Post	26%	14%
Wall Street Journal	11%	15%
BBC News	28%	19%
New York Post	16%	14%
Politico	16%	12%
Drudge Report	13%	11%
Breitbart News	9%	15%
Daily Caller	5%	11%
Radio News	25%	29%
Talk Radio	10%	16%

Source: CERL Georgetown University 2020 Election Survey, 1,327 respondents.

44 percent watching frequently compared to 25 percent of Trump followers. In fact, the gap in CNN viewership based on candidate preference was the largest among the sources considered here. Biden voters (28 percent) also tuned into MSNBC more often than Trump voters (18 percent). The regular audience for Fox News was composed of 28 percent Trump backers and 21 percent Biden voters. Only slightly more of the frequent readers of print newspapers backed Biden. However, the regular online news audience was notably more disposed toward Biden (53 percent) than Trump (44 percent). The differences in reliance on local newspapers and print magazines were small and nonsignificant. In terms of specific sources, Biden backers were far more likely than Trump supporters to frequently consult the *New York Times*, the *Washington Post*, and BBC News. They were also slightly more inclined to read *Politico*. Trump voters were more likely to read the *Wall Street Journal* than Biden voters by a small margin. Regular audiences for the conservative sites *Breitbart News* and the *Daily Caller* were small, with frequent readers favoring Trump. The difference in regular readership of the *New York Post* and the Drudge Report based on candidate preference was negligible. Trump voters were somewhat more inclined than Biden voters to listen regularly to radio news and talk radio during the election.

SOCIAL MEDIA IN THE CAMPAIGN

While Trump still held large-scale campaign rallies, the Democratic ticket respected social distancing requirements and limited in-person events to smaller drive-in gatherings. The two presidential campaigns adopted divergent social media strategies in keeping with their goals, resources, and personal styles.

American voters were heavily invested in social media during the campaign. The number of active users on social media platforms increased markedly during the election. Over 70 percent of the electorate actively used some form of social media to follow campaign news.[9] More than half of Americans regularly got their news from social media sites, with one-third relying on Facebook, one-quarter on YouTube, and 15 percent on Twitter.[10] Facebook was an essential campaign and press tool because it reached a wider swath of the voting population than other platforms, and its networks included people that users knew personally and trusted. Commensurate with the high level of interest in the election, social media users were extremely active in expressing opinions and spreading information. The CERL Georgetown University survey found that close to half of voters online participated in political discussions, expressed an opinion about politics knowing others may disagree, followed those with opposing political views, and shared or reposted information, pictures, or videos about candidates on social media. According to the Pew Research Center, 36 percent of voters showed their support for a candidate on social media.[11] CERL found that 43 percent of users indicated that they had voted on a social media platform.[12]

THE CANDIDATES' SOCIAL MEDIA STRATEGIES

Developing an effective social media game plan was vital to the Biden campaign. Biden's social media goals were to introduce himself to the electorate with positive messaging about his empathy and faith, reach out to first-time voters and undecideds, and generate press coverage. Posting on social media also helped Biden to avoid gaffes to which he was prone during live conversations. Due to his limited social media presence, Biden relied heavily on surrogates, celebrities, and influencers, and also employed platforms beyond Facebook and Twitter—including TikTok, Instagram, Cameo, Reddit, and online games—to become "digitally omnipresent."[13] His campaign trained hundreds of volunteers in digital organizing and content creation. In this way, Biden's message was amplified in unconventional venues like sports talk, entertainment fan sites, and gossip sites. Biden-Harris campaign signs and Biden HQ, a virtual island complete with a field office, trains, ice cream, and "no malarkey," were integrated into Animal Crossing, a popular video game on social media.[14]

Trump's social media strategy during the campaign differed little from his well-established digital activity. He vocally assailed Big Tech companies as adversaries, accusing them of attempting to silence him and rig the election in favor of Biden. These concerns, however, did not curb the prolific posting on social media that characterized his previous presidential bid and his time in office. Trump's messages were targeted narrowly to feeding his base and trolling his haters.[15] His posts were mostly incendiary in tone and content, as they were designed to stir controversy that would make headlines. As such, Trump garnered notably more attention than Biden for his Twitter activity among media and political elites. Trump's messages were riddled with misinformation about his opponent and the electoral process. Several posts were taken down or had fact-checking labels applied to them during the campaign by Facebook and Twitter. His account and those of some of his allies were banned for posting inflammatory rhetoric in the wake of the insurrection against the U.S. Capitol on January 6, 2021, by Facebook, Twitter, Instagram, YouTube, Snapchat, Reddit, Twitch, LiquidWeb, and Amazon Web Services, which hosted Parler.[16]

VOTER ENGAGEMENT WITH SOCIAL MEDIA

Biden began the campaign as a social media underdog with far fewer followers than his opponent. He gained followers continuously over the course of the election but was not able to overcome the initial deficit. By October, Trump had more than 30 million followers on Facebook and 85 million on Twitter; Biden had 3 million Facebook followers and 9 million Twitter followers.[17] The sheer number of social media posts by Trump far outnumbered Biden's posts. Trump's social media activity accelerated notably over the course of the campaign, especially when he was hospitalized for COVID-19. Data from Crowdtangle, a Facebook tool for tracking and analyzing public content on social media, pointed to a significant "engagement gap" favoring Trump in the raw number of reactions, shares, and comments that posts received during a 30-day period in October at the height of the campaign that was primarily a function of Trump's much larger number of social media followers (see table 10.2). Users engaged with Trump's official Facebook page 130 million times compared to 18 million for Biden. Trump garnered 60 million Instagram "likes" and comments to Biden's 34 million. The gap was greatest for YouTube video views, with 207 million views for Trump and 29 million for Biden—a difference of 178 million views.

The raw amount of social media activity associated with a candidate, however, is not a proxy for electoral success.[18] A closer examination of the social media metrics indicated that, while Trump may have had more followers than Biden, their enthusiasm for Trump's posts had diminished significantly since the 2016 campaign. Biden's smaller group of social media followers was far more active than Trump's base. Biden's "interaction rate"—a measure of engagement that factors in the number of followers of an account—was more than twice as high as Trump's rate.[19] Biden's supporters were far more likely to retweet and reply to his posts. Further, many of the posts on Trump's social media were negative reactions, while messages in Biden's feed were mostly positive. By the end of the campaign, Biden was handily outperforming Trump in terms of Twitter interactions.[20]

Table 10.2. User Engagement with Trump and Biden Social Media Over 30 Days in October 2020

	Trump	*Biden*
Facebook Reactions	130 Million	18 Million
Instagram "Likes" and Comments	60 Million	34 Million
Youtube Video Views	207 Million	29 Million

Source: Compiled from Kevin Roose, "Trump Still Miles Ahead of Biden in Social Media Engagement," *New York Times*, October 22, 2020, https://www.nytimes.com/2020/10/22/technology/trump-facebook.html.

NANO-INFLUENCERS

Celebrities have long engaged as social media influencers in campaigns. A-listers actively endorsed their candidates on the 2020 digital campaign trail. Among the celebrities posting their support for Biden were Beyoncé, Lady Gaga, Cardi B, Taylor Swift, Jennifer Aniston, Brad Pitt, Tom Hanks, Jennifer Lawrence, Mariska Hargitay, Keegan-Michael Key, Jim Gaffigan, Cher, Dwayne "The Rock" Johnson, and Tracee Ellis Ross. Trump's celebrity social media boosters included former NFL quarterbacks Jay Cutler and Brett Favre, Kid Rock, Jon Voight, Kirstie Alley, Stacey Dash, 50 Cent, Trace Adkins, Dean Cain, and Ted Nugent. In addition to the celebrities, Trump had in place an expansive network of conservative personalities, such as Alex Jones and Ben Shapiro, who had been priming his social media and amplifying his messages for years.[21]

A novel development that emerged in 2020 was the use of nano-influencers for campaign outreach to voters and the press. Nano-influencers generally are associated with social media accounts of 10,000 followers or less and reach small, targeted audiences that are typically nonpolitical, such as community groups in swing states, parenting groups, and beauty vloggers. Their political capital is vested in the perception that they are authentic and trustworthy. Some nano-influencers are paid by marketing organizations, political strategy and communications groups, such as Main Street One and NextGen, and candidates' campaigns, while others are uncompensated.[22]

The Biden campaign, with its smaller social media footprint and desire to galvanize untapped voter blocs, embraced nano-influencers. The campaign was the first ever to hire a firm to assist with influencer outreach. Biden himself regularly chatted with nano-influencers who asked him open-ended questions that he answered off-the-cuff. He discussed his approach to leadership, plans for police reform, and ways of combating systemic racism. Biden's granddaughters, Finn, Maisy, Naomi, and Natalie, hosted livestreams with nano-influencers that were popular with young voters. The interviews were streamed on Instagram Live and shared to Facebook and YouTube.[23]

NEW VOTERS, NEW SOCIAL MEDIA STRATEGIES

Young voters were markedly more politically active during the 2020 presidential election than they have been since 18 year olds first could vote in 1972. They were motivated largely by racial unrest and the government's mishandling of the COVID-19 pandemic. Voter turnout among 18 to 24 year olds, estimated at over 53 percent, was more than 10 percentage points higher than it was in 2016.[24] Their engagement in the campaign revolved heavily around social media. Young voters typically have been less likely than older voters to follow election news closely, especially in traditional venues like television.[25] The situation was no different in 2020. According to the Knight Foundation, social media was young adults' primary source of campaign news, with 40 percent mostly accessing information in their social media feeds.[26] Almost half of college and technical students in a Best Colleges survey indicated that social media directly impacted their vote.[27]

Young voters were drawn to platform alternatives to Facebook and Twitter, like Instagram, TikTok, and Twitch. They formed groups, such as Future Coalition and Gen-Z for Change, to organize youth phone banking and text banking efforts. They met online via Zoom to train volunteers in how to create and post content that would reach and appeal to young voters. They disseminated video and audio clips of candidates showing their personal sides, such as the inside of Georgia Democratic Senate candidate Jon Ossoff's home showcasing his "snack closet." They also employed online gaming as a tool for voter mobilization. New York Democratic Representative Alexandria Ocasio-Cortez used Twitch to stream herself playing the game "Among Us" while directing viewers to go to IWillVote.com and pledge to turn out in the election. Over 5.4 million people, whose average age was 21, viewed the video, with many visiting the voting site.[28]

MISINFORMATION

Elite-driven misinformation campaigns fueled by Trump, right-wing media, and political influencers were rampant. Trump capitalized on his position as newsmaker-in-chief to dominate mass media with coverage of even his most outrageous lies and augmented this coverage with tweets, press conferences, and television interviews on Fox News. This messaging was reinforced institutionally by the Republican National Committee, his presidential campaign committee, and right-wing media such as Newsmax.[29] His false missives were spread further online by Trump supporters as well as algorithms and bots. Misinformation also originated on user-generated social media posts. Rumors that initially included a grain of truth often were exaggerated and gained velocity on social media.[30]

Misinformation was spread inordinately online by people on the ideological extremes who distrusted the mainstream news media.[31] The propagation of falsehoods was most obvious among the right wing, which has a history of using online communities and messaging boards to organize dating back to the Tea Party movement in 2009. When Facebook and Twitter began labeling and deleting posts that they found dangerously misleading, Republicans and conservatives switched to niche sites, like Parler, MeWe, Gab, and the video-sharing site Rumble, that promised not to monitor political content.[32] Facebook became a conduit to these sites when users clicked on a post and were directed to them.

A disproportionate number of false posts were dispersed by a small group of "superspreaders" online. In the aftermath of his father's defeat at the polls, Eric Trump posted a request on Facebook that his followers report cases of voter fraud using the hashtag #StoptheSteal. Within a week, there were over 3.5 million posts referencing #StoptheSteal, which became a catalyst for rallies and protests, including the insurrection at the U.S. Capitol. Twenty-five "superspreaders" were responsible for almost 30 percent of content that people interacted with about voter fraud.[33]

While less prominent, left-wing conspiracy theories on social media increased after Trump entered the White House. Popular claims asserted that Trump's travel ban was a "trial balloon for a coup d'état,"[34] Vladimir Putin had salacious dirt on Trump, and Senate Majority Leader Mitch McConnell was funneling campaign funds to Trump via Russia.

"Trojan horse sites" that masquerade as independent journalism were responsible for generating and spreading incalculable numbers of false stories. These sites, which operate largely under the radar, have grown in number and influence since the 2016 election. They have the appearance of legitimate news platforms, which enhances their ability to traffic in lies and conspiracy theories. Hundreds of "countermedia" sites were prominent in the shadowy media ecosystem where heavily biased, hyperpartisan content about the election flourished.[35] In the run-up to the presidential contest, wealthy conservatives set up bogus local news websites across the country to push out stories that would damage Democratic candidates.[36] More than 1,800 local newspapers have closed since 2004, leaving a void that increasingly has been filled by "trojan horse sites." Websites made to emulate local news platforms, such as the Arizona Monitor and the Kalamazoo Times, emerged in news deserts where legitimate local news organizations had disappeared. The sites were run by ideological activists and companies with masked political agendas, such as Locality Labs in Arizona.[37] While they operate in the subterfuge of the digital world, the reach of these sites is hard to ignore. A study conducted during the presidential primaries found that the top 100 stories on these sites debunked by fact-checking organizations received over 158 million views. The 10 most popular sham news sites posted over 1,000 fake stories a week to over one million followers, who spread them through their personal networks.[38]

DOMINANT NARRATIVES

The effectiveness of misinformation in influencing hearts and minds is contingent upon "narrative laundering," where a story is legitimized through repetition across different media.[39]

Amidst the vast amount of misinformation circulated during the 2020 campaign were several dominant narratives. Trump's well-worn attacks on the "liberal" media and "fake news" were intensified. False claims about Biden's son, Hunter, were rampant. Trump's attempts to downplay his administration's questionable handling of the pandemic prompted story lines claiming that the virus was a hoax and that COVID-19 was no worse than the flu. Researchers at Cornell University found that Trump was the largest driver of misinformation about the pandemic, accounting for 38 percent of the falsehoods in circulation.[40]

Prominent misinformation narratives proliferated around the demonstrations against racial injustice sparked by the deaths of George Floyd and Breonna Taylor. The Black Lives Matter movement was characterized as synonymous with Antifa, a loosely associated group of left-wing antifascists who sometimes employ tactics used by anarchists that Trump wanted to declare a terrorist organization.[41] Peaceful BLM protests were described as violent riots and participants labeled terrorists, thugs, and worse. Protesters were alleged to be out to murder police officers. Anti-Biden rhetoric was embedded in this narrative. Biden was portrayed inaccurately as condoning violence and an advocate of defunding the police, interpreted as dismantling law enforcement, neither of which was true.[42]

Long-running narratives were resurrected for the misinformation campaign in 2020. Trump's supporters launched a "birther" conspiracy attack on Democratic vice presidential candidate Kamala Harris, claiming erroneously that she was ineligible to hold the office because she was not born in the United States. A similar conspiracy theory was spread against Barack Obama by Trump during Obama's presidential bids and while he was in office.[43] Another resuscitated theme purported that elites were running an international pedophile sex trafficking ring. During the 2016 election, the "Pizzagate" conspiracy theory alleged that leaked emails of high-ranking Democratic Party officials included coded messages leading to a child sex ring in a pizzeria in Washington, D.C. The QAnon conspiracy theory claimed during the 2020 campaign that Trump was waging a secret war against elite Satan-worshipping pedophiles in government, business, and the media. Adherents believed that a day of reckoning would come when Hillary Clinton, Trump's Democratic rival in the 2016 election, would be arrested and executed.[44]

UNDERMINING THE ELECTION

Among the most virulent of the misinformation narratives was the allegation that the election was rigged in favor of Biden and the Democrats. The fact that states had to rely heavily on mail-in ballots and other novel procedures due to the pandemic along with the high voter turnout widened the opportunities to sow mistrust. Backed by some prominent Republicans, claims of institutional voting fraud gained legitimacy despite the fact that FBI Director Christopher Wray stated publicly that the agency had not seen "any kind of coordinated national fraud effort . . . by mail or otherwise."[45] Trump exacerbated the purported danger to electoral integrity by repeatedly threatening not to recognize the results of the election if he lost—a threat on which he made good.[46] The election fraud misinformation campaign influenced opinions, as postelection surveys consistently found that between 70 percent and 80 percent of Republicans disputed the outcome of the presidential contest.[47]

Demonstrably false claims of voter fraud were backed up by photos and videos manipulated to document the alleged transgressions. Photos of long lines at in-person polling places and confusing ballots as well as a video of ballot stuffing from Russia were widely circulated as evidence. Relentless attacks levied at the postal system's inability to handle the large influx of mail-in ballots were accompanied by images of discarded mail. Claims that Republican observers were not allowed into the TCF Center in Detroit, where votes were being counted, gained national news attention until they were discredited. An image of a man wheeling a wagon into the TCF Center purportedly full of votes was actually a news photographer bringing in his equipment. Unsubstantiated reports of massive numbers of dead people voting in battleground states, including Arizona, Michigan, and Pennsylvania, were used as evidence of "the steal."[48] Dominion Voting Systems, a company that provided electronic voting machines and tabulators to states, was falsely charged with engaging in an international plot to steal the election from Trump by transferring millions of votes to Biden. Allegedly, the fraud was perpetrated by deep state operatives using a nonexistent supercomputer with the codename Hammer and a program called Scorecard to change votes nationally. Dominion subsequently filed a $1.3 billion defamation suit against Sidney Powell, a lawyer in Trump's inner circle, to counter the "malicious campaign of lies."[49] These unsubstantiated claims were promoted by Trump himself in a postelection phone call to the secretary of state of Georgia in an attempt to change the vote count.

#Sharpiegate was a conspiracy theory used to raise doubts about Biden's narrow margin of victory in Arizona. It began as a claim in small, pro-Trump Facebook groups that voters in Arizona who filled out paper ballots with

Sharpie pens could not scan their ballots. In fact, Sharpies were the best choice for filling out ballots because of their fast-drying ink and the clear impression they leave. The rumor caught on in forums frequented by MAGA influencers on TikTok and 4Chan, and then made its way to the mainstream media. #Sharpiegate was validated by Fox News and covered but debunked by CNN and MSNBC. The conspiracy theory sparked offline action, as a QAnon-supporting candidate for governor organized a protest outside the Arizona state capitol asking followers to "Bring your Sharpies and hold them high!" It became the basis for Trump's lawyers to challenge Arizona's votes in the election, which was unsuccessful.[50]

CONCLUSION

The days when media coverage meant fact-based reporting on elections by professional journalists are long gone. Legacy print media are still producing quality copy, but their ranks have diminished, their audiences have narrowed to a particular segment of the electorate that is largely liberal and Democratic, and their influence as agenda setters for other content-producers has waned. New media trends initiated in the late 1990s have evolved to the point where voters are getting a large amount of their election information from social media and alternative news sources with questionable pedigrees. Social media influencers have attracted millions of devoted followers. These developments raise concerns about the quality of news that people are receiving, especially stories and information fragments that are not subject to editorial oversight of any kind.

Social media's appeal—and its power—lies in their audiences' ability to be active participants in seeking, producing, and distributing messages. Voters are encouraged by social media influencers to react to and act on their messages. Positive outcomes can result, such as getting people to vote. Studies in the recent past have found limited evidence of a connection between partisan media messages and political action.[51] The events of the 2020 presidential election, however, should prompt scholars to revisit this assumption. Against a backdrop of the pandemic, racial unrest, and economic distress, Trump was unwilling to admit defeat and deflected his anger to a significant following that fed off his discontent and was emboldened by his lies. The flames of his digital rants were fanned by influencers motivated by extreme political allegiances and amplified throughout the media ecosystem. The role of the media in fomenting the siege of the U.S. Capitol as the country prepared for a transition of power from Trump to Biden should not be underestimated.

NOTES

1. Nic Newman, Richard Fletcher, Anne Schultz, Simge Andi, and Rasmus Kleis Nielsen, *Reuters Institute Digital News Report 2020*, Research Report, Reuters Institute for the Study of Journalism, University of Oxford, 2020. https://reutersinstitute.politics.ox.ac.uk/digital-news-report-2020.

2. Michael Barthel, Katerina Eva Matsa, and Kirsten Worden, "Coronavirus-Driven Downturn Hits Newspapers Hard as TV News Thrives," Pew Research Center, October 29, 2020, https://www.journalism.org/2020/10/29/coronavirus-driven-downturn-hits-newspapers-hard-as-tv-news-thrives/.

3. Penelope Muse Abernathy, "The News Landscape in 2020: Transformed and Diminished," UNC Hussman School of Journalism, https://www.usnewsdeserts.com/reports/news-deserts-and-ghost-newspapers-will-local-news-survive/the-news-landscape-in-2020-transformed-and-diminished/.

4. Megan Graham, "Media Companies Expect a Tough Quarter for TV Advertising, with No Live Sports and Spending Delayed," CNBC, May 8, 2020, https://www.cnbc.com/2020/05/08/tv-advertising-bracing-for-tough-quarter-amid-coronavirus-pandemic.html.

5. Stuart Soroka, "News Coverage of the 2020 Presidential Election," University of Michigan Institute for Social Research Center for Political Studies, October 16, 2020, https://cpsblog.isr.umich.edu/?p=2871.

6. Michael M. Grynbaum and John Koblin, "Biden Beats Trump in Ratings Battle of the Network Town Halls," *New York Times*, October 16, 2020, https://www.nytimes.com/2020/10/16/business/media/biden-trump-town-hall-ratings.html.

7. Mark Jurkowitz, Amy Mitchell, Elisa Shearer, and Mason Walker, "U.S. Media Polarization and the 2020 Election: A Nation Divided," Pew Research Center, January 24, 2020. https://www.journalism.org/2020/01/24/u-s-media-polarization-and-the-2020-election-a-nation-divided/.

8. The data were collected between November 9 and 15, 2020, immediately following the presidential election. The survey was administered to a national sample of voters online using MTurk by the Civic Education Research Lab (https://cerl.georgetown.edu/) at Georgetown University. For additional information, contact Dr. Diana Owen at owend@georgetown.edu.

9. Peter Suciu, "Social Media Could Determine the Outcome of the 2020 Election," *Forbes*, October 26, 2020, https://www.forbes.com/sites/petersuciu/2020/10/26/social-media-could-determine-the-outcome-of-the-2020-election/?sh=1c0d265a26f6.

10. Elisa Shearer and Amy Mitchell, "News Use Across Social Media Platforms," Pew Research Center, January 12, 2021, https://www.journalism.org/2021/01/12/news-use-across-social-media-platforms-in-2020/.

11. Andrew Daniller and Hannah Gilberstadt, "Key Findings About Voter Engagement in the 2020 Election," Pew Research Center, December 14, 2020, https://www.pewresearch.org/fact-tank/2020/12/14/key-findings-about-voter-engagement-in-the-2020-election/.

12. Diana Owen and Wenyuan Deng. "Generational Differences in Digital Electoral Engagement in the 2020 Presidential Campaign," in Jody Baumgartner and Terri Towner, eds., *The Internet and Campaign 2020* (New York: Lexington Books, 2021).

13. Anna Bredava, "Biden's and Trump's Election Campaigns: A Social Media Analysis," *Social Media Management*, November 2, 2020. https://awario.com/blog/elections-2020-social-media/.

14. Makena Kelly, "The Official Biden HQ in Animal Crossing Has Poll Booths, Ice Cream, and No Malarkey," *The Verge*, October 16, 2020. https://www.theverge.com/2020/10/16/21519505/joe-biden-animal-crossing-new-horizons-biden-hq-campaign-election.

15. Jacob Jarvis, "Donald Trump, 'King of Twitter,' Is Being Outperformed by Joe Biden," *Newsweek*, September 29, 2020. https://www.newsweek.com/donald-trump-joe-biden-twitter-facebook-comparison-1534671.

16. Hannah Denham, "These Are the Platforms that Have Banned Trump and His Allies," *Washington Post*, January 13, 2021. https://www.washingtonpost.com/technology/2021/01/11/trump-banned-social-media/.

17. Tristan Hotham, "Trump vs. Biden: Who Is Engaging the Most Followers on Facebook?" IPR, University of Bath, October 19, 2020. https://blogs.bath.ac.uk/iprblog/2020/10/19/trump-vs-biden-who-is-engaging-the-most-followers-on-facebook/.

18. Jonathan Bright, Scott Hale, Bharath Ganesh, Andres Bulovsky, Helen Margetts, and Phil Howard, "Does Campaigning on Social Media Make a Difference? Evidence From Candidate Use of Twitter During the 2015 and 2017 U.K. Elections," *Communication Research*, 47, no. 7 (2020), 988-1009.

19. Kevin Roose, "Trump Still Miles Ahead of Biden in Social Media Engagement," *New York Times*, October 22, 2020. https://www.nytimes.com/2020/10/22/technology/trump-facebook.html.

20. Jacob Jarvis, "Donald Trump, 'King of Twitter,' Is Being Outperformed by Joe Biden," *Newsweek*, September 29, 2020. https://www.newsweek.com/donald-trump-joe-biden-twitter-facebook-comparison-1534671.

21. Mark Scott, "Despite Cries of Censorship, Conservatives Dominate Social Media," *Politico*, October 26, 2020. https://www.politico.com/news/2020/10/26/censorship-conservatives-social-media-432643.

22. Anastasia M. Goodwin, Katie Joseff, and Samuel C. Woolley, "Social Media Influencers and the 2020 U.S. Election," Center for Media Engagement, the University of Texas at Austin, 2020, https://mediaengagement.org/wp-content/uploads/2020/10/Social-Media-Influencers-and-the-2020-U.S.-Election-1.pdf.

23. Peter Suciu, "Social Media Could Determine the Outcome of the 2020 Election," *Forbes*, October 26, 2020. https://www.forbes.com/sites/petersuciu/2020/10/26/social-media-could-determine-the-outcome-of-the-2020-election/?sh=1c0d265a26f6.

24. CIRCLE, "Youth Voter Turnout Increased in 2020," Tufts Tisch College, November 25, 2020, https://circle.tufts.edu/latest-research/election-week-2020#youth-voter-turnout-increased-in-2020.

25. John B. Holdbein and D. Sunshine Hillygus. *Making Young Voters* (New York: Cambridge University Press, 2020).

26. Ashley Zohn, "Media, Democracy and the Emerging Electorate of Young Voters," Knight Foundation, October 21, 2020, https://knightfoundation.org/articles/media-democracy-and-the-emerging-electorate-of-young-voters/.

27. Reece Johnson and Anne Dennon, "College Students Call COVID-19, Racial Inequality Top Election Issues," Best Colleges, October 27, 2020, https://www.bestcolleges.com/research/college-student-voter-survey-covid-19-racial-inequality/

28. Imad Khan, "AOC's Twitch Get-Out-the-Vote Efforts Will Help Democrats in 2020—and Beyond," NBC News, October 29, 2020, https://www.nbcnews.com/think/opinion/aoc-s-twitch-get-out-vote-efforts-will-help-democrats-ncna1245318.

29. Yochai Benkler, Casey Tilton, Bruce Etling, Hal Roberts, Justin Clark, Rob Faris, Jonas Kaiser, and Carolyn Schmitt, "Mail-In Voter Fraud: Anatomy of a Disinformation Campaign," Working Paper, Berkman Klein Center for Internet & Society at Harvard University, 2020, https://cyber.harvard.edu/publication/2020/Mail-in-Voter-Fraud-Disinformation-2020.

30. Kate Starbird, Michael Caulfield, Renee DiResta, Jevin West, Emma Spiro, Nicole Buckley, Rachel Moran, and Morgan Wack, "Uncertainty and Misinformation: What to Expect on Election Night and Days After," Election Integrity Partnership, October 26, 2020, https://www.eipartnership.net/news/what-to-expect.

31. Toby Hopp, Patrick Ferrucci, and Chris J. Vargo, "Why Do People Share Ideologically Extreme, False, and Misleading Content on Social Media? A Self-Report and Trace Data-Based Analysis of Countermedia Content Dissemination on Facebook and Twitter," *Human Communication Research* 46, no. 1, (2020), 357-84.

32. Mike Isaac and Kellen Browning, "Fact-Checked on Facebook and Twitter, Conservatives Switch Their Apps," *New York Times*, November 11, 2020, https://www.nytimes.com/2020/11/11/technology/parler-rumble-newsmax.html.

33. Sheera Frenkel, "How Misinformation 'Superspreaders' Seed False Election Theories," *New York Times,* November 23, 2020, https://www.nytimes.com/2020/11/23/technology/election-misinformation-facebook-twitter.html.

34. Brendan Nyhan, "Why More Democrats Are Now Embracing Conspiracy Theories," *New York Times*, February 15, 2017, https://www.nytimes.com/2017/02/15/upshot/why-more-democrats-are-now-embracing-conspiracy-theories.html?_r=1.

35. Toby Hopp, Patrick Ferrucci, and Chris J. Vargo, "Why Do People Share Ideologically Extreme, False, and Misleading Content on Social Media? A Self-Report and Trace Data-Based Analysis of Countermedia Content Dissemination on Facebook and Twitter," *Human Communication Research* 46, no. 1, (2020), 357-84.

36. Sarah Fisher, "2020's Homegrown Fake News Crisis," *Axios*, March 4, 2020, https://www.axios.com/fake-news-local-outlets-2020-presidential-election-1144b4ee-d4b9-40f9-9d14-9fdc43793867.html.

37. McKay Coppins, "Billion-Dollar Disinformation Campaign to Reelect the President," *The Atlantic*, March 2020, https://www.theatlantic.com/magazine/archive/2020/03/the-2020-disinformation-war/605530/.

38. Karen Kornbluth, Ellen P. Goodman, and Eli Weiner, "Safeguarding Digital Democracy," The German Marshall Fund of the United States, 2020, https://www.gmfus.org/sites/default/files/Safeguarding%20Democracy%20against%20Disinformation_v7.pdf.

39. Karen Kornbluth, Ellen P. Goodman, and Eli Weiner, "Safeguarding Digital Democracy," The German Marshall Fund of the United States, 2020. https://www.gmfus.org/sites/default/files/Safeguarding%20Democracy%20against%20Disinformation_v7.pdf.

40. Sheryl Gay Stolberg and Noah Weiland, "Study Finds 'Single Largest Driver' of Coronavirus Misinformation: Trump," *New York Times*, October 22, 2020, https://www.nytimes.com/2020/09/30/us/politics/trump-coronavirus-misinformation.html.

41. Nicholas Bogel-Burroughs and Sandra E. Garcia, "What Is Antifa, the Movement Trump Wants to Declare a Terror Group?" *New York Times*, September 28, 2020. https://www.nytimes.com/article/what-antifa-trump.html.

42. Cooper Gatewood and Ciaran O'Connor, "Disinformation Briefing: Narratives around Black Lives Matter and Voter Fraud," Research Report, ISD, 2020. https://www.isdglobal.org/isd-publications/disinformation-briefing-narratives-around-black-lives-matter-and-voter-fraud/.

43. Jasmine Wright, "Harris Responds to Trump's Birther Attacks: 'They're Going to Engage in Lies," CNN, August 16, 2020. https://www.cnn.com/2020/08/16/politics/harris-trump-birther-attacks/index.html.

44. Barbara Guitierrez, "Conspiracy Theories Abound This Election Season," News@TheU, University of Miami, October 7, 2020, https://news.miami.edu/stories/2020/10/conspiracy-theories-abound-this-election-season.html; Mike Wendling, "QAnon: What Is It and Where Did It Come From?" BBC News, January 7, 2021, https://www.bbc.com/news/53498434.

45. Cooper Gatewood and Ciaran O'Connor, "Disinformation Briefing: Narratives around Black Lives Matter and Voter Fraud," Research Report, ISD, 2020. https://www.isdglobal.org/isd-publications/disinformation-briefing-narratives-around-black-lives-matter-and-voter-fraud/.

46. Yochai Benkler, Casey Tilton, Bruce Etling, Hal Roberts, Justin Clark, Rob Faris, Jonas Kaiser, and Carolyn Schmitt, "Mail-In Voter Fraud: Anatomy of a Disinformation Campaign," Working Paper, Berkman Klein Center for Internet & Society at Harvard University, 2020, https://cyber.harvard.edu/publication/2020/Mail-in-Voter-Fraud-Disinformation-2020.

47. Emily Badger, "Most Republicans Say They Doubt the Election. How Many Really Mean It?" *New York Times*, November 30, 2020. https://www.nytimes.com/2020/11/30/upshot/republican-voters-election-doubts.html.

48. Kate Starbird, Michael Caulfield, Renee DiResta, Jevin West, Emma Spiro, Nicole Buckley, Rachel Moran, and Morgan Wack, "Uncertainty and Misinformation: What to Expect on Election Night and Days After," Election Integrity Partnership, October 26, 2020, https://www.eipartnership.net/news/what-to-expect.

49. Tonya Riley, "The Cybersecurity 2020: Dominion Lawsuit Could Be Just Start of Legal Action Against Trump Allies," *Washington Post*, January 11, 2021, https://

www.washingtonpost.com/politics/2021/01/11/cybersecurity-202-dominion-lawsuit-could-be-just-start-legal-action-against-trump-allies/.

50. Kate Starbird, Michael Caulfield, Renee DiResta, Jevin West, Emma Spiro, Nicole Buckley, Rachel Moran, and Morgan Wack, "Uncertainty and Misinformation: What to Expect on Election Night and Days After," Election Integrity Partnership, October 26, 2020, https://www.eipartnership.net/news/what-to-expect; Tina Nguyen and Mark Scott, "How 'SharpieGate' Went From Online Chatter to Trump-world Strategy in Arizona," *Politico*, November 5, 2020. https://www.politico.com/news/2020/11/05/sharpie-ballots-trump-strategy-arizona-434372.

51. Markus Prior, "Media and Political Polarization," *Annual Review of Political Science* 16, (2020), 101-27.

11

Defending Democracy during a Pandemic

Grace Panetta

On the evening of Monday, March 16, 2020, Ohio's Republican governor, Mike DeWine, had a major dilemma on his hands. With cases of the highly threatening coronavirus rising dramatically, DeWine had already taken a number of decisive actions: declaring a state of emergency, halting in-person learning in schools, and barring indoor service at restaurants and bars.[1] Yet Ohio was still scheduled to hold its primary election the next day, with thousands of Ohioans and poll workers ready to head to the polls. DeWine was concerned that an in-person election would conflict with guidance from the Centers for Disease Control and Prevention that gatherings should be limited to 50 people at most.

"It is my recommendation that we postpone in-person voting until June 2, 2020," DeWine tweeted that evening.[2] "We cannot tell people to stay inside, but also tell them to go out and vote." In a notably bold move, DeWine announced that the state's health director, Dr. Amy Acton, would formally order counties not to hold in-person voting the following day, under the state of emergency that he had declared a week earlier.

After Acton duly issued the order, DeWine and Secretary of State Frank LaRose filed suit to change the date of the election. After several late-night court decisions and ample confusion all around, the Ohio Supreme Court ultimately upheld DeWine and LaRose's move to cancel in-person voting on March 17.[3] Yet rescheduling of the election still hung in the balance. Within a week, DeWine and LaRose managed to reach an unprecedented agreement with the Ohio legislature to hold the primary election almost entirely via mail-in ballots, continuing through April 28. LaRose's office, which was not authorized to distribute actual mail ballots or even ballot applications to all registered voters, sent out postcards instead that instructed voters on how to vote by mail.[4] On the 28th, Ohio held limited in-person voting, but only for certain disabled and homeless citizens.

As DeWine and Acton had hoped, Ohio's directives and procedures for the spring election seem to have achieved the goal of preventing significant COVID-19 outbreaks. Yet the election saw disappointingly low voter turnout,[5] and it triggered widespread anxieties and questions over how November's election process (and also the primary races still to come) might unfold.[6] The virus had begun to spread through the nation at an alarming pace, leaving no place or demographic group untouched. Would President Donald Trump use the circumstances of the pandemic to justify delaying or canceling the November election? (In point of fact, he could do no such thing.)[7] More immediately, would it even be possible to hold further primary elections? While voting by mail allows voters to cast a ballot safely from home without venturing out to a polling location, it also presents novel challenges. Would a sudden spike in voting by mail overwhelm election offices and render them unable to follow sound election procedures? Would voters understand how to vote by mail? If not, would many more ballots than usual be rejected?[8]

In the end, the story of the 2020 election was of a country and its election systems withstanding extraordinary stress tests. The election unfolded successfully in spite of a global pandemic, unprecedented strains on state and local budgets, and sweeping changes in how Americans chose to vote. All this transpired even as the president sought to undermine the integrity of the results by spreading dangerous misinformation about early and absentee balloting,[9] false contentions that were repeated over many months in right-wing echo chambers,[10] and which ultimately resulted in a violent insurrection on Capitol Hill as Congress gathered to count electoral votes.[11]

2020 ACCELERATED A LONG-PERCOLATING TREND TOWARD VOTING BY MAIL

Election administration in the United States is heavily decentralized, controlled largely at the local level: approximately 10,000 distinct jurisdictions are charged with carrying out elections.[12] As a result, election and voting policies vary notably between states and even within states.

Nevertheless, some element of absentee and early voting has been a feature of American elections since the Civil War. The two world wars in the first half of the twentieth century actually fostered the creation of the absentee voting system that we know today. As time advanced, states began to offer absentee voting as an option available not only to military personnel, but also to civilians.[13]

Since the late 1980s, the share of voters casting their ballots in person has steadily dropped, while the percentage of voters choosing to vote before Election Day has increased—all as states have consistently expanded the availability of both mail and early voting. In the 2004 presidential election, nearly 80 percent of voters voted in person on Election Day, with around 12 percent voting absentee and 8 percent voting early in person—making for approximately 24.9 million people voting prior to Election Day, according to the U.S. Election Assistance Commission. By the 2016 election, the share of Election Day in-person voters had fallen to 60 percent, with 23 percent voting absentee or by mail and 17 percent voting early in person. In total, 57.2 million voters cast a ballot before Election Day.[14] It is important to note, however, that a large proportion of the individuals voting by mail were from all-mail election states (including Colorado, Oregon, and Washington), or from states like Arizona and Montana that do not hold all-mail elections but routinely see more than half of the electorate voting by mail. In fully half of U.S. states in the 2016 presidential election, fewer than 10 percent of voters cast their ballots by mail, according to the U.S. Census Bureau.[15] In other words, prior to 2020, only a handful of states had significant experience in processing high volumes of mail ballots.

The COVID-19 pandemic greatly accelerated the gradual shift from voting in person on Election Day to voting early or by mail. As of the beginning of 2020, three states (Colorado, Oregon, and Washington) had been holding their elections entirely by mail for years, and Hawaii and Utah were at that time moving to an all-vote-at-home model. In addition, 28 states and the District of Columbia allowed any voter to vote by mail without an excuse. During the year 2020, 29 Democratic and Republican-controlled states passed a total of 79 bills further expanding voting access and making it easier for voters to cast a ballot other than by appearance at a polling place, according to an analysis by the Brennan Center for Justice at New York University Law School.[16]

For the 2020 presidential election, 10 states and the District of Columbia sent most or all registered voters a vote-from-home ballot while also offering various in-person voting options. Thirty-five more states allowed voters to vote by mail, either without a documented excuse (being away from the county of residence on Election Day, having a disability, being over the age of 65, etc.), or by citing a fear of contracting COVID-19. That left only five states that required a justification beyond fear of viral infection for voting by mail: Indiana, Louisiana, Mississippi, Tennessee, and Texas.[17] More than 40 states also held some form of early in-person voting prior to Election Day, either regular in-person voting at a polling place (just as a voter would experience on Election Day itself), or through a process called "in-person absentee" voting, in which a voter fills out a mail ballot at a local election office.[18] Such ballots must be processed by the same regulations as ballots sent in through the mail. Some states, including Kentucky, Pennsylvania, and Virginia, held in-person early voting for the first time in 2020. Others, like Texas, expanded early voting dates.

In addition to augmenting voting options, the pandemic pushed many legislatures to enact procedural reforms intended to make the entire process easier for voters and election officials alike. Those included expanding the availability of ballot drop boxes and drop-off locations as an alternative to the U.S. Postal Service, allowing voters to correct or "cure" problems with their mail ballots, providing prepaid postage for ballots, and most crucially, affording election officials more time before Election Day to authenticate and process mail ballots.

These changes resulted in a record number of voters nationwide choosing to cast their ballots prior to Election Day. They brought an increase in the share of the electorate choosing to do so in every single state, even in states restricting voting by mail to specific groups.[19] In 2020, the number of voters voting prior to Election Day, either by mail or early in-person, nearly doubled to 101 million. According to state data compiled by the U.S. Elections Project at the University of Florida, the number who voted by mail also doubled from 33.1 million to 66.5 million—out of approximately 160 million total votes cast.

Importantly, not all states distinguish mail votes from in-person early or in-person absentee votes.[20] Comprehensive national survey data from the Survey of the Performance of Elections (SPAE) also documented this shift. Run by the Massachusetts Institute of Technology's Election Data Science Lab, the survey asks voters about their voting experiences and levels of satisfaction and trust in the voting process. The 2020 survey was administered through YouGov and interviewed more than 18,000 voters throughout the United States. Of those surveyed, 26 percent said they voted early in-person, while 46 percent reported voting by mail—up substantially from the 21 percent who reported doing so in 2016. Just 28 percent reported voting in-person on Election Day, down 32 percentage points from the 60 percent of voters who reported voting in-person on Election Day in 2016.[21]

PRESIDENT TRUMP POLITICIZED THE ACT OF VOTING ITSELF

While the share of the electorate voting by mail in 2020 greatly increased overall in comparison to 2016, just how Americans would and did cast their ballots became a topic of deep partisan division. Democratic and Democratic-leaning voters largely drove the shift toward mail voting after President Donald Trump had spent months spreading misinformation and lies about the reliability of mail voting.[22] After frightening his base away from voting by mail during the election itself, which he lost, Trump and his allies then embarked upon an unprecedented campaign to subvert the results of the election itself—filing dozens of flawed and ultimately unsuccessful lawsuits, unsuccessfully pressuring election officials to delay certification of results, and attempting in vain to get state legislatures involved.[23] After those efforts failed, Trump pressured Republican members of Congress to challenge certain slates of presidential electors from states that had voted for President-elect Joe Biden.[24]

Trump was no stranger to leveraging conspiracy theories about voting and elections to undermine his political foes. In the past, he had accused presidential primary rival Ted Cruz of rigging the 2016 Iowa caucuses (which take place in full view of television cameras),[25] and had also falsely claimed that he would have won the national popular vote in 2016 if not for millions of spurious votes supposedly cast by undocumented immigrants.[26] He even convened a presidential commission, headed by controversial then-Kansas Secretary of State Kris Kobach, to find evidence of illegal voting. That inquiry eventually petered out when states refused to hand over the voter data requested by the commission, which disbanded without producing a report.[27]

In the 19 states that report mail ballots returned by party registration in the U.S. Election Project's dataset, Democrats both requested and returned ballots in 2020 at higher rates than Republicans. In those states, 48 percent of mail ballots were returned by registered Democrats, 27 percent by registered Republicans, and 24 percent by unaffiliated voters. In the 2008 SPAE survey, 19 percent of Republicans reported voting by mail compared to 18 percent of Democrats, a gap that widened slightly in the next two presidential elections—largely due to the fact that blue states were the ones running all-mail elections. In 2016, 26 percent of Democrats and 21 percent of Republicans said they voted by mail, a five percentage point difference. In 2020, however, 59 percent of Democrats reported casting their ballots by mail compared to 30 percent of Republicans, a 29-point gap.

A Pew Research Center survey conducted in November 2020 yielded results remarkably similar to those of the 2020 SPAE: 46 percent of voters reported casting their ballots by mail, with 54 percent voting in person. In Pew's survey, 58 percent of Biden voters reported voting by mail compared to 32 percent of Trump voters, a 26-point gap. Conversely, 37 percent of Trump voters reported voting in person on Election Day, compared to 17 percent of Biden voters.[28] In view of these trends, Trump's words may have influenced how partisans decided to vote, and perhaps Trump even suppressed some of his own voters by questioning voting by mail with such vehemence and persistence (although the overall turnout was so high that both Biden and Trump voters had to have turned out in force).

In the spring of 2020, as many states announced plans to expand eligibility for mail voting and began to send out mail ballot application forms to voters, Trump pointedly critiqued the intentions of some states to reschedule their primaries owing to the pandemic.[29] From there he went on to begin spreading full-fledged misinformation designed to undermine the perceived integrity of the election months before it began. In particular, Trump falsely claimed that mail voting was rife with high levels of fraud and malfeasance, and that expanding mail voting would mean "you'd never have a Republican elected in this country again."[30] Some of Trump's assertions were absurd, including claims that foreign countries would flood the U.S. postal system and election offices with forged, counterfeit mail ballots.[31] In a similarly unhinged vein, he warned that bands of juvenile delinquent children in California would steal ballots out of mailboxes,[32] and even suggested that ballot drop boxes were vectors for COVID-19,[33] despite the CDC's conclusion that surface transmission of COVID-19 is extremely rare.[34]

Trump's wild claims regarding voting procedures admittedly lacked intellectual coherence, yet his all-out war on absentee and mail voting represented a stark reversal for the GOP because it upended decades of Republican get-out-the-vote strategy—in the process baffling and upsetting numerous Republican candidates and operatives.[35] In states including Arizona, Georgia, Florida, Ohio, Pennsylvania, and Wisconsin, laws establishing no-excuse mail voting had in fact been enacted by Republican-controlled state legislatures—and in some cases signed into law by Republican governors. Indeed, Republican candidates and strategists had long since concluded that mail voting is particularly convenient for retired and elderly voters, who make up a significant portion of the electorate in states like Arizona and Florida, and who ordinarily wish to vote at their own convenience rather than waiting in a long line on Election Day.[36] Furthermore, from a strategic standpoint, campaigns in general seek to "bank" as many votes as possible before Election Day. Every voter whose vote is recorded prior to Election Day is a voter that campaigns can cross off their lists, a voter who needs no follow-up to ensure that he or she actually gets to the polls on Election Day itself.

It is in fact the case that in 2020, the Trump campaign itself, along with the Republican National Committee and other state and local Republican party organizations, actually sent out mail ballot application forms, in addition to mailers and texts urging voters to request their mail ballots as soon as possible. These activities introduced a marked discordance between Trump's charged rhetoric and actual GOP strategy on the ground.[37] In the 2000s and 2010s, as Republican lawmakers and activists pushed to restrict voting access, they mainly focused on lobbying state legislatures to pass voter ID laws, which only prevent one kind of voter fraud: in-person voter impersonation. For the most part, those same Republicans did not argue for additional restrictions on absentee voting. Even though fraud in either category is exceptionally rare, absentee and mail ballot fraud occurs at a higher rate than does voter impersonation.[38] Indeed, in the 2000 election dispute in Florida, it was the Democrats who filed for recounts of ballots cast in person in heavily Democratic counties, while Republicans fought hard for absentee and military ballots of questionable validity to be counted.[39] By 2020, Republicans were litigating court battles to limit third-party ballot collection. In many venues, they also sought to enjoin state officials from expanding the eligibility criteria for voting by mail, to block them from giving voters more time to correct errors with their ballots, and in particular, to keep them from extending the deadlines for arrival of ballots postmarked by Election Day.[40]

Although Trump's aggressive efforts to overturn the election ultimately failed, they were highly traumatic for American democracy, and threatened to jeopardize the integrity of future elections. Even though the overwhelming majority of voters reported satisfaction with their voting experiences in the SPAE survey, they did not express similar confidence in the results. The share of overall voters who said they were very or somewhat confident that votes nationwide were counted as intended fell from 84 percent in 2016 to 77 percent in 2020. In 2016, 80 percent of Republicans said they were confident that votes were counted as intended, compared with 69 percent of Democrats. By 2020, that discrepancy both reversed and widened dramatically to a remarkable 70-point gap: 93 percent of Democrats were very or somewhat confident in the vote count, but only 23 percent of Republicans.

CHAOTIC PRIMARIES IN SOME STATES FOLLOWED BY A NOTABLY SMOOTH NOVEMBER NATIONWIDE

State and local election administrators are surely among the most overworked, underpaid, and least appreciated of all public servants. Stories of election dysfunction frequently make headlines, and TV news crews never seem to tire of documenting long lines snaking around voting sites. Yet the vast majority of election administrators, who consistently oversee well-run elections with no lines or other difficulties, rarely receive attention or credit. Their challenges were greatly compounded in 2020, when every aspect of the voting process underwent an especially grueling test.

Congress allotted $400 million in election assistance to states and counties as part of the CARES Act, signed into law in March 2020.[41] These funds, however, fell far short of the $4 billion in funding that the Brennan Center had recommended as being necessary in order for states to be able to hold fully pandemic-safe elections.[42] Moreover, many jurisdictions used the bulk of their funds in administering their primary contests, leaving little left over for the general election in November.

Three weeks after Ohio canceled in-person voting in its primary, Wisconsin forged ahead and held its regularly scheduled April 7 spring election, which included the presidential primary and a high-stakes state Supreme Court race—despite a marked surge in COVID-19 cases in the state. Democratic Governor Tony Evers, much like his Republican colleague Mike DeWine, wanted to replace in-person voting on the appointed day with an election held entirely by mail, a request the Republican-controlled Wisconsin legislature immediately rejected as logistically unfeasible.[43] The result was an uncommonly chaotic election. Several last-minute court decisions regarding the rules surrounding voting by mail were immediately appealed, confusing countless voters in the process. In addition, jurisdictions struggled to find enough poll workers to staff voting locations. Milwaukee, which ordinarily has 180 polling stations open, was able to staff only 5 on April 7.[44] Even states like Georgia, Maryland, and Pennsylvania, all of which postponed their primaries from the spring to June, experienced difficulties in scaling up mail voting and ensuring a smooth in-person voting experience. Pennsylvania's election officials in particular suffered the double blow of having to run a statewide election with no-excuse mail voting and also in-person absentee voting, both for the very first time and during a global pandemic. Counties struggled to keep up with the demand for voting by mail amid a rush of over 2 million mail ballot applications, with many voters receiving their ballots too late and others not receiving ballots at all.[45]

In various Pennsylvania cities and also in Washington, D.C., voters had to contend as well with prominent law enforcement and National Guard presence at polling places, all in response to the nationwide protests over the death of George Floyd and racial inequities in policing. Officials in D.C. took the step of issuing a citywide curfew an hour before the polls closed. Even though the curfew technically exempted voters and essential workers, the messaging still confused and intimidated many voters, contributing to long lines at the already-reduced number of polling places that the District had managed to staff and operate.[46]

In Georgia, which postponed its presidential and congressional elections until June 9, some voters reported not receiving the mail ballots they had requested. Officials and poll workers also struggled with the learning curve of running their first election with the state's brand-new Dominion Voting Systems ballot-marking devices, which the state had purchased to replace aging direct-recorder electronic machines. On a ballot marking device, voters mark their choices on an electronic touchscreen, which prints out a paper ballot that is then scanned. As workers struggled to get the machines working properly, confusion and delays gave rise to hours-long wait times—and even near-chaos at some voting locations in the metro Atlanta area.[47]

The rocky spring and summer elections inspired keen concern on the part of experts and critics, some of whom questioned whether America's election infrastructure could in fact withstand the strains of the pandemic and the skyrocketing demand for voting by mail.[48] Yet despite the conspicuous lack of financial support from Congress, states and counties learned much from the missteps of the spring. The great majority pulled off a remarkable feat in November, averting many of the nightmare scenarios that had included predictions of mass disorder with mail ballots, long lines at polling places due to a lack of election workers, and vote-counting dramas nationwide. There were certainly scattered instances of difficulties in the fall, including mail ballots sent to the wrong voters in some Ohio, Pennsylvania, and New York counties, owing to printing errors. Some voting locations had long wait times, while others failed to open on time—such problems, however, are par for the course in every election and did not deviate significantly from the norm.[49]

Overall, from the moment the first general election ballots were sent out to domestic and civilian voters in North Carolina on September 4, the 2020 general election was one of the best-executed, smoothest, secure, and peaceful elections in the nation's history, even amid record voter turnout. The success of the November election was a true team effort, jointly accomplished by election officials, nonprofit organizations, and media outlets, all of whom devoted considerable resources to educating voters, disseminating factual information about the voting process, and providing voters with the resources overall to cast their ballots and make their votes count. The nonprofit and private sectors also stepped in to fill the void left by a general lack of government action in the areas of voter outreach efforts and grant funding.[50] Even professional sports teams became involved, offering up their pandemic-idled arenas and stadiums for use as in-person voting locations or mail ballot counting centers.[51]

The election was also a success thanks to the voters themselves, who heeded the advice to settle on their voting plans well in advance, request mail ballots as early as possible, and exercise care in filling out and submitting ballots.[52] A record number of voters, including young people, also stepped up to serve their communities as poll workers, ensuring that voting locations were adequately staffed and did not have long wait times.[53] Significantly, voters reported remarkably high levels of satisfaction with their voting experiences in the SPAE survey whether they voted by mail or in-person, levels almost exactly on par with the results of the 2016 version of the survey.

As it turned out, the election brought no violence or voter intimidation on the part of Trump supporters or other agitators, as many observers feared would occur given the sheer quantities of misinformation and vitriol that Trump and his allies had directed against the electoral process.[54] In addition, media outlets and election officials pulled back the curtain to explain the ballot-counting process, helpfully setting expectations that the election would probably not be called on Election Night itself owing to the substantial increase in mail ballots, which take longer to count than in-person votes.

Aside from the overall administrative success of voting by mail in November 2020, the election was the most secure in American history, thanks in part to cybersecurity improvements at the federal, state, and local levels. Also significant in many voting jurisdictions was the transition from voting machines producing no voter-verifiable paper trails to hand-marked ballots, ballot-marking devices, or voting machines with voter-verifiable and auditable paper trails.[55]

VOTER TURNOUT SIGNIFICANTLY INCREASED BY COMPARISON TO 2016

More than 159.6 million voters turned out in the 2020 presidential election, representing 66.7 percent of the nation's voting-eligible population. The 2020 turnout rate marked the highest voter turnout in a presidential election since 1900, when 73 percent of the voting-eligible population participated, according to Michael McDonald's U.S. Elections Project.[56] In the 2016 presidential election four years earlier, 138.8 million voters turned out to vote, representing 59.2 percent of the voting-eligible population.[57] According to McDonald's calculations, voter turnout increased not only nationwide, but also in every single state. The state with the highest voting-eligible population turnout was Minnesota at 80 percent, followed by Colorado at 76.4 percent, Maine at 76.3 percent, Wisconsin at 75.8 percent, and Washington at 75.7 percent.[58] By comparison to 2016, the voting-eligible population voter turnout rate increased by the greatest margins in Hawaii and Utah, both of which fully transitioned in 2020 to the procedure of sending a mail ballot to every registered voter. Even in the states that posted the lowest voting-eligible population voter turnout rates—including West Virginia, Arkansas, Mississippi, and Texas—voter turnout still improved over 2016 levels.[59]

"There is no doubt in my mind that Donald Trump was the reason why we had record turnout in 2020," McDonald asserted in a November 20, 2020, webinar hosted by Nonprofit VOTE.[60] McDonald pointed to the record-high turnout in the midterm elections of 2018, which followed a meager turnout in 2014, citing this as evidence that the Trump presidency was the main driver of turnout even before the pandemic struck, even though Trump himself was not on the ballot in 2018. "Our laws did not change; there was a little more competition, but not a lot. The only major change we had in our politics was the Donald Trump presidency. Whether you love him or hate him, he drives passions, and he drives people to vote," McDonald stated.

While correlation does not mean causation, the high turnout in 2020 was also foretold by previous scholarly research, which established that enhancing the availability of voting by mail increases turnout across the board. Four out of the top 10 states with the highest turnouts of the voting-eligible population sent a mail ballot to every registered voter, as did five out of the top 10 states that saw the biggest increases in voter turnout between 2016 and 2020 (see table 11.1). Conversely, the states that restricted mail voting to those with excuses other than COVID-19 concerns, or otherwise imposed burdens on voting by mail (like requiring notarization or a photocopy of the voter's ID), were at the bottom of the pack in both turnout rates and improvement over 2016.

In the same address, McDonald remarked: "It may be that conducting an all-mail ballot election in the midst of a pandemic particularly enabled voters to participate in the election where they would have otherwise found barriers and decided not to vote." He added, however, that sending every voter a mail

Table 11.1. States with the Greatest Voter Turnout Increases

State	*2016 VEP Turnout, Total Ballots Counted*	*2020 VEP Turnout, Total Ballots Counted*	*Percentage Point Changes*	*All-Mail State in 2020?*
Hawaii	43.2%	57.5%	+14.3	Yes
Utah	57.9%	69.2%	+11.3	Yes
California	58.2%	68.5%	+10.3	Yes
Washington	65.7%	75.7%	+10	Yes
Arizona	56.1%	65.9%	+9.8	No
New Jersey	65.8%	75.3%	+9.5	Yes
Vermont	64.8%	74.2%	+9.4	Yes
Texas	51.4%	60.4%	+9	No
Montana	64.3%	73.1%	+8.8	Yes
Michigan	65.7%	73.9%	+8.2	No

Source: U.S. Elections Project as of January 28, 2021.

ballot does not necessarily guarantee that a state will see high voter turnout, noting that Hawaii, Nevada, and Washington, D.C. all had voting-eligible population turnout below the overall national rate of 66.7 percent.

What does the future hold for voting and election policy? Voting is ultimately a consumer choice, and the sheer number of voters exposed to voting by mail and early voting in 2020 strongly suggests that more people will consistently choose those voting methods going forward. In the SPAE survey, 81 percent of all voters who voted by mail said they were likely to do so again in the future, with 60 percent saying they were very likely to do so and 21 percent indicating they were somewhat likely to do so. While Republican voters continue to distrust mail voting at higher rates than Democrats, 68 percent of the Republicans who did vote by mail in 2020 nonetheless stated that they were very or somewhat likely to continue doing so moving forward.

These trends indicate that on the whole, the era of most voters actually voting on Election Day itself may be over. "Election Week" rather than Election Day may be with us to stay. And despite the lopsided partisan breakdown in how Americans chose to cast their ballots, the nearly two-fold increase in the proportion of the electorate voting by mail by no means doomed Republicans across the board. Indeed, Republicans who were not named Donald Trump did quite well in congressional and state legislative races,[61] contravening the optimistic scenarios for Democrats that pre-election polls and fund-raising numbers had suggested. Republicans held their own in several key U.S. Senate races, won back roughly a dozen seats on net in the House of Representatives,[62] and flipped more than 80 seats on net in state legislatures nationwide.[63]

To be sure, the fraught election environment that Trump and his allies inflamed means that partisan struggles over electoral policy and voting restrictions are likely to continue to fester in state legislatures across the country. Yet some lawmakers may nonetheless arrive at a bipartisan consensus on nonpartisan, common-sense reforms, like allowing more time for counties to process and count mail ballots ahead of Election Day. The swing states of Pennsylvania and Wisconsin, for example, did not allow officials to begin processing or counting mail-in ballots before the polls opened on Election Day, leaving officials in the position of having to run an in-person election and count many thousands of ballots all at once.[64] In Michigan, where the legislature passed a one-time bill allowing large jurisdictions a one-day head start on processing ballots, Republican leaders later acknowledged that they should have granted municipal clerks even more time.[65]

In the 2020 election, America's voters, election officials, and institutions withstood both an unrelenting global pandemic and prodigious quantities of misinformation and disinformation to produce record levels of participation.

State officials from around the country also stood to defend the results of the election when they came under question. Yet the unprecedented attacks on certified results, both rhetorical and physical, left the system more vulnerable than ever in many respects. At the time of this writing, the grand experiment of American democracy has arrived at a worrisome inflection point. America's voters and institutions must now decide whether to build upon the resounding successes of 2020, or instead to permit disinformation and armed confrontation to carry the day.

NOTES

1. Laura A. Bischoff and Kristen Spicker, "Coronavirus Timeline: A Look at the Orders Changing Life in Ohio," *Dayton Daily News*, May 13, 2020, https://www.daytondailynews.com/news/local/timeline-coronavirus-prompts-orders-changing-everyday-life-ohio/gpnVSADPxZxMltlDVyqKEP/.

2. Tweet from Mike DeWine, March 16, 2020, https://twitter.com/GovMikeDeWine/status/1239627744570421253□□□□.

3. Grace Panetta, "The Ohio Supreme Court Issued a Last-minute Ruling Allowing the State to Postpone its March 17 Primary," *Business Insider*, March 16, 2020, https://www.businessinsider.com/ohio-postpones-march-17-primary-until-june-cancels-in-person-voting-2020-3.

4. Zach Montellaro, "Ohio to Run All-Mail Primary through April 28," *Politico*, March 25, 2020, https://www.politico.com/news/2020/03/25/ohio-vote-by-mail-primary-election-149012.

5. Jim Nelson, "Low Voter Turnout and Confusion Highlight Ohio's Delayed Primary Election," 19 News Cleveland, April 29, 2020, https://www.cleveland19.com/2020/04/29/low-voter-turnout-confusion-highlight-ohios-delayed-primary-election/.

6. Darrel Rowland and Rick Rouan, "After a Problem-Plagued Primary, Ohio Leaders Disagree about November Election Plan," *Columbus Dispatch*. April 28, 2020, https://www.dispatch.com/news/20200428/after-problem-plagued-primary-ohio-leaders-disagree-about-november-election-plan.

7. Grace Panetta, "No, Trump Can't Cancel or Delay the November General Election Over His Covid-19 Diagnosis," *Business Insider*, October 2, 2020, https://www.businessinsider.com/trump-cant-cancel-or-postpone-the-november-election-over-coronavirus-2020-3.

8. Derek Thompson, "How Voting by Mail Could Cost Biden the Election," *The Atlantic*, September 30, 2020, https://www.theatlantic.com/ideas/archive/2020/09/the-democrats-vote-by-mail-conundrum/616535/.

9. Grace Panetta, "Trump's Claims about US Election Security in the First Debate were as Wildly False as They Were Incoherent," *Business Insider*, September 30, 2020, https://www.businessinsider.com/point-by-point-fact-check-trump-debate-answers-voting-elections-2020-9.

10. Lois Beckett and Julia Carrie Wong, "The Misinformation Machine Amplifying Trump's Election Lies," *The Guardian*, November 10, 2020, https://www.theguardian.com/us-news/2020/nov/10/donald-trump-us-election-misinformation-media.

11. Marc Fisher et al., "The Four-Hour Insurrection," *Washington Post*, January 7, 2021, https://www.washingtonpost.com/graphics/2021/politics/trump-insurrection-capitol/.

12. Elizabeth Howard, "5 Things You May Not Know About Local Election Officials," Brennan Center for Justice, October 26, 2020, https://www.brennancenter.org/our-work/research-reports/5-things-you-may-not-know-about-local-election-officials.

13. Alex Seitz-Wald, "How Do You Know Voting by Mail Works? The U.S. Military's Done it Since the Civil War," NBC News, April 19, 2020, https://www.nbcnews.com/politics/2020-election/how-do-you-know-voting-mail-works-u-s-military-n1186926.

14. "EAVS Deep Dive: Early, Absentee, and Mail Voting," US Election Assistance Commission, October 17, 2017, https://www.eac.gov/documents/2017/10/17/eavs-deep-dive-early-absentee-and-mail-voting-data-statutory-overview.

15. 2016 Current Population Survey Voting & Registration Supplement, https://www.census.gov/data/tables/time-series/demo/voting-and-registration/p20-580.html; https://docs.google.com/spreadsheets/d/1KS74w98eI59gYUiY_qoI7FKfZIDTuCHGZhv6YWdNXjc/edit#gid=0.

16. "Voting Laws Roundup 2020," Brennan Center for Justice, December 8, 2020, https://www.brennancenter.org/our-work/research-reports/voting-laws-roundup-2020-0.

17. Grace Panetta and Yuqing Liu, "Vote By Mail Rules Differ By State. Here's A Map Showing How It Works Where You Live," *Business Insider*, September 17, 2020, https://www.businessinsider.com/states-where-you-can-vote-by-mail-map-2020-8.

18. Shayanne Gal and Grace Panetta, "When Early Voting Starts and Ends in Each State," *Business Insider*, October 30, 2020, https://www.businessinsider.com/when-is-early-voting-in-each-state-2020-8.

19. Lazaro Gamio et al., "Record-setting Turnout: Tracking Early Voting in the 2020 Election," *New York Times*, November 12, 2020, https://www.nytimes.com/interactive/2020/us/elections/early-voting-results.html.

20. U.S. Elections Project. 2020 General Election Early Vote Statistics, November 23, 2020. https://electproject.github.io/Early-Vote-2020G/index.html.

21. Charles Stewart III, "How We Voted in 2020: A First Look at the Survey of the Performance of American Elections," MIT Election Science and Data Lab, December 15, 2020, http://electionlab.mit.edu/sites/default/files/2020-12/How-we-voted-in-2020-v01.pdf.

22. MaryAlice Parks and Kendall Karson, "A Step-by-Step Look at Trump's Falsehoods on Mail-in Voting: Analysis," *ABC News*, October 1, 2020, https://abcnews.go.com/Politics/step-step-trumps-falsehoods-mail-voting-analysis/story?id=73354979.

23. Ann Gerhart and Jake Crump, "Election Results Are Under Attack: Here Are the Facts," *Washington Post*, January 5, 2021, https://www.washingtonpost.com/elections/interactive/2020/election-integrity/.

24. Charles Davis and Lauren Frias, "A Timeline of How Trump Incited His Followers yo Storm yhe Capitol and Attempt a Coup," *Business Insider*, January 7, 2021, https://www.businessinsider.com/how-trump-in-final-weeks-incited-his-followers-to-storm-the-capitol-2021-1.

25. Tom McCarthy, "Donald Trump Claims Ted Cruz 'Stole' Iowa Caucuses and Calls for New Election," *The Guardian*, February 3, 2016, https://www.theguardian.com/us-news/2016/feb/03/donald-trump-ted-cruz-stole-iowa-caucuses-new-election.

26. Tom LoBianco, "Trump Falsely Claims 'Millions of People Who Voted Illegally' Cost Him Popular Vote," CNN, November 28, 2016, https://www.cnn.com/2016/11/27/politics/donald-trump-voter-fraud-popular-vote/index.html.

27. Eli Rosenberg, "The Most Bizarre Thing I've Ever Been a Part Of': Trump Panel Found No Widespread Voter Fraud, Ex-member Says," *Washington Post*, August 3, 2018, https://www.washingtonpost.com/news/politics/wp/2018/08/03/the-most-bizarre-thing-ive-ever-been-a-part-of-trump-panel-found-no-voter-fraud-ex-member-says/.

28. "Sharp Divisions on Vote Counts, as Biden Gets High Marks for His Post-Election Conduct," Pew Research Center, November 20, 2020, https://www.pewresearch.org/politics/2020/11/20/the-voting-experience-in-2020/.

29. Sonam Sheth and Eliza Relman, "Trump says it's 'Unnecessary' to Postpone Primary Eections Shortly after Discouraging Gatherings of More Than 10 People," *Business Insider*, March 16, 2020, https://www.businessinsider.com/coronavirus-trump-says-unnecessary-to-postpone-elections-2020-3.

30. Grace Panetta, "Trump Baselessly Claimed that Expanding Voting Access Would Lead to a Republican Never Being Elected in America Again," *Business Insider*, March 30, 2020, https://www.businessinsider.com/trump-falsely-claims-expanding-voting-access-would-hurt-republicans-2020-3.

31. Grace Panetta, "Trump is Pushing a Dubious Theory that Foreign Countries Will Interfere in the 2020 Election by Mass Producing Counterfeit Ballots," *Business Insider*, June 22, 2020, https://www.businessinsider.com/ag-barr-floats-theory-that-foreign-countries-could-make-counterfeit-ballots-2020-6.

32. Sarah Ruiz-Grossman, "Trump Makes Baseless Claim About Children Stealing Vote-by-Mail Ballots," *Huffington Post*, May 28, 2020, https://www.huffpost.com/entry/trump-kids-steal-ballots-mailboxes_n_5ed04b24c5b69af10d23db93.

33. Nina Golgowski, "Twitter Flags Trump Tweet Claiming Ballot Boxes are a COVID-19 Risk," *Huffington Post*, August 24, 2020, https://www.huffpost.com/entry/trump-tweets-ballot-boxes-covid-risk_n_5f42c291c5b6305f32590b99.

34. Jacey Fortin, "Surfaces Are 'Not the Main Way' Coronavirus Spreads, C.D.C. Says," *New York Times*, May 22, 2020, November 19, 2020, https://www.nytimes.com/2020/05/22/health/cdc-coronavirus-touching-surfaces.html.

35. Amy Gardner and Josh Dawsey, "Trump's Attacks on Mail Voting are Turning Republicans Off Absentee Ballots," *Washington Post*, July 7, 2020, https://www.washingtonpost.com/politics/trumps-attacks-on-mail-voting-are-turning-republicans-off-absentee-ballots/2020/07/07/640b6126-bbd4-11ea-80b9-40ece9a701dc_story.html.

36. Greg Allen, "Even as Trump Denounces Vote by Mail, GOP in Florida And Elsewhere Relies On It," NPR. April 11, 2020, https://www.npr.org/2020/04/11/831978099/even-as-trump-denounces-vote-by-mail-gop-in-florida-and-elsewhere-relies-on-it.

37. Russell Berman, "The Republicans Telling Their Voters to Ignore Trump," *The Atlantic*, June 5, 2020, https://www.theatlantic.com/politics/archive/2020/06/trump-republicans-vote-mail-arizona-florida/612625/.

38. Natasha Khan and Corbin Carson, "Election Fraud Not As Common As Recent Voter ID Laws Suggest," *Center for Public Integrity*, August 13, 2012, May 19, 2014, https://publicintegrity.org/politics/election-fraud-not-as-common-as-recent-voter-id-laws-suggest/.

39. Rick Hasen, *The Voting Wars* (New Haven: Yale University Press, 2012), 25–35.

40. "Voting Rights Litigation 2020." Brennan Center for Justice, July 28, 2020, https://www.brennancenter.org/our-work/court-cases/voting-rights-litigation-2020.

41. Amy Gardner and Mike DeBonis, "Senate Stimulus Package Includes $400 Million to Help Run Elections Amid the Pandemic," *Washington Post*, March 25, 2020, https://www.washingtonpost.com/politics/senate-stimulus-package-includes-400-million-to-help-run-elections-amid-the-pandemic/2020/03/25/4d0db91e-6ebe-11ea-b148-e4ce3fbd85b5_story.html.

42. Lawrence Norden et al., "Estimated Costs of Covid-19 Election Resiliency Measures," Brennan Center for Justice, March 19, 2020, https://www.brennancenter.org/our-work/research-reports/estimated-costs-covid-19-election-resiliency-measures.

43. Grace Panetta, "Wisconsin Officials Are Moving Full-speed-ahead With Holding the State's April 7 Presidential Primary Despite Rising Coronavirus Cases," *Business Insider*, March 30, 2020, https://www.businessinsider.com/coronavirus-wisconsin-april-7-primary-as-others-postpone-2020-3.

44. Nick Corasaniti and Stephanie Saul, "Inside Wisconsin's Election Mess: Thousands of Missing or Nullified Ballots," *New York Times*, April 9, 2020, https://www.nytimes.com/2020/04/09/us/politics/wisconsin-election-absentee-coronavirus.html.

45. Jonathan Lai, "Pennsylvania's Mail Ballot Problems Kept Tens of a Thousands from Voting in a Pandemic Primary," *Philadelphia Inquirer*, June 30, 2020, https://www.inquirer.com/politics/election/pa-mail-ballot-deadlines-disenfranchisement-20200730.html.

46. Grace Panetta, "Long Lines, Missing Mail-in Ballots and Confusion This Week Exposed the Problems that Could Plague the November Election," *Business Insider*, June 6, 2020, https://www.businessinsider.com/missing-ballots-long-lines-foreshadow-november-election-problems-2020-6.

47. Danny Hakim, Reid J. Epstein, and Stephanie Saul, "Anatomy of an Election 'Meltdown' in Georgia," *New York Times*, July 25, 2020, https://www.nytimes.com/2020/07/25/us/politics/georgia-election-voting-problems.html.

48. Norm Ornstein, "The November Election is Going to be a Mess," *The Atlantic*, July 22, 2020, https://www.theatlantic.com/ideas/archive/2020/07/november-election-going-be-mess/614296/.

49. Grace Panetta and Sonam Sheth, "The 2020 Election Catastrophe That Wasn't," *Business Insider*, November 4, 2020, https://www.businessinsider.com/2020-election-administration-was-successful-not-a-disaster-2020-11.

50. Geoff Hing et al., "How Private Money Helped Save the Election," *American Public Media*, December 7, 2020, https://www.apmreports.org/story/2020/12/07/private-grant-money-chan-zuckerburg-election.

51. Kate Brumback and Larry Lage, "Arenas, Stadiumes Find New Life as Safer Options for Voting," *Associated Press*, October 22, 2020, https://apnews.com/article/election-2020-nfl-nba-virus-outbreak-primary-elections-365602551b8fa01deca154ffd3d490c84.

52. Pam Fessler, "A 2020 Surprise: Fewer Absentee Ballot Rejections Than Expected," NPR, December 31, 2020, https://www.npr.org/2020/12/31/951249068/a-2020-surprise-fewer-absentee-ballots-rejections-than-expected.

53. Barbara Sprunt, "Poll Worker Numbers Have Many Election Officials Breathing Sigh of Relief," NPR, October 29, 2020, https://www.npr.org/2020/10/29/928225412/on-poll-workers-many-election-officials-breathe-sigh-of-relief.

54. Barry Yeoman et al., "After a Season of Fear, America's Election Day Voting Passes Mostly in Peace," *Washington Post*, November 3, 2020, https://www.washingtonpost.com/national/unrest-fears-election-day/2020/11/03/9f4852f2-1e18-11eb-ba21-f2f001f0554b_story.html.

55. Jen Kirby, "Trump's Own Officials Say 2020 Was America's Most Secure Election In History," *Vox*, November 13, 2020, https://www.vox.com/2020/11/13/21563825/2020-elections-most-secure-dhs-cisa-krebs.

56. McDonald calculates voting-eligible population as the total population age 18 or older, minus those who are ineligible to vote in their states due to being in prison or on probation or parole. McDonald also adds the estimated number of voting-eligible U.S. citizens living abroad to the denominator determining the national turnout rate.

57. "November 2016 General Election Turnout Rates," US Elections Project, https://docs.google.com/spreadsheets/u/1/d/1VAcF0eJ06y_8T4o2gvIL4YcyQy8pxb1zYkgXF76Uu1s/edit#gid=2030096602.

58. "November 2020 General Election Turnout Rates," U.S. Elections Project, https://docs.google.com/spreadsheets/d/1h_2pR1pq8s_I5buZ5agXS9q1vLziECztN2uWeR6Czo0/edit#gid=2030096602.

59. Michael McDonald, "Voting in the 2020 Election," U.S. Elections Project, November 11, 2020, https://www.nonprofitvote.org/documents/2020/11/voter-turnout-2020-elections-presentation.pdf/?link_id=2&can_id=4afcd3944340012c4a628ab1e3a2768b.

60. "WEBINAR: Voter Turnout in the 2020 Elections with Michael McDonald," Nonprofit VOTE, November 20, 2020, https://www.youtube.com/watch?v=_BFvnjkXI_M.

61. Ally Mutnick and Sabrina Rodriguez, "'A Decade of Power': Statehouse Wins Position GOP to Dominate Redistricting," *Politico*, November 4, 2020, https://www.politico.com/news/2020/11/04/statehouse-elections-2020-434108.

62. Aaron Navarro, "Democrats 'Devastated' and Reflective After House GOP Exceeds Expectations," CBS News, November 7, 2020, https://www.cbsnews.com/news/democrats-devastated-and-reflective-after-house-gop-exceeds-expectations/.

63. "2020 State Legislative Results," CNAlysis, https://cnalysis.com/maps/2020-state-legislative-results.

64. Grace Panetta, "The Key Swing States of Michigan, Pennsylvania, and Wisconsin Could Take Longer to Report Election Results. Here's Why," *Business Insider*, November 6, 2020, https://www.businessinsider.com/election-results-may-take-longer-in-michigan-pennsylvania-wisconsin-2020-10.

65. Tim Alberta, "The Inside Story of Michigan's Fake Voter Fraud Scandal," *Politico*, November 24, 2020, https://www.politico.com/news/magazine/2020/11/24/michigan-election-trump-voter-fraud-democracy-440475.

12

The $14 Billion Election

Emerging Campaign Finance Trends and Their Impact on the 2020 Presidential Race and Beyond

Michael E. Toner and Karen E. Trainer

The 2020 presidential and congressional election was the most expensive election in American history, shattering previous fund-raising and spending records. Total spending on the 2020 election totaled an estimated $14 billion, which was more than double the amount spent during the 2016 cycle and more than any previous election in U.S. history.[1] The historic 2020 spending tally was more than was spent in the previous two election cycles *combined*.[2]

Moreover, former Vice President Joseph Biden and Senator Kamala Harris made fund-raising history in 2020 as their presidential campaign became the first campaign in history to raise over $1 billion in a single election cycle, with a total of $1.1 billion.[3] For their part, President Trump and Vice President Pence raised in excess of $700 million for their presidential campaign, more than double the amount that they raised in 2016.[4]

The record amount of money expended on the 2020 election was also fueled by a significant increase in spending by outside groups such as Super PACs as well as enhanced congressional candidate fund-raising. Political party expenditures increased in 2020, but constituted a smaller share of total electoral spending.

Of the $14 billion total, approximately $6.6 billion was spent in connection with the presidential race and $7.2 billion was expended at the congressional level.[5] To put those spending amounts into perspective, the $7.2 billion tally at the congressional level nearly equals the GDP of Monaco.[6] More than $1 billion of the $14 billion was spent for online advertising on platforms such as Facebook and Google.[7]

2020 PRESIDENTIAL CAMPAIGN FUND-RAISING BROKE ALL RECORDS AND INCLUDED THE FIRST BILLION-DOLLAR PRESIDENTIAL CAMPAIGN

To properly understand contemporary presidential campaign fundraising trends, it is necessary to briefly discuss the creation of the presidential public financing system in the 1970s and the gradual abandonment of that system by leading presidential candidates during the last two decades.

The presidential public financing system was established after the Watergate scandal and first went into effect for the 1976 presidential election. Under the system, presidential candidates have the option of accepting public funds for their primary election or general election campaigns, or both. For the primaries, presidential candidates can receive matching funds from the government of up to $250 for each individual contribution they receive. For the 2020 primaries, each presidential candidate could receive a maximum of approximately $51 million in matching funds.[8] However, candidates electing to receive matching funds for the 2020 presidential race were subject to a nationwide spending limit during the primaries of approximately $51 million, as well as state-by-state spending limits based upon the population of each state. Under federal election laws, the primary season runs from the time a person legally becomes a presidential candidate through the national nominating conventions, a period of time that can last 18 months or even longer. The national and state-by-state spending limits apply throughout this period of time. By contrast, candidates who decline to take matching funds are not subject to any spending limits for the primaries and are free to raise as much money as they can, subject to the contribution limits.[9] For the general election, presidential candidates have the option of accepting a public grant to finance all of their political activities and be subject to a nationwide spending limit, or candidates can turn down public funds and raise private contributions subject to the contribution limits and operate without any spending restriction. The public grant for the general election in 2020 was approximately $103.7 million.[10]

The presidential public financing system has become obsolete during the last 20 years as more and more presidential candidates decided to operate their campaigns outside of the system in order to free themselves of the spending limits that come with the acceptance of public funds. In the 2000 presidential race, George W. Bush raised $100 million for his primary campaign and became the first candidate to turn down matching funds for the primaries and be elected president when he defeated Al Gore. In 2004, both major party nominees turned down matching funds for the primaries for the first time, as George W. Bush raised $270 million and John Kerry raised $235 million for the primary season. Significantly, both Bush and Kerry in 2004 accepted the $75 million public grant for the general election, joining every major party nominee since 1976 in doing so. However, the historical practice of accepting public funds for the general election was shattered in 2008 when Barack Obama became the first presidential candidate to be elected president who turned down public funds for both the primaries and the general election, which helped clear the way for Obama to raise a record-shattering $750 million for his campaign, including $414 million for the primaries alone. By contrast, John McCain in 2008 raised $221 million for the primaries, but opted to accept the $85 million public grant for the general election, which provided McCain with a total of only $306 million for his entire campaign—barely 40 percent of the total funds that the Obama campaign had at its disposal.[11] In 2012, both Obama and Mitt Romney opted out of the public financing system for the primaries and the general election. In total, their campaigns raised $1.22 billion, which was a 16 percent increase over the $1.05 billion raised by the major party nominees in 2008.[12] In 2016, Hillary Clinton and President Trump also opted out of public funding and raised a combined $928 million.

The 2020 election cycle began with a significant cash and fundraising advantage for the Trump campaign. President Trump started raising funds for the 2020 election shortly after his inauguration, becoming the first president to actively fundraise for his reelection campaign during the first two years of his term. By the fall of 2018, Trump had already raised in excess of $100 million for his reelection campaign and associated fund-raising committees,[12] and the president continued to raise tens of millions of dollars for his reelection campaign through the fall and winter of 2018-2019.

By the time Biden became the presumptive Democratic nominee in June, the Trump campaign and the Republican National Committee had raised approximately $200 million. As of late August, the Biden campaign and Democratic National Committee had a combined cash-on-hand total of $466 million, which was an advantage of $141 million over the Trump campaign and the RNC.[13] By the end of September, the RNC and the Trump campaign raised a combined $1.1 billion and spent almost $800 million.[14]

In addition to setting a record for the total amount raised in a single election cycle, the Biden campaign also broke records with several of its monthly fund-raising totals. In September 2020, the Biden campaign and the DNC raised a combined total of $384 million, breaking their previous record of $365 million set in August 2020. By comparison, the Obama campaign raised $202 million in September 2008 ($240 million in 2020 dollars when adjusted for inflation).[15]

Table 12.1. Summary of Party Nominee Fundraising Totals (2008-2020)

Candidate	*Total Campaign Funds*
2020	
Biden	$1.1 Billion
Trump	$717 Million
2016	
Trump	$329 Million*
Clinton	$569 Million
2012	
Obama	$738 Million
Romney	$483 Million
2008	
Obama	$750 Million
McCain	$306 Million**

Note: *$66 million of this amount represents contributions or loans made by Trump to his campaign. **Candidate accepted public funds.
Source: Federal Election Commission data.

Although President Trump loaned or contributed a total of $66 million to his 2016 campaign, only $8,000 of the $717 million raised by the Trump campaign in 2020 represented Trump's personal funds.

Table 12.1 above outlines the totals raised by the major party presidential nominees from 2008 through 2020.

The 2020 presidential race also broke records on the spending side. Through late October, $1.8 billion was spent on television advertisements in connection with the presidential race. By comparison, the 2016 presidential election cost a total of $2.4 billion, including expenditures other than advertising costs.[16] In Florida alone, an estimated $250 million was spent on television advertising in connection with the 2020 presidential race. This is $100 million more than was spent on television advertising in Florida in connection with the 2016 election.[17]

In total, the Biden campaign in 2020 spent approximately $13 per vote received. This is comparable to amounts spent by Democratic presidential nominees in previous election cycles. The Trump campaign spent approximately $10 for each vote received.[18]

Some 2020 presidential primary candidates spent significant personal funds on their campaigns. For example, billionaire Tom Steyer spent $340 million on his own campaign[19] before ending his run without winning any delegates.[20] Former New York City Mayor Michael Bloomberg spent over $1 billion on his campaign, which lasted less than four months; Bloomberg won only 55 delegates.[21] A total of 1,991 delegates were needed to win the nomination, and Biden won a total of 2,687.[22]

This follows a historical trend of failed self-funded presidential campaigns. For example, Republican Steve Forbes spent a total of $69 million in losing the Republican nomination in 1996 and 2000.[23] Similarly, Republican John Connally's losing 1980 presidential campaign spent $11 million during the Republican primaries, including $500,000 of his own funds, and Connally famously ended up winning only one Republican delegate.[24]

CONGRESSIONAL FUND-RAISING ALSO BROKE RECORDS AND INCLUDED SO-CALLED "RAGE DONATING" TO UNSUCCESSFUL CAMPAIGNS

Spending in congressional elections totaled $7.2 billion in 2020, up from only $4 billion in 2016.[25] Democratic candidates as a whole raised $1.2 billion, while their Republican counterparts raised $691 million.[26] However, at the congressional level, the candidate that raised the most money did not always win.

At the Senate level, the campaign that spent the most funds only won 72 percent of the time.[27] For example, in South Carolina's Senate race, Senator Lindsey Graham's campaign spent $97.6 million compared to opponent Jaime Harrison's $129.8 million; despite the campaign resource disparity, Graham won the race by 10 points.[28] The Graham-Harrison race was the most expensive Senate election in history based on candidate spending, although it was not the most expensive if outside group spending is also included.[29] Some analysts have referred to contributions to long-shot candidates such as Harrison as "Rage Donating."[30]

This "rage-donating" trend continued at the House level for a number of Republicans that challenged incumbent Democrats in safe Democratic districts. For example, in Maryland's Seventh Congressional District, Republican challenger Kimberly Klacik spent $4.8 million. Klacik was soundly defeated by Democrat Kweisi Mfume, who spent only $620,000.[31]

A significant amount of contributions at the congressional level were from contributors who lived outside of the candidate's state. For example, candidates in Arizona, North Carolina, and Iowa raised the majority of their funds from out-of-state donors. In the aforementioned South Carolina Senate race, 93 percent of Jaime Harrison's funds came from outside of South Carolina. A total of 87 percent of funds raised by Lindsey Graham also came from out of state. Amy McGrath, Senator Mitch McConnell's opponent in the Kentucky Senate race, also raised over 90 percent of her funds from out-of-state donors.

In total, Democratic Senate candidates raised 80 percent of their funds from out-of-state donors in 2020, compared to only 57 percent in 2016.[32]

In total, the Senate candidates with the top 10 fund-raising totals raised over $1 billion during the 2020 election cycle. Notably, the four candidates in the Georgia Senate runoff elections collectively raised $447 million, which made for the most expensive Senate runoff in American history. In fact, Jon Ossoff's $140 million fundraising total in his Georgia Senate race exceeded the $133 million raised by Al Gore nationally during his 2000 presidential run.[33]

SPENDING BY OUTSIDE GROUPS LIKEWISE SHATTERED RECORDS

The passage of the McCain-Feingold campaign finance law in 2002, combined with court decisions permitting unlimited corporate, union, and individual contributions to finance independent expenditures sponsored by outside organizations such as Super PACs and 501(c) organizations, has led to a proliferation of outside groups in recent years that are having a growing impact on federal elections. These outside groups, which have flourished on both the right and the left, have become increasingly engaged in political activities that were once the province of political parties, such as voter registration drives, absentee ballot programs, get-out-the-vote, voter identification, and political advertising and issue advocacy efforts.

The McCain-Feingold law, which took effect during the 2004 presidential election cycle, prohibits the RNC, DNC, and the other national political party committees from raising or spending soft-money funds for any purpose. "Soft money" is defined as funds raised outside of the prohibitions and limitations of federal law, including corporate and labor union general treasury funds and individual contributions in excess of federal limits. Funds raised in accordance with federal law come from individuals and from federally registered PACs and are harder to raise; hence, these funds are commonly referred to in campaign finance parlance as "hard money." Prior to McCain-Feingold, the national political parties were legally permitted to accept unlimited corporate, union, and individual soft-money contributions and could use these funds to help underwrite a wide variety of political and electoral activities, including voter registration efforts, absentee ballot drives, GOTV activities, slate cards, and similar ticket-wide political activities. Prior to McCain-Feingold, the two parties were also able to use soft-money contributions to help finance issue advertisements supporting and opposing federal candidates. "Issue advertisements" are public communications that frequently attack or promote federal candidates and their records, but which refrain from expressly advocating the election or defeat of any candidate (which is referred to as "express advocacy").

In *Citizens United v. FEC*, the U.S. Supreme Court in 2010 struck down the long-standing prohibition on corporate independent expenditures in connection with federal elections. That same year, in *SpeechNow v. FEC*, a federal appeals court invalidated limits on contributions from individuals to political committees that fund only independent expenditures for or against federal candidates. In advisory opinions issued after the *SpeechNow* decision, the Federal Election Commission (FEC) concluded that political committees formed strictly to make independent expenditures supporting or opposing federal candidates could accept unlimited contributions from individuals, corporations, and labor organizations.[34] These relatively new kinds of political committees, which are prohibited from making contributions to federal candidates and to other federal political committees, are commonly referred to as "Super PACs."

501(c) entities are organized and operate under Section 501(c) of the Internal Revenue Code, and include social welfare organizations established under Section 501(c)(4), labor organizations established under Section 501(c)(5), and trade associations and business leagues organized under Section 501(c)(6). Section 501(c)(4), 501(c)(5), and 501(c)(6) entities are permitted to accept unlimited corporate, union and individual contributions and may engage in partisan political activities, provided such political activities are not their primary purpose. By contrast, as political committees registered with the FEC, Super PACs are by definition partisan entities and may spend all of their funds on partisan political activities. Super PACs are required to publicly disclose their donors, whereas 501(c) organizations are generally not.

In October 2020 alone, election-related spending by Super PACs and other outside groups such as unions and 501(c) organizations totaled approximately $1.2 billion.[35] This amount nearly matched the $1.3 billion spent by outside groups throughout the entire 2016 election cycle. In total, outside groups other than political party committees spent $2.7 billion in the 2020 election cycle. As figure 12.1 illustrates, this amount nearly doubled the $1.3 billion spent by outside groups in the 2016 election. Outside spending in connection with the presidential race favored Biden by nearly two to one.[36]

Of the $2.7 billion spent by non-political party outside groups, nearly $1.4 billion was expended by the 10 biggest spenders of the election cycle. These entities are listed in table 12.2. Of these 10 outside entities, four were among the biggest spenders of the 2015-2016 election cycle.

Because Super PACs and 501(c) organizations may not make contributions to federal campaign committees, traditional PACs—which can only accept

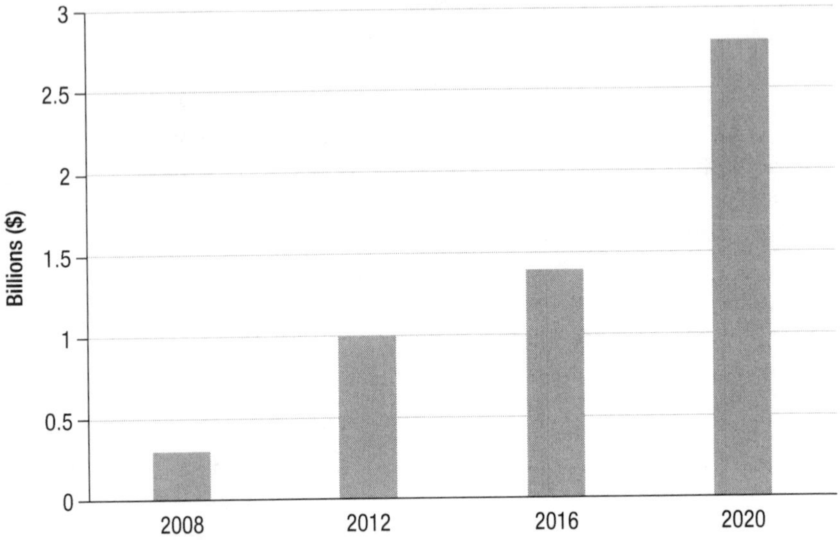

Figure 12.1. Outside Spending by Election Cycle (Excluding Political Party Committees)
Source: "2020 Outside Spending, by Group," Open Secrets, https://www.opensecrets.org/outsidespending/summ.php?cycle=2020&chrt=V&disp=O&type=P.

donations subject to federal contribution limits and source prohibitions—remain an important vehicle as well for supporting federal candidates.[37] Table 12.3 lists the 10 largest PACs based upon the total amounts contributed to candidates during the 2020 election cycle. Almost all of these PACs are "connected" PACs associated with corporations, trade associations, labor organizations, and membership organizations.[38] A number of connected PACs

Table 12.2. Largest Non-Party Outside Spenders (2020 Election Cycle)

Name	*Entity Type*	*2019–2020 Disclosed Spending*
Senate Leadership Fund	Super PAC	$263,994,674
Senate Majority PAC	Super PAC/501(c)	$232,957,574
Congressional Leadership Fund	Super PAC/501(c)	$142,623,572
House Majority PAC	501(c)	$139,826,774
Priorities USA Action	Hybrid PAC	$135,834,454
America First Action	Super PAC	$133,819,985
Future Forward USA	Hybrid PAC	$114,774,178
Preserve America PAC	Super PAC	$102,990,134
Club for Growth	PAC/Super PAC/501(c)	$62,701,807
American Crossroads	Super PAC	$56,386,457

Source: "2020 Outside Spending, by Group," Open Secrets, https://www.opensecrets.org/outsidespending/summ.php?cycle=2020&chrt=V&disp=O&type=P.

Table 12.3. Largest PACs by Total Contributions Made (2020 Election Cycle)

PAC Name	*2019–2020 Total Contributions*
National Association of Realtors PAC	$3,556,195
National Beer Wholesalers Association PAC	$2,923,500
Credit Union National Association PAC	$2,701,800
AT&T Inc PAC	$2,625,500
American Crystal Sugar PAC	$2,607,500
Comcast Corporation PAC	$2,565,000
American Bankers Association PAC	$2,553,200
Operating Engineers Union PAC	$2,535,200
Majority Committee PAC	$2,480,100
Sheet Metal, Air, Rail & Transportation Union PAC	$2,392,950

Source: "Top 2020 PACs to Candidates," Open Secrets, https://www.opensecrets.org/political-action-committees-pacs/top-pacs/2020?type=C.

disseminated advertisements supporting or opposing federal candidates in addition to making direct contributions to candidates.

SMALL DONORS, "MEGADONORS," AND WOMEN CONTRIBUTED IN RECORD AMOUNTS DURING THE 2020 ELECTION

Small donors—defined as those contributing less than $200 per candidate within the election cycle—contributed in record amounts in 2020. These small donors provided 27 percent of the total funds contributed to federal candidates, an increase from the 2016 total of 21 percent.[39] Small donors provided 22 percent of the funds raised in connection with the 2020 election as a whole, an increase from the 2016 total of 15 percent.

Small donors represented an even bigger percentage of the total fundraising pie at the presidential level. In total, 49 percent of the Trump campaign's funds came from donors giving $200 or less. By contrast, 38 percent of the Biden campaign's funds came from donors in this category.[40] However, Democratic candidates as a whole outraised Republicans in small donor contributions during the 2020 election cycle, raising $1.7 billion compared to $1 billion for Republicans.[41]

Continuing a trend that has been consistent over the last several election cycles, a number of wealthy individuals made enormous contributions in connection with the 2020 election. For example, Sheldon and Miriam Adelson contributed $75 million to pro-Trump organizations.[42] In addition, Tom Steyer contributed $340 million to his own campaign before dropping out of the race for the Democratic nomination.

Table 12.4. Top Individual Donors to Outside Groups, 2019-2020 Cycle

Donor Name	*Total*	*Ideology*
Sheldon and Miriam Adelson	$215,100,000	100% Republican
Michael Bloomberg	$151,336,446	100% Democrat
Tom Steyer	$67,390,015	100% Democrat
Richard Uihlein	$64,817,100	100% Republican
Kenneth Griffin	$60,250,000	100% Republican
Timothy Mellon	$60,005,555	100% Republican
Cari Tuna	$47,040,000	100% Democrat
Stephen Schwarzman	$33,500,000	100% Republican
Jeffrey Yass	$29,368,000	100% Republican
Karla Jurvetson	$24,687,042	100% Democrat

Source: "2020 Top Donors to Outside Spending Groups, Open Secrets, https://www.opensecrets.org/outsidespending/summ.php?disp=D.

Table 12.4 above identifies the top 10 Super PAC donors of the 2020 election cycle. The top 10 individual donors gave $642 million to federal political committees in the 2020 election cycle, with nearly all of the money going to various outside groups, including 501(c) organizations and Super PACs.[43] Of the individuals listed, three were also among the top 10 individual donors to outside groups in the 2016 election cycle.

Women contributed to federal candidates in historic amounts in 2020: $1.4 billion, which comprised 41 percent of total candidate fund-raising during the election cycle. By comparison, women contributed $590 million to federal candidates in 2016, which comprised 36 percent of total candidate fund-raising at that time.[44]

POLITICAL PARTY FUND-RAISING INCREASED IN 2020, BUT PARTY SPENDING REPRESENTED A SMALLER SHARE OF TOTAL OUTSIDE SPENDING

There are growing indications that national political party committees are struggling to remain as relevant as they once were in federal elections as spending increasingly shifts to Super PACs and other outside groups that are not subject to the hard-dollar fund-raising requirements that apply to the national political party committees.

Congress passed an appropriations bill in 2014 that included provisions allowing national political party committees to establish separate subaccounts with additional contribution limits. Contributions made to these accounts may be used to pay for office building expenditures, expenses incurred in recounts and other legal proceedings, and national convention expenses. Individuals and PACs may make contributions to these separate subaccounts in addition to making contributions to a national political party's main political account. For example, an individual may contribute up to $35,500 per year to the DNC's main political account, plus up to $35,500 per year to each of the DNC's office building, recount, and national convention subaccounts. Accordingly, an individual may contribute up to $142,000 per year to the DNC or RNC.

In 2020, total political party fund-raising increased markedly over previous election cycles, reversing a previous downward trend over several election cycles. The RNC and DNC collectively raised a total of $1.3 billion in the 2019-2020 election cycle, compared to $770 million in 2012 and $790 million in 2016. Figure 12.2 shows total election cycle fund-raising for the RNC, DNC, and both combined over the last four presidential election cycles.

Despite significantly higher fundraising totals during the 2020 election cycle, national political party spending nevertheless represented a smaller portion of outside spending as a whole compared with previous election cycles. In 2016, 14 percent of outside spending was by party committees. In 2020, this percentage dropped to just 11 percent. This change was driven by an increase in spending by "other" groups, such as corporations and individuals. By contrast, spending by Super PACs remained steady at 64 percent. Figure 12.3 illustrates the changes in outside group spending between 2016 and 2020.

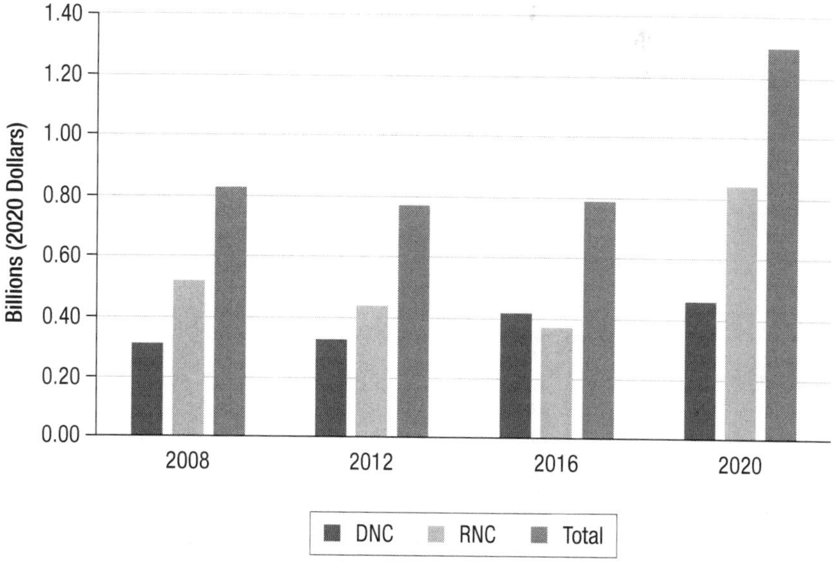

Figure 12.2. Political Party Fundraising in Presidential Election Cycles (2020 Dollars)
Source: Federal Election Commission data.

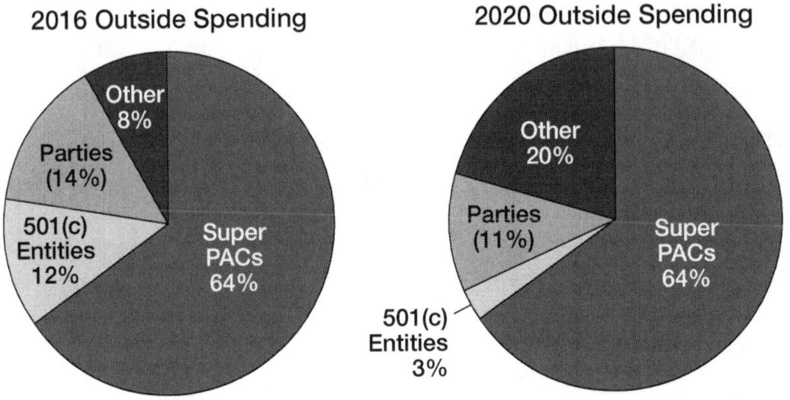

Figure 12.3. Comparison of 2016 and 2020 Outside Group Spending by Entity Type

Note: Percentages do not add up to 100 percent due to rounding.

Source: Open Secrets, https://www.opensecrets.org/outsidespending/fes_summ.php?cycle=2020, https://www.opensecrets.org/outsidespending/summ.php?cycle=2016&chrt=V&disp=O&type=P.

As a whole, 501(c) organizations spent significantly less on the 2020 election than they did on the 2016 and 2012 elections. In 2016, 501(c) groups collectively spent approximately $181 million, compared to over $308 million in 2012. In 2020, the total spent by these groups dropped to just $112 million.[45]

Given the fund-raising advantages outside groups currently enjoy over national political party committees, the outside group-political party spending imbalance may become even more pronounced in the future unless campaign finance laws are changed to allow the national political parties to raise and spend the same kinds of funds as outside groups are legally able to do.

Political party committees continued to engage in extensive joint fund-raising activities in 2020. Under FEC regulations, candidates and political parties may simultaneously raise hard-dollar funds through joint fundraising committees (“JFCs”), which permit candidates and political parties to combine the per-recipient contribution limits and thereby solicit greater amounts of money from donors at any one time.[46] The Biden Victory Fund, which was comprised of the Biden campaign committee, the DNC, and 47 state Democratic party committees, raised $659 million. By comparison, the Trump Make America Great Again Committee, which was comprised of the Trump campaign committee and the RNC, raised $821 million[47] and was the largest joint fund-raising committee of the 2020 election cycle.[48] Trump Victory, a joint fund-raising committee comprised of the Trump campaign, the RNC, and 46 state Republican party committees, raised an additional $366 million.

ACTBLUE AND WINRED HELPED FACILITATE THE RECORD-BREAKING FUND-RAISING WITNESSED DURING THE 2020 ELECTION

In 2018, a significant amount of contributions to Democratic congressional candidates—including 55 percent of contributions made by individuals—were processed through ActBlue, which describes itself as "a nonprofit, building fundraising technology for the left" with the goal of "help[ing] small-dollar donors make their voices heard in a real way."[49] ActBlue allows donors to save their credit card information when making a contribution, which makes additional contributions easier and allows candidates to raise funds for each other. Since 2012, the volume of donations processed by ActBlue has doubled during every election cycle.[50]

In previous election cycles, on the Republican side there were multiple for-profit online fund-raising firms that raised funds for campaigns and other political committees. The fragmentation between different vendors limited the ability of the various vendors to provide conveniences such as saved credit card numbers and fundraising by one candidate for another. In 2019, the firm WinRed was launched as a Republican response to ActBlue. In its first 18 months of existence, $1.2 billion was raised through WinRed. To put that fund-raising figure in perspective, ActBlue surpassed $1.2 billion in total contributions in 2016.[51]

In the third quarter of 2020 alone, ActBlue raised $1.6 billion in contributions from 6.8 million donors. This matched the $1.6 billion that was raised through ActBlue during the entire 2017-2018 election cycle.[52] By comparison, WinRed raised $620 million within the third quarter of 2020.[53] In total, ActBlue raised $4.8 billion in online contributions in the 2020 election cycle,[54] compared to $1.9 million raised by WinRed.[55]

SOME SUPER PACS DELAYED PUBLIC DISCLOSURE OF THEIR DONORS UNTIL AFTER THE ELECTION

A number of Super PACs structured their activities such that their donors were not publicly disclosed until after the election; these PACs have come to be known as "pop-up PACs" in campaign finance parlance. This trend began with a small number of Super PACs in 2016, and more Super PACs followed this strategy in 2018 and 2020. During the 2016 election cycle, approximately $9 million in primary election spending corresponded to incoming contributions disclosed after the election. During the 2018 election cycle, this total increased to $15.6 million in spending on primary and special elections with donor disclosure delayed until after the election.[56]

One strategy that a number of these so-called pop-up Super PACs used to delay public disclosure of their donors was registering with the FEC after the close of books for the last disclosure report due before Election Day. These Super PACs were required to disclose information about certain independent expenditures within 24 hours of disseminating the independent expenditures, but were not required to disclose information concerning their donors until after the election. Specifically, Super PACs that followed this strategy for the 2020 general election registered on or after October 14, 2020, and were not required to disclose their donors until December 3, 2020—a month after Election Day.

For example, the Super PAC True Kentucky Patriots was launched to support libertarian Kentucky Senate candidate Brad Barron. The PAC registered with the FEC on October 13 and began making independent expenditures on October 19. The PAC spent nearly $2 million on independent expenditures supporting Barron in the 2020 general election, but was not required to disclose its donors until December 3. The PAC had ties to other committees that supported the Democratic nominee, and may have supported Barron in order to siphon votes away from Senate Majority Leader Mitch McConnell, who was ultimately reelected.[57]

Pop-up Super PACs were also present in the 2020 primaries. For example, two pop-up PACs, Sunflower State and Plains PAC, spent a total of $8.6 million in connection with the Kansas Senate Republican primary. When the donors to these groups were disclosed after the primary, it became clear that the PACs were funded by party-aligned donors. For example, Plains PAC received several transfers from Senate Leadership Fund, a Super PAC associated with Senator McConnell. Similarly, Sunflower State received transfers from SMP (Senate Majority PAC), a Super PAC associated with the Democratic Senate leadership.[58] As was noted in table 12.2, Senate Leadership Fund and Senate Majority PAC were the two largest nonpolitical party outside group spenders of the 2020 election cycle.[59]

EARLY VOTING RATES INCREASED DRAMATICALLY DUE TO THE PANDEMIC AND CAUSED MAJOR SHIFTS IN CAMPAIGN STRATEGY

For many years, voters who expected to be absent from their home communities on Election Day could apply for an absentee ballot and could cast it prior to the election. However, in order to obtain an absentee ballot, many jurisdictions required voters to show cause or otherwise explain why they were not able to vote on Election Day in their local precincts, which reduced the number of people who voted absentee.[60] In 1980, California amended its laws to permit voters for the first time to cast ballots before Election Day without providing any excuse or showing any cause.[61] In succeeding decades, many more states changed their laws to permit voters to vote prior to Election Day without cause, either in person or by mail. Some states today allow voters to become permanent absentee voters and automatically receive absentee ballots for each election without having to submit a request. As of late 2020, 34 states and the District of Columbia had some form of early voting without requiring voters to provide an excuse.[62] Additional states temporarily allowed no-excuse early voting for the 2020 election due to the coronavirus pandemic.[63] Grace Panetta explores these changes in more detail in her chapter in this book.

Some election analysts have concluded that it is unclear whether the rising popularity of early voting impacts voter turnout overall or has an effect on the outcome of elections. However, the extraordinary increase in early voting has had a profound impact on the strategies and tactics employed by modern campaigns. For many years, the last 72 hours before Election Day were the primary focus for GOTV efforts, but now those campaign operations must be performed for a month or even longer in certain states. For example, encouraging early voting can help campaigns ensure that their candidate goes into Election Day with a significant vote lead. It also allows campaigns to focus their final GOTV efforts on a smaller group of individuals who have not voted prior to Election Day.

TEXT MESSAGING WAS AN IMPORTANT GET-OUT-THE-VOTE AND FUND-RAISING TOOL

In 2020, campaigns, political parties, and outside groups used text messaging to remind supporters to vote and to raise funds. The Trump campaign alone reportedly sent over a billion text messages during the 2020 election season,[64] and MoveOn.org sent approximately 350 million texts.[65] This phenomenon caused some analysts to identify the 2020 presidential race as the first "texting election."[66] Texting efforts were aided by new technologies that allowed volunteers to send texts to phone numbers pulled from voter registration records. Because such texts are initiated by a person, they are not subject to laws prohibiting robocalls and robotexts.[67]

LOOKING AHEAD TO 2024

Biden's victory over Trump in the 2020 presidential election marked only the third time since Franklin Roosevelt's presidency that an elected incumbent president was defeated in a bid for a second term. In doing so, Biden overcame significant fundraising challenges, first during the primaries—in which his campaign was significantly outspent for months by Bernie Sanders, Michael Bloomberg, and Pete Buttigieg—and then later during the early stages of the general election season, when the Trump-Pence campaign enjoyed a huge cash-on-hand advantage over the Biden-Harris campaign, which was achieved through four years of nonstop campaign fund-raising by Trump.[68] However, the Biden-Harris campaign ultimately outraised and outspent the Trump-Pence campaign and became the first presidential campaign in history to amass over $1 billion for a single election.

The $64,000 question for 2024 is whether Biden will seek a second term. If Biden does decide to run for reelection, it is inconceivable that he would be denied the Democratic presidential nomination given the power of incumbency in modern presidential politics. If Biden declines to run, Kamala Harris would be the clear front-runner for the nomination and would likely have a significant campaign fund-raising advantage over any potential Democratic challengers; indeed, every sitting vice president who has sought their party's nomination over the last 60 years has won the nomination.

On the Republican side, the primary field will be unsettled until Trump decides whether to run for president again.[69] If Trump does not run, Mike Pence could be the candidate best situated to inherit much of Trump's fund-raising base and combine it with the support of key elements of the Republican establishment. Other potential top-tier Republican candidates with national fund-raising bases include Senators Ted Cruz, Marco Rubio, and Tom Cotton, former U.N. Ambassador Nikki Haley, and Florida Governor Ron DeSantis.

Regardless of whether Biden runs again, the stage is set for the 2024 presidential contest to be highly competitive and fiercely contested with continued campaign finance innovations and developments.

NOTES

1. Stacy Montemoyer, Pete Quist, Karl Evers-Hillstrom, and Douglas Weber, "Joint Report Reveals Record Donations in 2020 State and Federal Races," Follow The Money, November 19, 2020, https://www.followthemoney.org/research/institute-reports/joint-report-reveals-record-donations-in-2020-state-and-federal-races.

2. "2020 Election to Cost $14 Billion, Blowing Away Spending Records," Open Secrets, October 28, 2020, https://www.opensecrets.org/news/2020/10/cost-of-2020-election-14billion-update/.

3. Karl Evers-Hillstrom, "Biden Campaign Becomes First to Raise $1 Billion from Donors," Open Secrets, December, 7, 2020, https://www.opensecrets.org/news/2020/12/biden-campaign-1billion-from-donors/.

4. Ibid.

5. Ciara Torres-Spelliscy, "The Most Expensive Election Ever," Brennan Center, November 11, 2020, https://www.brennancenter.org/our-work/analysis-opinion/most-expensive-election-ever.

6. Reid Wilson, "US Election Spending Exceeds GDP of Numerous Countries." *The Hill,* December 7, 2020, https://thehill.com/homenews/campaign/529080-us-election-spending-exceeds-gdp-of-numerous-countries.

7. "2020 Election to Cost $14 Billion, Blowing Away Spending Records," Open Secrets, October 28, 2020, https://www.opensecrets.org/news/2020/10/cost-of-2020-election-14billion-update/.

8. "Presidential Spending Limits for 2020," Federal Election Commission, https://www.fec.gov/help-candidates-and-committees/understanding-public-funding-presidential-elections/presidential-spending-limits-2020/.

9. Individuals could contribute up to $2,800 per election to presidential candidates for the 2020 election and federal multicandidate PACs could contribute up to $5,000 per election, with the primary and general elections considered separate elections. The individual contribution limits are adjusted for inflation each election cycle.

10. "Public Funding of Presidential Elections," Federal Election Commission, https://www.fec.gov/introduction-campaign-finance/understanding-ways-support-federal-candidates/presidential-elections/public-funding-presidential-elections/.

11. The Obama campaign had a remarkable resource advantage over the McCain campaign in 2008, including a nearly 4-to-1 edge during the general election phase of the campaign. The Obama campaign's broad resource advantage was particularly pronounced in the final weeks of the 2008 campaign. In September 2008 alone the Obama campaign raised over $150 million, and between October 15 and November 24 the Obama campaign raised an additional $104 million and spent $136 million. To put these Obama campaign fund-raising and spending figures in perspective, the McCain campaign received only $85 million of public funds to finance all of its political activities during the entire general election campaign.

12. Michelle Ye Hee Lee and Anu Nrayanswamy, "Trump Tops $100 Million for His Own Reelection," *Washington Post,* October 15, 2018, https://www.washingtonpost.com/politics/trump-tops-100-million-in-fundraising-for-his-own-reelection/2018/10/15/9ee33594-d094-11e8-83d6-291fcead2ab1_story.html.

13. Shane Goldmacher, "Biden Has $466 Million in Bank, and a Huge Financial Edge on Trump," *New York Times,* September 20, 2020, https://www.nytimes.com/2020/09/20/us/politics/20biden-trump-election-finance.html.

14. Shane Goldmacher and Maggie Haberman, "How Trump's Billion-Dollar Campaign Lost Its Cash Advantage," *New York Times,* September 7, 2020, https://www.nytimes.com/2020/09/07/us/politics/trump-election-campaign-fundraising.html.

15. "Presidential Fundraising Soars Again," Follow The Money, October 21, 2020, https://www.followthemoney.org/news/news-releases/show/456.

16. Shane Goldmacher, "The 2020 Campaign Is the Most Expensive Ever (by a Lot)," *New York Times,* October 28, 2020, https://www.nytimes.com/2020/10/28/us/politics/2020-race-money.html.

17. Gary Fineout, "A TV Ad Tidal Wave in Florida: Nearly $250M and Counting," *Politico,* October 1, 2020, https://www.politico.com/states/florida/story/2020/10/01/a-tv-ad-tidal-wave-in-florida-nearly-250m-and-counting-1319503.

18. Darragh Roche, "Joe Biden's Billion-Dollar Campaign Spent $13 for Every Vote." *Newsweek,* December 8, 2020, https://www.newsweek.com/joe-biden-billion-dollar-campaign-spent-13-every-vote-1553058.

19. Julie Bykowicz and Tarini Parti, "Big Donors Spent Heavily on Failed Election Efforts," *Wall Street Journal,* November 23, 2020, https://www.wsj.com/articles/big-donors-spent-heavily-on-failed-election-efforts-11606147552.

20. Sean McMinn, "How Many Delegates Do the Democratic Presidential Candidates Have?" NPR, https://www.npr.org/2020/02/10/799979293/how-many-delegates-do-the-2020-presidential-democratic-candidates-have.

21. Benjamin Siegel and Soo Rin Kim, "Mike Bloomberg Spent More Than $1 Billion on Four-Month Presidential Campaign According to Filing," ABC News, April 20, 2020, https://abcnews.go.com/Politics/mike-bloomberg-spent-billion-month-presidential-campaign-filing/story?id=70252435.

22. Sean McMinn, "How Many Delegates Do the Democratic Presidential Candidates Have?" NPR, https://www.npr.org/2020/02/10/799979293/how-many-delegates-do-the-2020-presidential-democratic-candidates-have.

23. Leslie Wayne, "THE 2000 CAMPAIGN: THE END; Forbes Spent Millions, but for Little Gain," *The New York Times,* February 10, 2000, https://www.nytimes.com/2000/02/10/us/the-2000-campaign-the-end-forbes-spent-millions-but-for-little-gain.html.

24. Bill Peterson and Tom Curtis, "Connally Quits Race," *Washington Post,* March 10, 1980, https://www.washingtonpost.com/archive/politics/1980/03/10/connally-quits-race/2eed323d-9081-4cc3-8ea6-73474222b42b/.

25. Ollie Gratzinger, "GOP Challengers Spent Big in Blue Districts, Lost Bids for House Seats," *Open Secrets,* https://www.opensecrets.org/news/2020/11/gop-challengers-safebluedistricts-lost-bids/.

26. Stacy Montemayer, Pete Quist, Karl Evers-Hillstrom, and Douglas Weber, "Joint Report Reveals Record Donations in 2020 State and Federal Races," Follow the Money, November 19, 2020, https://www.followthemoney.org/research/institute-reports/joint-report-reveals-record-donations-in-2020-state-and-federal-races.

27. Julie Bykowicz and Tarini Parti, "Big Donors Spent Heavily on Failed Election Efforts." *Wall Street Journal,* November 23, 2020, https://www.wsj.com/articles/big-donors-spent-heavily-on-failed-election-efforts-11606147552.

28. Eliana Miller, "Nine of the 10 Most Expensive Senate Races of All Time Happened in 2020," *Open Secrets,* December 9, 2020, https://www.opensecrets.org/news/2020/12/most-expensive-races-of-all-time-senate2020/.

29. "Most Expensive Races," Open Secrets, https://www.opensecrets.org/elections-overview/most-expensive-races?housespentcycle=2020&display=allcandsout&senatespentcycle=2020.

30. Eitan Hersh, "Rage Donating Only Made Democrats Feel Better," *The Atlantic,* November 12, 2020, https://www.theatlantic.com/ideas/archive/2020/11/folly-just-throwing-money-political-candidates/617074/.

31. Ollie Gratzinger, "GOP Challengers Spent Big in Blue Districts, Lost Bids for House Seats," Open Secrets, November 10, 2020, https://www.opensecrets.org/news/2020/11/gop-challengers-safebluedistricts-lost-bids/.

32. Stacy Montemayer, Pete Quist, Karl Evers-Hillstrom, and Douglas Weber, "Joint Report Reveals Record Donations in 2020 State and Federal Races," Follow the Money, November 19, 2020, https://www.followthemoney.org/research/institute-reports/joint-report-reveals-record-donations-in-2020-state-and-federal-races.

33. Stef W. Kight, "2020 Senate Fights Spark Breathtaking Fundraising Totals," *Axios,* January 3, 2021, https://www.axios.com/2020-senate-elections-fundraising-66a15b67-ea03-4941-afa6-1d380a2681cf.html?utm_campaign=organic&utm_medium=socialshare&utm_source=email.

34. FEC Advisory Opinions 2010-09, https://www.fec.gov/updates/ao-2010-09-corporate-sponsored-ie-only-committee-may-solicit-and-accept-unlimited-individual-contributions/; FEC Advisory Opinions 2010-11, https://www.fec.gov/updates/ao-2010-11-contributions-to-an-independent-expenditure-committee.

35. "2020 Election to Cost $14 Billion, Blowing Away Spending Records," Open Secrets, October 28, 2020, https://www.opensecrets.org/news/2020/10/cost-of-2020-election-14billion-update/.

36. "Outside Spending," Open Secrets, https://www.opensecrets.org/outside-spending/fes_summ.php.

37. A hybrid PAC can act as both a Super PAC and a traditional PAC and maintains separate bank accounts for conducting Super PAC and traditional PAC activities. Traditional PACs, unlike Super PACs, may make contributions to federal candidates and other federal political committees. Traditional PACs are prohibited from accepting corporate and labor union contributions and may accept contributions from individuals up to $5,000 per calendar year. Traditional PACs are referred to herein as "PACs."

38. Majority Committee PAC is a leadership PAC.

39. Stacy Montemayer, Pete Quist, Karl Evers-Hillstrom, and Douglas Weber, "Joint Report Reveals Record Donations in 2020 State and Federal Races," Follow the Money, November 19, 2020, https://www.followthemoney.org/research/institute-reports/joint-report-reveals-record-donations-in-2020-state-and-federal-races.

40. Karl Evers-Hillstrom, "Biden Campaign Becomes First to Raise $1 Billion from Donors," Open Secrets, December, 7, 2020, https://www.opensecrets.org/news/2020/12/biden-campaign-1billion-from-donors/.

41. "2020 Election to Cost $14 Billion, Blowing Away Spending Records," Open Secrets, October 28, 2020, https://www.opensecrets.org/news/2020/10/cost-of-2020-election-14billion-update/.

42. Julie Bykowicz and Tarini Parti, "Big Donors Spent Heavily on Failed Election Efforts," *Wall Street Journal,* November 23, 2020, https://www.wsj.com/articles/big-donors-spent-heavily-on-failed-election-efforts-11606147552.

43. "2020 Election to Cost $14 Billion, Blowing Away Spending Records," Open Secrets, October 28, 2020, https://www.opensecrets.org/news/2020/10/cost-of-2020-election-14billion-update/.

44. Stacy Montemayer, Pete Quist, Karl Evers-Hillstrom, and Douglas Weber, "Joint Report Reveals Record Donations in 2020 State and Federal Races," Follow the Money, November 19, 2020, https://www.followthemoney.org/research/institute-reports/joint-report-reveals-record-donations-in-2020-state-and-federal-races.

45. "Outside Spending," Open Secrets, https://www.opensecrets.org/outside spending/; Stacy Montemayer, Pete Quist, Karl Evers-Hillstrom, and Douglas Weber, "Joint Report Reveals Record Donations in 2020 State and Federal Races," Follow the Money, November 19, 2020, https://www.followthemoney.org/research/institute-reports/joint-report-reveals-record-donations-in-2020-state-and-federal-races.

46. For example, if a JFC included a presidential campaign, a national political party committee and two state political party committees, individual donors could contribute up to $61,100 to the JFC—up to $5,600 to the presidential campaign ($2,800 for the primary and $2,800 for the general election), $35,500 to the main account of the national political party, and $10,000 each to the two state political parties. Any prior contributions that individual donors made to any of the entities participating in the JFC would count against what could be contributed to the JFC. Federal Election Commission data.

47. In Mid-November, the Trump Make America Great Again Committee amended its FEC Statement of Organization to include Save America as a participant.

48. "Joint Fundraising Committees," Open Secrets, https://www.opensecrets.org/jfc/.

49. Carrie Levine and Chris Zubak-Skees, "How ActBlue is Trying to Turn Small Donations into a Blue Wave," Public Integrity, October 25, 2018, https://publicintegrity.org/federal-politics/how-actblue-is-trying-to-turn-small-donations-into-a-blue-wave/.

50. Elena Schneider, "How ActBlue has Transformed Democratic Politics," *Politico,* October 30, 2020. https://www.politico.com/news/2020/10/30/democrats-actblue-fundrasing-elections-433698.

51. Ibid.

52. Elena Schneider, "ActBlue's Stunning Third Quarter: $1.5 Billion in Donations," *Politico,* October 15, 2020. https://www.politico.com/news/2020/10/15/actblues-stunning-third-quarter-15-billion-in-donations-429549.

53. Zach Montellaro, "GOP Raises Over $620M Through WinRed in Third Quarter," *Politico,* October 12, 2020, https://www.politico.com/news/2020/10/12/gop-raises-over-620m-through-winred-in-third-quarter-428983.

54. Karl Evers-Hillstrom, "Biden Campaign Becomes First to Raise $1 Billion from Donors," Open Secrets, December, 7, 2020, https://www.opensecrets.org/news/2020/12/biden-campaign-1billion-from-donors/.

55. Julia Musto, "Republicans Raise $804M on WinRed in Two Months." Fox News, December 4, 2020, https://www.foxnews.com/politics/republicans-raise-804m-on-winred-in-first-two-months-of-fourth-quarter.

56. Derek Willis and Maggie Severns, "The Hidden Money Funding the Midterms," *Politico,* October 15, 2018, https://www.politico.com/interactives/2018/hidden-money-funding-midterms-superpacs.

57. Karl Evers-Hillstrom, "Pop-Up Super PACs Meddle in Key Races and Hide Donors from Voters," Open Secrets, October 29, 2020, https://www.opensecrets.org/news/2020/10/pop-up-super-pacs-key-races/.

58. Ibid.

59. "2020 Outside Spending, by Super PAC," Open Secrets, October 29, 2020, https://www.opensecrets.org/outsidespending/summ.php?chrt=V&type=S.

60. For example, scholars estimate that only about 5 percent of the nation's voters cast absentee ballots in 1980. June Krunholz, "Forget Election Day – Early Voting for President Has Started," *Wall Street Journal*, September 23, 2008.

61. Michael P. McDonald, "Early Voting in 2012: What to Expect," *The Huffington Post*, https://www.huffpost.com/entry/early-voting-in-2012-what_b_1773768.

62. "States with No-Excuse Absentee Voting," *National Conference of State Legislatures,* https://www.ncsl.org/research/elections-and-campaigns/vopp-table-1-states-with-no-excuse-absentee-voting.aspx.

63. "Absentee and Mail Voting Policies in Effect for the 2020 Election," *National Conference of State Legislatures,* https://www.ncsl.org/research/elections-and-campaigns/absentee-and-mail-voting-policies-in-effect-for-the-2020-election.aspx.

64. Jim Zarroli, "Getting Lots Of Political Messages On Your Phone? Welcome To 'The Texting Election,'" NPR, October 7, 2020, https://www.npr.org/2020/10/07/920776670/getting-lots-of-political-messages-on-your-phone-welcome-to-the-texting-election.

65. Devin Dwyer and Jacqueline Yoo, "Tidal Wave of Political Text Messages Hits Campaign Home Stretch," ABC News, October 31, 2020, https://abcnews.go.com/Politics/tidal-wave-political-text-messages-hits-campaign-home/story?id=73795827.

66. Jim Zarroli, "Getting Lots Of Political Messages On Your Phone? Welcome To 'The Texting Election,'" NPR, October 7, 2020, https://www.npr.org/2020/10/07/920776670/getting-lots-of-political-messages-on-your-phone-welcome-to-the-texting-election.

67. Devin Dwyer and Jacqueline Yoo, "Tidal Wave of Political Text Messages Hits Campaign Home Stretch," ABC News, October 21, 2020, https://abcnews.go.com/Politics/tidal-wave-political-text-messages-hits-campaign-home/story?id=73795827.

68. Trump was a campaign finance innovator throughout his four years in office. Trump's innovations began the day after he was inaugurated in 2017 when he formed a presidential reelection campaign and began actively raising funds to seek a second term. In doing so, Trump became the first president in the modern era to actively fund-raise for his reelection campaign during the first two years of his term. It will be interesting to see if Biden and other newly elected presidents continue this practice in the future.

69. No matter what Trump decides to do in the years ahead, there is no question he will remain a fund-raising force within the Republican Party. Indeed, just days after the 2020 presidential election, Trump formed a Leadership PAC, which could be a precursor to creating a 2024 presidential campaign committee. Published reports

indicate that Trump's PAC had already raised over $70 million by the end of 2020, which was an astonishing fundraising figure just weeks after a presidential election. Maggie Haberman and Reid J. Epstein, "As Trump Seeks to Remain a Political Force, New Targets Emerge," *New York Times*, January 25, 2021, https://www.nytimes.com/2021/01/25/us/politics/trump-portman-ohio-sarah-sanders.html?smid=em-share.

13

Was Trump Worth It for Republicans?

Sean Trende

On the morning of January 6, in the waning days of his administration, President Donald Trump gave a fiery speech on the National Mall. The speech itself wasn't that unusual for a Donald Trump speech. He accused "radical-left Democrats" of stealing the election from him and said he would never concede because "[y]ou don't concede when there's theft involved." He urged protestors on to the Capitol: "I know that everyone here will soon be marching over to the Capitol building to peacefully and patriotically make your voices heard," and concluded by asking the crowd to pressure Republican senators to overturn the results of the 2020 election: "[W]e're going to try and give our Republicans, the weak ones because the strong ones don't need any of our help. We're going to try and give them the kind of pride and boldness that they need to take back our country. So let's walk down Pennsylvania Avenue."[1]

The "walk" down Pennsylvania Avenue quickly became a march, and the crowd quickly turned into a mob. While Trump was still speaking, the mob breached the outer perimeter of the Capitol building, just as senators and representatives gathered to count the electoral votes. As protestors from Trump's rally continued to trickle down the mall, the mob grew in size, and occupied the Capitol steps as the senators debated the objections that Republican representatives and senators had raised to the counting of the electoral votes. Shortly thereafter, the Capitol interior was breached, and senators and representatives were evacuated. During this mayhem, Trump continued to press his claims of a stolen election on Twitter, criticized Vice President Mike Pence for failing to overrule the Electoral College himself, and repeatedly reaffirmed the righteousness of the protestors while asking them to go home.[2]

Within days, the fallout was severe. Democrats called for the Trump cabinet to invoke the 25th Amendment, which would have removed Trump from power immediately.[3] When this failed, Trump was swiftly impeached, becoming the first president in history to be impeached twice.[4] Unlike Trump's first impeachment, this time 10 House Republicans joined ranks to impeach him.[5]

As of this writing, I do not know how this will turn out in the short-term. It seems unlikely that Trump will be convicted by the Senate, which would bar Trump from ever seeking federal office again, but some important Republican senators have signaled that they may support conviction.[6] Perhaps more significantly, his job approval has declined even among Republicans; in a CNN poll issued in the wake of the attack, his job approval within the GOP had slipped to 80 percent, down from 94 percent before the election.[7]

It is even less clear how this will play out in the medium-to-long term. If Trump is removed from office, will Trump-supporting Republicans hold it against the Republican Party as a whole? Will they more narrowly target senators who vote for removal? And if Trump is not convicted, will his opponents move on? In the lead-up to the 2010 midterms, many commentators expressed disbelief that the country would turn the reins of power over to the party that had, just a few years earlier, presided over a disastrous war in the Middle East and a financial crisis that precipitated the worst economic recession since the 1930s. Yet Americans proved to have extremely short memories; even Trump's 2019 impeachment barely served as a blip on the radar screen in 2020. Will Trump fade into the background, as is very much not his wont? Will he be able to thrust himself into the public debate with his presence on social media very much diminished?

Against this background, it is difficult to press the claim that Trump was worth it for the Republican Party. Simply put, more so than with any other president, this story is still being written. Because of this, the bulk of this chapter will take things as they stood on the morning of January 6. It will conclude with some thoughts on how things might go based on the events that unfolded in the subsequent weeks, and why Trump may have managed to deal a serious blow to his party's—and his own—political prospects.

THE COALITIONAL PERSPECTIVE ON DONALD TRUMP'S PRESIDENCY

In 2002, Ruy Teixeira and John Judis published one of the most important books on elections of the past 20 years: *The Emerging Democratic Majority*.[8] The content of the book was less strident than the name implied: It suggested not that a Democratic majority was immediately coming, but rather that a different Democratic coalition was emerging. This coalition was based in fast-growing demographic groups and threatened to seriously constrain the ability of conservative Republicanism to continue if Democrats governed well.

The Judis and Teixeira thesis was modest in its claims, and quite reasonable—it was even arguably indisputable. We might call this the "weak" version of the Emerging Democratic Majority theory. What followed, however, was not. In the wake of the Democratic wave elections in 2006 and 2008, the "Democrats have a solid coalition if they govern well" argument mutated into a new argument: The "demographics is destiny" argument frequently heard from progressive flacks during the Obama years. We might call this the "strong" version of the argument. Some Democrats explicitly talked about a permanent majority that would end conservatism.[9] Michael Lind proclaimed the rebirth of a New American Republic, and immediately lumped Barack Obama in with George Washington, Abraham Lincoln, and Franklin Roosevelt.[10] The great James Carville even penned a book entitled *40 More Years*, whose theme the reader can readily identify.[11] Dylan Loewe published a book entitled *Permanently Blue*,[12] while Sam Tanenhaus' *The Death of Conservatism* bolstered similar claims.[13]

This came to a head in the wake of Obama's 2012 reelection. By now, commentators had seen enough: Republicans had to get on board with large portions of the Democratic agenda to neutralize them as issues and transform their coalition into a more upscale, modernized American party. The Republican National Committee published a now-infamous "autopsy" that prominently demanded that the GOP endorse comprehensive immigration reform to bolster its standing among nonwhite voters as a price for continuing to win elections.[14]

This was a debate in which I was intimately involved, penning a controversial article entitled "The Case of the Missing White Voters, Revisited."[15] The gist of the article was simple: The Republican Party actually had two paths to victory. One was the "autopsy" path, a path to citizenship and outreach (this was the approach that I personally wanted the GOP to take). But the other approach was the "Missing Whites" argument, which noted that in 2012, millions of blue collar non-Hispanic white voters simply opted not to vote. They may not have liked Barack Obama, but they also saw little appeal in Mitt Romney, the GOP nominee who owned car elevators. This theory seemed well borne out by the results of the 2016 election, when Donald Trump rode massive blue-collar support to the Oval Office.

The article was actually part of a four-part series. The second and third pieces garnered less attention, but offer important insights into the 2020 election. The third article in particular focused on the Hispanic vote, and the GOP's potential with that group.[16] It noted that the long-term trend of the Hispanic vote in America had been toward Republicans for quite some time.

It questioned whether immigration reform was as important to Hispanic voters as commentators suggested; when asked, Hispanics indicated that, like most Americans, health care and the economy topped their list of important considerations; on immigration, they don't look dissimilar from the United States as a whole (in 2020, 59 percent of Hispanics labeled immigration as important, versus 52 percent of U.S. adults).[17] It noted that George H.W. Bush had been part of an administration that signed comprehensive immigration reform, yet put up one of the worst performances among Hispanics on record. It concluded that there might have been a variety of reasons for George W. Bush's impressive showing among Hispanics in 2004, including Bush's support of increased government spending, his relatively "blue collar persona" (at least for a very wealthy individual), his experience governing a state with a large Hispanic population, and his status as a wartime president. In short, the piece was optimistic about the future of the GOP with Hispanics.

If Donald Trump did nothing else, he laid to rest the idea that demographic change would drive Democrats inexorably toward the presidency. From a coalitional perspective, he was something of a mixed bag for Republicans, but his success demonstrated that there was, in fact, more than one way to skin the electoral cat. Whatever the Emerging Democratic Majority theory might have predicted, it did not predict that a 70-year-old reality television host with a penchant for saying things like, "When Mexico sends its people . . . [t]hey're sending people that have lots of problems, and they're bringing those problems with us. They're bringing drugs. They're bringing crime. They're rapists," would win the presidency by the year 2016 and come close in 2020 (though Trump did allow that "some, I assume, are good people.")[18] It certainly did not predict that he would have one of the strongest showings among Hispanic voters of any Republican in recent history.

There's little doubt that Donald Trump represented a different kind of Republican, and that his presidential coalition looked significantly different than the coalition of other presidential candidates. We can see this most readily from examining exit polling from 2012 and 2020, summarized in table 13.1. I have also included data from the AP VoteCast poll. While not an apples-to-apples comparison in terms of methodology and biases with earlier exit polls, it nevertheless provides a somewhat different gloss on the same data.

I chose 2012 because the Democratic popular vote margin in that election was virtually identical to the margin in 2020. That alone is interesting; Donald Trump almost won the Electoral College, while Mitt Romney very much did not. A coalition grounded in blue-collar voters is much more efficiently distributed than a coalition grounded in nonwhite voters and college educated voters, at least for now, and Trump's coalition maximizes that advantage.

But digging deeper into the exit polls, we see some of the profound shifts that Trump brought to the GOP, and a validation of some theories about

Table 13.1. Republican Share of Vote, 2012 vs. 2020 Exit Polls

	2012	*2020 (Exits)*	*2020 (AP)*
Race			
White	60%	59%	56%
Black	6%	12%	8%
Hispanic	28%	33%	36%
Asian	26%	36%	30%
Age			
18-29	38%	38%	37%
30-44	46%	47%	44%
45-64	52%	51%	52%
65+	60%	53%	52%
Education			
College	49%	44%	42%
Non-College	48%	51%	52%
Income			
Under $50,000	39%	44%	45%
$50,000-$99,000	54%	42%	50%
$100,000+	55%	56%	48%

demographic change. Note that Donald Trump actually did worse among whites than Romney, marginally according to the exit polls, and substantially according to the AP. Trump made up with this, however, with an overperformance among nonwhite voters. Trump's showing among Black voters in the exit polls was actually the strongest for a Republican since 1996, and one of the strongest since the GOP stopped routinely winning 30 percent of the Black vote in the 1960s. His showing among Hispanics was also one of the better performances for a Republican in recent years, and reflected a substantial improvement from Romney's.

While the Democratic lean of the youth vote had been a substantial concern for Republicans in the early 2010s, those voters seem to have lost some of their Democratic bona fides as they aged. That cohort barely gave Mitt Romney a third of the vote in 2012; by 2020 they had largely aged into the next age bracket (the same is true if you take Barack Obama's 2008 win as a baseline) which, while not Republican in 2020, was also not far off from the national average in either the AP VoteCast or the exit polling. At the same time, Trump saw a substantial ebb in support from older voters, both vis-à-vis his 2016 showing and Romney's in 2020. That ebb likely cost him the presidency, but the fact that age polarization decreased significantly in this election blunts concerns about the Republicans' demographic future.

But looking at income and education gives a clearer picture of the tradeoffs involved. Trump improved the GOP's fortunes among lower income voters and those without college educations. They nosedived, however, among voters with college education and middle-to-upper income voters.

This all resulted in tradeoffs that we can see by examining three states: Georgia, Texas, and Ohio. In 2012, Mitt Romney carried Georgia by eight points, even as he was losing the popular vote by four. In 2020, Trump narrowly lost it. We can see why in map 13.1:

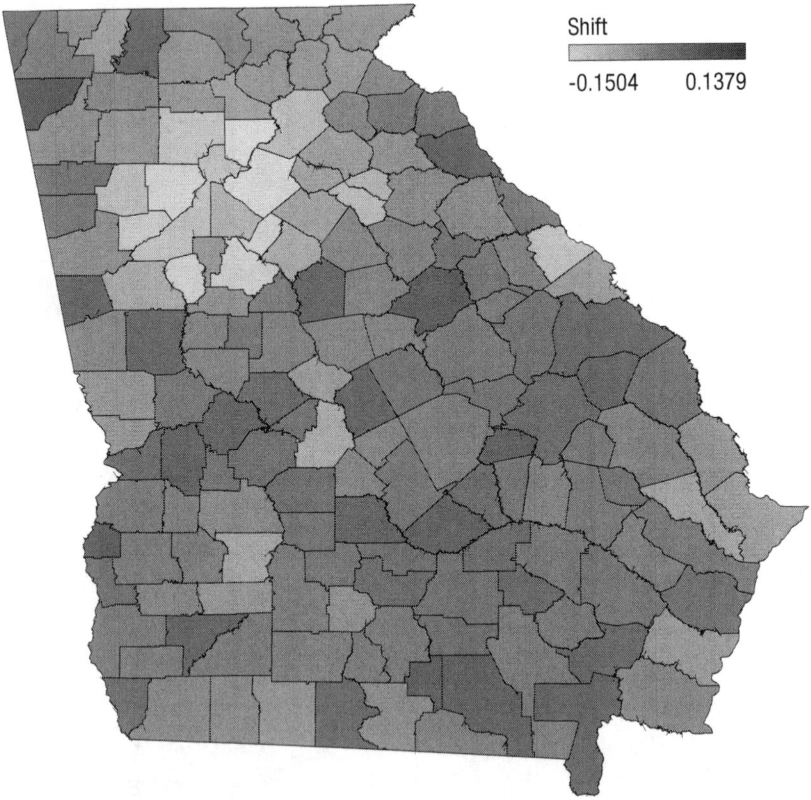

Map 13.1. Shift in Republican Performance in Georgia, 2012-2020

This shows the shift in Republican performance in Georgia from 2012 to 2020. Note that, to keep the color scheme even, I have truncated the scale at -15 percent and positive 15 percent. In some of these states, particularly Texas, the shift is substantially more than this, so much so that a few counties with particularly large shifts would overwhelm the color scheme and obscure smaller, but important shifts.

If you are familiar with Georgia's geography, this is an easy map to read: metro Atlanta, especially suburban Forsyth and Gwinnett counties, shifted heavily against Republicans; Augusta moved to a lesser extent. The rest of the state, in particular the rural areas, swung toward Trump.

We see similar movement in Texas:

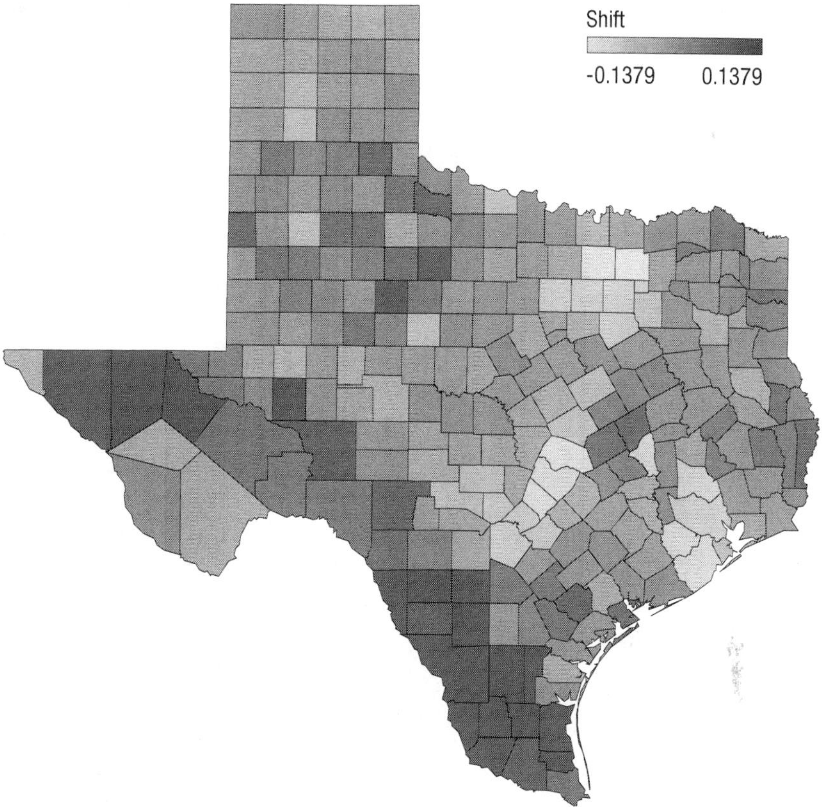

Map 13.2. Shift in Republican Performance in Texas, 2012-2020

The wealthy north Dallas suburbs of Collin and Denton counties moved toward Democrats, as did, to a lesser extent, Montgomery County, to the north of Houston. The I-35 corridor counties surrounding Austin likewise swerved leftward, with Williamson County (to the north of Austin) being particularly pronounced.

But we can also see the large shift in rural counties in Texas and along the Rio Grande Valley. Trump's successes here were nothing short of astounding. Starr County moved 34 percentage points toward Donald Trump from 2012 to 2020. Joe Biden became the first Democratic presidential candidate since 1920 to lose Zapata County. Had Republicans spent money in the congressional races, Democrats likely would have lost the Fifteenth Congressional District.

What makes this all the more stunning is that Donald Trump's nativism would seemingly have the most impact in the heavily Mexican-American border counties. But as one Hispanic strategist explained to me anonymously, most immigrants, legal or otherwise, are fiercely patriotic, having come to this country by choice, rather than by birth. Many border patrol agents are Hispanic-American. Most of the police and police chiefs in border towns are Mexican-American. It is only a theory, of course, and one that demands additional proof, but it does suggest that perhaps the cultural realignment of politics seemingly under way works out in strange and unforeseeable ways.

Finally, we look at Ohio:

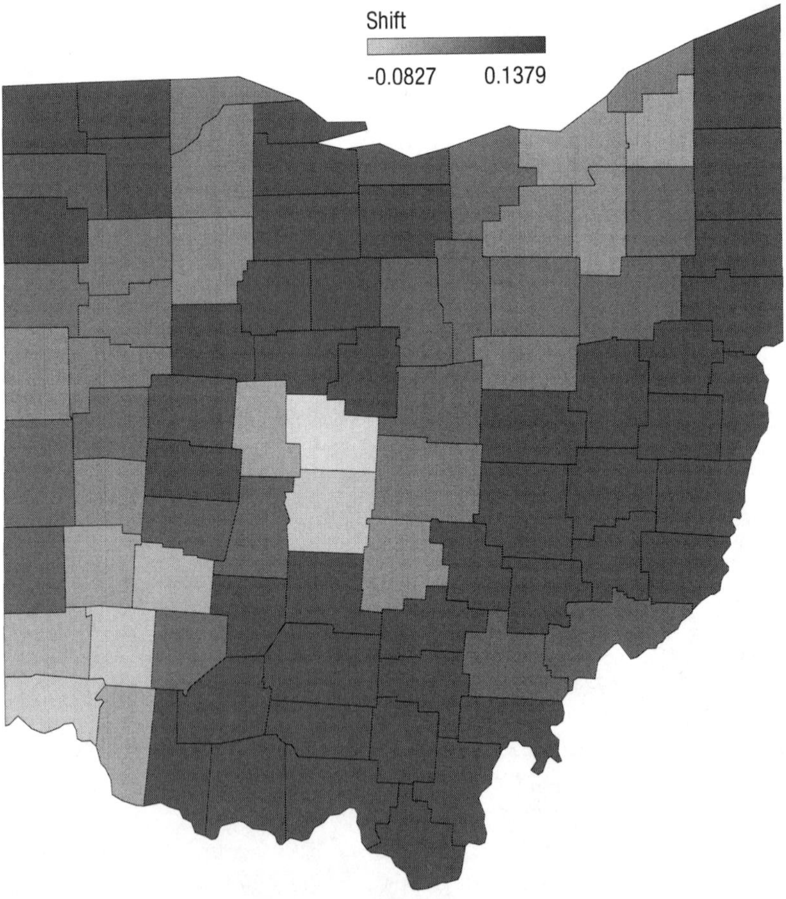

Map 13.3. Shift in Republican Performance in Ohio, 2012-2020

Here we see dramatic shifts in the vote allegiances of rural voters, particularly in Appalachia. The "new economy" hub of Columbus in central Ohio stands out for its Democratic shift, particularly in upscale Delaware County; metro

Table 13.2. Trump 2020 Percentage Vote Share in Georgia, Ohio, and Texas by Area Type

Type of Area	*Ohio*	*Georgia*	*Texas*
Rural	78.06	70.82	79.66
Small Town	70.55	67.74	72.68
Big Town	66.15	54.72	64.23
Small City	50.55	56.33	36.41
Big City	47.14	N/A	42.28
Mega City	N/A	42.18	49.62

Cincinnati in the southwest demonstrates less of a swing, while blue-collar northeastern Ohio has swung even less.

That these states have similar shifts should seem obvious from the maps, but it is even more striking when we look at the outcomes in these states by type of place. In table 13.2, I have categorized every county in each state by the type of metropolitan area to which it belongs (metro areas are determined by the U.S. Census Bureau; size of the metro area determines how I classified the area). It shows Donald Trump's vote share in each state by the type of metro area.

As you can see, the similarities are quite pronounced. Trump does a little worse in "big towns" in Georgia than elsewhere (a function of the University of Georgia), and did particularly poorly in small cities in Texas (some of the border town areas). But otherwise, the different areas performed more-or-less the same regardless of the state.

So why did these states swing in different directions? Why has Ohio become unusually Republican, while Texas became a purplish-red state and Georgia became the lightest shade of blue? The answer is found in the two "NA"s in the table. Ohio lacks a "Mega City" on the order of Dallas or Atlanta, that would counteract the red shift in rural areas. Columbus has shifted leftward, but there aren't yet enough votes to do what Atlanta did in Georgia. Likewise, Georgia lacks medium-sized cities that are moving leftward, but are still fertile ground for Republicans. We can see this better in table 13.3, which shows the percentage of votes cast in each state in each grouping:

Table 13.3. Percentage of Votes Cast in Georgia, Ohio, and Texas by Area Type

Type of Area	*Ohio*	*Georgia*	*Texas*
Rural	3.57	7.35	5.49
Small Town	13.85	9.96	5.78
Big Town	9.71	18.4	14.77
Small City	21.76	5.25	4.33
Big City	51.11	N/A	18.51
Mega City	N/A	59.05	51.13

As you can see, Atlanta dominates Georgia in a way that even Dallas and Houston combined do not dominate Texas. Ohio in particular has a lot of small cities and towns that are fairly Republican that, combined with a lack of mega cities, pushed the state rightward.

On balance, Donald Trump's coalition was something of a mixed bag for Republicans. His 2020 reelection bid resulted in a much less polarized electorate than we have seen in quite some time, in terms of age, race, and income—an almost ironic outcome for such a polarizing presidency. He grew Republican strength in growing demographic groups. Overall, this allowed him to slow the Democrats' advance in places like Texas, and to break through in places like Wisconsin, Michigan, and Pennsylvania that had played Lucy-with-the-football to the GOP's Charlie Brown for years.

At the same time, there are causes for concern for Republicans. The weakening of Republican strength among upscale white voters threatens their

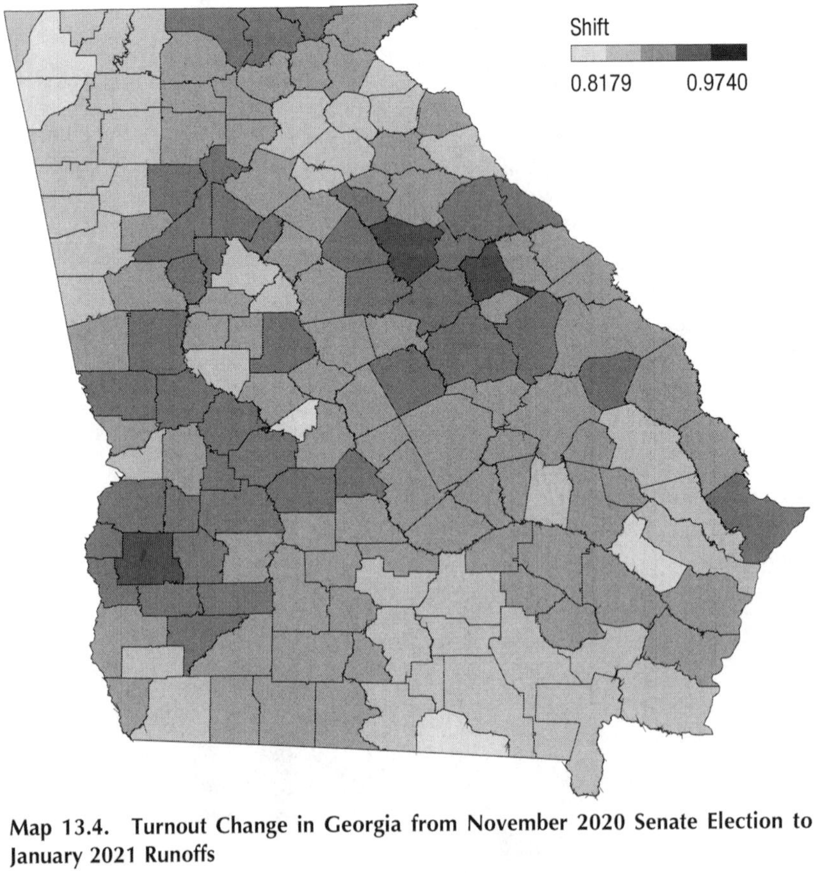

Map 13.4. Turnout Change in Georgia from November 2020 Senate Election to January 2021 Runoffs

hold on places like Arizona, Georgia, and Texas, which are increasingly dominated by these types of voters. More importantly, Trump's appeal may be entirely personal to him. Map 13.4 shows the changes in turnout from the November Senate races in Georgia to the January 5 runoff election in the same state.

Areas with greater drop-offs in turnout are lighter colored, while areas with small drop-offs in turnout are darker colored. As you can see, turnout remained robust in Democratic areas, particularly metro Atlanta and the "Black Belt" that stretches across the center of the state. Turnout was down significantly in the northwestern and southeastern portions of the state, which are bastions of Trumpism.

If Republicans can figure out ways to hold on to the gains Trump made among nonwhite voters and blue-collar voters, while also bringing suburbanites back into the fold, they will have a very strong governing coalition. That task, however, is easier than it sounds, as some of Trump's progress is likely Trump-specific. But the fact that we are having a conversation about different options facing the Republican Party moving forward represents a substantial improvement of its fortunes vis-à-vis where it found itself after the last presidential election that it lost.

THE ELECTORAL PERSPECTIVE ON DONALD TRUMP'S PRESIDENCY

Measures of partisan strength in the United States are decidedly president-centric. A party that controls the presidency but nothing else—as was the case for Republicans for most of the time period from 1952 to 1992—is nevertheless considered in healthy shape, while a party that controls much else but narrowly misses winning the presidency—as was the case for Republicans in 2012—is often considered in need of a major overhaul.

This seems wrong. A party that holds the presidency but cannot move its agenda forward has no real strength; this is in part why, despite making 10 consecutive Supreme Court appointments from 1969 to 1992, the GOP was unable to make good on its promises to shift the federal judiciary radically rightward; that occurred only after it had taken control of the Senate. Likewise, most legislating in this country still occurs at the state level; holding significant power there is meaningful, even if a party is shut out of the federal government.

To address this, in 2015, David Byler and I created an index that would measure party strength in Washington.[19] This index, which I used in the 2019 book *The Blue Wave* to evaluate claims that 2018 was a wave election, looks at five basic pillars of electoral strength in the country: the presidency, House, Senate, governorships, and state legislatures.

To calculate the index, we look at the Republican share of the popular vote for the presidency, excluding third parties (as we do for all other portions of the metric). We could have looked at the Electoral College as well, which would seem appropriate given that this is how we actually elect presidents in America, and the concept of a "popular vote" is something of a myth. Given, however, that parties can easily rack up wins approaching 100 percent of the electoral vote, we decided to exclude that metric as it would too easily skew the index.

We calculate separately a party's share of seats in the Senate. In the House, we proceed a little bit differently. We look at a party's share of seats in the House, but also look at the popular vote. We chose to look at both of these metrics because, unlike the Electoral College, parties rarely approach 100 percent of either metric. They do tend to be closely related, so the difference isn't that important.

Finally, we examine power in the states. Governorships are crucial in developing law in our states, and they often provide a "farm team" for senators and presidents; we look at a party's share of each. Power in the state legislatures is calculated by averaging the share of state Senates and state Houses controlled by a party with the *share* of seats in state Houses and state Senates.

These five metrics are then added together, providing a scale that would theoretically range from 0 to 500, although no party has ever approached either extreme. We then subtracted 250 from the score, which centers the index on zero (which would reflect perfect parity). Using this metric then allows us to evaluate claims made about the strength of parties. For example, the Republican Party scored -34.5 after the 2008 elections. While this was definitely a strong showing by the Democrats, it did not approach the -75.4 we saw after the 1976 elections or the -119.5 Republicans were at post-1936. This, perhaps, should have tempered predictions about the Republican Party's demise. Similarly, the Republican score of 35.9 post-2016 showed the party in its strongest position since 1928.

Figure 13.1 shows the overall trend line.

The Republican Party did astonishingly well in the 1860s during the Reconstruction period, before sinking to parity in the late 1800s. In the aftermath of the Panic of 1893, the Republican Party once again opened a big advantage, before being decimated in the 1930s. Since then, one might fairly read the chart as showing a Republican Party gradually improving its position in the American political sphere.

This continued under Donald Trump. Although the GOP clearly lost ground over the course of his presidency, the narrow Democratic advantage

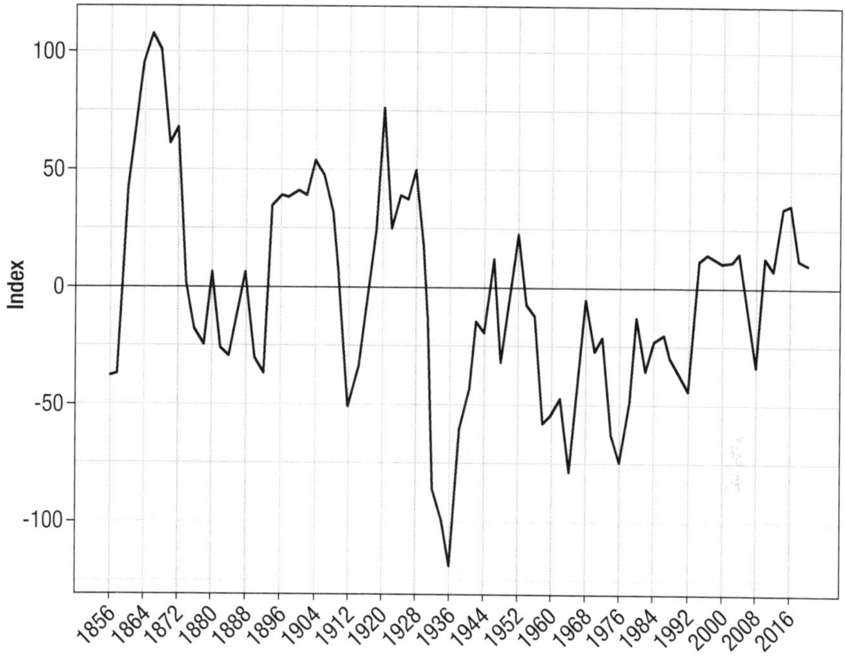

Figure 13.1. Index of Republican Party Strength, 1856-2020

in the House, Senate, and popular vote, combined with the Republican Party's strong position in the states, leaves it with an overall edge, with about as much strength as it had after the 2010 midterm elections.

Moreover, Trump's losses were not unusual. If we confine ourselves to first presidential terms (I include FDR's term in 1944 because Harry Truman served as president for almost all of it) the average loss in the term is 27.6 points. As we see in table 13.4, Republican losses in this term were similar.

Overall, from an electoral perspective, Trump's presidency was neutral-to-positive for the Republican Party. The party didn't suffer any unusual electoral losses, and likely saw its coalitional options multiply.

THE POLICY PERSPECTIVE ON DONALD TRUMP'S PRESIDENCY

One of the less positive aspects of Trump's presidency for Republicans, however, is the policy portfolio, or lack thereof. The GOP once was lauded by Democratic Senator Daniel Patrick Moynihan as "the party of ideas."[20] One

Table 13.4. Change in Index of Party Strength over Presidential First Terms

2016	Trump	–25.58
2008	Obama	–42.53
2000	Bush (W)	5.4
1992	Clinton	–58.36
1988	Bush (HW)	–13.65
1980	Reagan	–10.4
1976	Carter	–62.91
1968	Nixon	–17.64
1964	Johnson	–75.98
1960	Kennedy	25.81
1952	Eisenhower	–36.93
1944	Roosevelt/Truman	13.03
1932	Roosevelt	34.21
1928	Hoover	–137.16
1924	Coolidge	11.94
1920	Harding	–38.71
1912	Wilson	–45.73
1908	Taft	–87.54
1900	McKinley/Roosevelt	14.03
1896	McKinley	2.27
1892	Cleveland	–76.95
1888	Harrison	–45.97
1884	Cleveland	–37.78
1880	Garfield/Arthur	–36.33
1876	Hayes	25.12
1868	Grant	–31.86
1860	Lincoln	55.59
1856	Buchanan	–78.45

would be forgiven for failing to believe this ever happened today. Aside from tax cuts, a few miles of wall, and judges, there is remarkably little to show for the Trump years that cannot be undone with the flick of a pen by President Biden (and Biden got started as soon as he took office). Of course, those judges *are* important, particularly the three Supreme Court justices. There are precious few accomplishments for Trump advocates to weigh.

Still, Trump probably helped the Republican Party in other, more important ways. The GOP had been in thrall to what its critics called "Zombie Reaganism"—a policy portfolio growing out of the iconic president's term of office. This portfolio was increasingly unsuccessful in elections, in part because the GOP had won so many important fights. Consider what Ronald Reagan was elected to do: lower tax rates (a couple making around $85,000 per year in today's dollars faced a marginal tax rate of 37 percent, roughly the bracket that couples making over $400,000 per year paid today); tame inflation; slow the brakes on social change; and defeat the Soviet Union.

All of these changes were largely adopted by the Democratic Party by the 1990s. Bill Clinton opted only to raise taxes for high-income individuals, appointed the fiscally hawkish Alan Greenspan as Federal Reserve chairman, and was relatively hawkish. Even on social issues, Clinton promised to keep abortion "safe, legal, and rare," and reframed fights over gay rights in terms of middle class morality. "If it feels good, do it" morphed into "hate is not a family value."

With their most popular issues co-opted, Republicans were pushed further right and possessed less popular issues on which to run. It increasingly seemed to view a tax cut as a cure for every social ill. Democrats' reluctance to raise taxes on the middle class framed the debate as one over taxes on the rich, one which Republicans were on the unpopular side of. Even with those taxes on the wealthy operating at a lower rate, the supply side argument that they would pay for themselves was substantially weakened. With welfare transformed, Republicans were left trying to slow the growth of popular middle-class entitlements like social security. The Paul Ryan plan may have thrilled Republican policy wonks, but it offered little to blue collar voters in eastern Ohio, who simply went missing. Republicans projected their old hawkish Cold War framework onto the War on Terror, with catastrophic consequences for the party, the country, and the Middle East.

If nothing else, Donald Trump broke the "Zombie Reagan" mold, jettisoning GOP orthodoxies that had weakened its standing with working class voters, white, Black, and brown alike. It seems unlikely that all of "Trumpism" will be retained, and it is unclear whether "Trumpism" without "Trump" makes sense (see the Georgia Senate race above). At the same time, the old GOP policy portfolio isn't returning, either. There will be some sort of synthesis that emerges, but the important thing is that Donald Trump demonstrated that it was possible to win the GOP nomination without endorsing all of the old Republican nostrums about how government was supposed to work. Republicans have needed to have a conversation about what it means for a long time. If nothing else, now they will have a conversation and develop an agenda that a more competent Republican president might be able to work through Congress.

THE LONG-TERM PERSPECTIVE ON DONALD TRUMP'S PRESIDENCY

When I began writing this chapter, it had a different conclusion than it has today. After all, Republicans had come very, very close to winning a trifecta—complete control over all of the federal government—in 2020. Joe Biden's margin of victory in Arizona was just over 10,000 votes. In Georgia, it was just under 12,000 votes. In Wisconsin, it was just under 21,000 votes.[21] In the House of Representatives, the combined margin in the closest five Democratic wins was around 35,000 votes.[22] The Senate was even closer; just 13,471 votes separated David Perdue from winning a majority in November and avoiding a runoff, securing control of the Senate. At least as of the morning of January 6, there was fairly little cause for concern within the GOP. Given their overperformance in state legislatures, Republicans were slated to control redistricting for the 2020 cycle, likely giving them control of the House of Representatives in 2022.[23] That they were able to do this amidst a pandemic that has killed, as of this writing, 400,000 people, a summer of riots, and what was possibly the worst second quarter economic growth in history, is frankly astonishing.

As of the morning of January 6, Donald Trump was probably as well-positioned as any losing incumbent president in history to win a nonconsecutive reelection four years later. He oversaw a massive political movement with throngs of devoted fans, the Republican Party was still in his control, and he could dominate the political conversation with a 280-character tweet. The Republican Party's loss in the Georgia Senate runoffs seemed to demonstrate that Republicans needed Donald Trump on the ticket to post big wins.

By the end of the day, that had all been thrown away. He still had throngs of devoted fans, although many were disillusioned. The Republican Party began to fracture; as noted before, it seems likely that Mitt Romney would not be the sole Republican favoring his conviction in the Senate this time. His Twitter account was deactivated, limiting his ability to reach supporters. What some thought would be a massive political rally on the day of his departure turned into a small farewell at Andrews Air Force Base.

The long-term fallout remains to be seen. Obviously if Trump is convicted by the Senate in his eventual trial, a comeback bid in 2024 will be impossible. The trial is likely to split the Republican coalition further, heightening the tension between the populist base of the new Republican coalition and the suburban remnant of the old one, but we cannot say for certain how long memories will be. If Trump is acquitted, he will loom over the 2024 Republican nomination process, whether he chooses to run or not. Getting out the Trump-supporting base in 2022 could become more difficult. Whatever real benefits Trump conferred upon the Republican presidency during his tenure, it has a very real potential of being squandered.

There are reasons to believe that the Biden presidency may pose a particular challenge for Republicans going forward. In 2016, Barack Obama's former senior strategist observed that we tend to nominate and elect presidents that "cure" the weaknesses of the outgoing administration.[24] George H.W. Bush was presented as aloof and out of touch; Bill Clinton felt our pain. Clinton was presented as a corrupt philanderer; George W. Bush promised to restore dignity to the White House. Bush was presented as an anti-intellectual cowboy; Barack Obama was smooth and cerebral. Obama was a technocrat and progressive; Trump was, well, not those things.

So, what was Trump at the end of his presidency? It is certainly difficult to summarize what he meant for the 80 million voters who opposed him, but if I had to characterize him, I would say this: exhausting. The 2 a.m., tweets, the name-calling, the impeachments, the offer to buy Greenland, the pandemic response, the denouement in the sacking of the Capitol—all of this certainly took a toll on someone tasked to cover him. I imagine the effect is similar for the American people.

In this sense, Joe Biden is a reaction to Trump. His campaign was definitively boring, and his presidency promises to be much of the same: no overwhelmingly controversial cabinet nominees so far, nor pushes to pack the courts or for a single-payer health care system. The return to normalcy Biden promised was Harding-esque, and while Harding is remembered as something of a mediocrity, he holds the largest popular vote margin since our current two-party system was established in 1856. Harding's "return to normalcy" campaign wasn't just directed at Woodrow Wilson's administration—which had overseen a flurry of legislating in its early years, the conduct of a controversial war that it had campaigned on avoiding, a pandemic, a campaign of domestic terror, and runaway postwar inflation—but also against the norm-breaking presidency of Teddy Roosevelt.

Likewise, Biden's campaign seemed directed at a nation exhausted by its recent presidents. The relatively conservative nature of Bill Clinton's administration was overshadowed by a series of tawdry affairs; George W. Bush had two wars and a financial collapse; Barack Obama was determined to push the country as far leftward as he felt he could; Trump was Trump. It may seem like damning with faint praise to suggest that Biden's lack of panache may suit him well, but after the past 30 years, he seems like the man for the moment in a way that, frankly, none of the other Democratic presidential contenders could have been.

Finally, although one cannot time the business cycle, Democrats are taking over at the very beginning of an expansion. With trillions of dollars of stimulus pumping into the economy—in part because of Trump's reorientation of the Republicans as a pro-spending party—there's a chance we could be in for a lengthy economic expansion. If a typical business cycle lasts 12 years, Republicans may be shut out of the presidency for a decade, raising the prospect that their Supreme Court majority may evaporate (although their congressional majorities may actually be quite healthy at that point).

Which is to say, Donald Trump strengthened the Republican Party in many ways, but left Democrats with a golden opportunity. Twenty years ago, Judis and Teixeira suggested that a Democratic Party that governs well could wield power for a very, very long time. It would be ironic, although perhaps a touch appropriate, if a president who disproved the strong version of their theory ultimately helped prove the weak version.

NOTES

1. "Transcript Of Trump's Speech At Rally Before US Capitol Riot," *Associated Press,* January 13, 2021, https://apnews.com/article/election-2020-joe-biden-donald-trump-capitol-siege-media-e79eb5164613d6718e9f4502eb471f27.
2. Shelly Tan, Youjin Shin and Danielle Rindler, "How One Of America's Ugliest Days Unraveled Inside And Outside the Capitol," *Washington Post*, January 8, 2021, https://www.washingtonpost.com/nation/interactive/2021/capitol-insurrection-visual-timeline/.
3. Jacob Pramuk, "Pence Refuses to Invoke 25th Amendment as Democrats Work to Remove Trump," CNBC, January 12, 2021, https://www.cnbc.com/2021/01/12/us-capitol-riot-house-to-vote-on-25th-amendment-trump-impeachment.html.
4. "UPFRONT Recap: President Donald Trump Impeached Twice," WISN, January 17, 2021, https://www.wisn.com/article/trump-impeached-twice/35234696.
5. Domenico Montanaro, "These Are the 10 Republicans Who Voted to Impeach Trump," NPR, January 14, 2021, https://www.npr.org/2021/01/14/956621191/these-are-the-10-republicans-who-voted-to-impeach-trump.
6. Alan Fram, "McConnell Open to Convicting Trump in Impeachment Trial," *Associated Press*, January 13, 2021, https://apnews.com/article/joe-biden-donald-trump-impeachments-capitol-siege-mitch-mcconnell-29ca8c7dff7943c3daf2952d4a809097.
7. Trump approval among Republicans from SSRS polls conducted for CNN from January 9-14, 2021, http://cdn.cnn.com/cnn/2021/images/01/17/rel1a.-.trump,.impeachment.pdf, and October 23-26, 2020 http://cdn.cnn.com/cnn/2020/images/10/28/rel15.pdf.
8. John B. Judis and Ruy Teixeira, *The Emerging Democratic Majority*, (London, England: Simon & Schuster UK, 2002).
9. Andy Barr, "Dems Talk of 'Permanent Progressive Majority,'" *Politico*, November 7, 2008, http://www.politico.com/news/stories/1108/15407.html.
10. Michael Lind, "Obama and the Dawn of the Fourth Republic," *Salon*, November 7, 2008, https://www.salon.com/2008/11/07/fourth_republic/.
11. James Carville, *40 More Years: How the Democrats Will Rule the Next Generation* (New York: Simon & Schuster, 2009).

12. Dylan Loewe, *Permanently Blue: How Democrats Can End the Republican Party and Rule the Next Generation* (New York: Three Rivers Press, 2010).
13. Sam Tanenhaus, *The Death of Conservatism* (New York: Random House, 2009).
14. Shushannah Walshe, "RNC Completes 'Autopsy' on 2012 Loss, Calls for Inclusion not Policy Change," ABC News, March 18, 2013, https://abcnews.go.com/Politics/OTUS/rnc-completes-autopsy-2012-loss-calls-inclusion-policy/story?id=18755809.
15. Sean Trende, "The Case of the Missing White Voters, Revisited." *RealClearPolitics*, June 21, 2013, https://www.realclearpolitics.com/articles/2013/06/21/the_case_of_the_missing_white_voters_revisited_118893.html.
16. Sean Trende, "The GOP and Hispanics: What the Future Holds." *RealClearPolitics*, June 28, 2013, https://www.realclearpolitics.com/articles/2013/06/28/the_gop_and_hispanics_what_the_future_holds_119011.html.
17. Jens M. Krogstad and Mark H. Lopez, "Hispanic Voters Say Economy, Health Care and COVID-19 Are Top Issues in 2020 Presidential Election," Pew Research Center, September 11, 2020, https://www.pewresearch.org/fact-tank/2020/09/11/hispanic-voters-say-economy-health-care-and-covid-19-are-top-issues-in-2020-presidential-election/.
18. Michelle Ye Hee Lee, "Donald Trump's False Comments Connecting Mexican Immigrants and Crime," *Washington Post*, July 8, 2015, https://www.washingtonpost.com/news/fact-checker/wp/2015/07/08/donald-trumps-false-comments-connecting-mexican-immigrants-and-crime/.
19. Sean Trende and David Byler, "The GOP Is the Strongest It's Been in Decades," *RealClearPolitics*, May 19, 2015, https://www.realclearpolitics.com/articles/2015/05/19/the_gop_is_the_strongest_its_been_in_decades_126633.html.
20. Peter Wehner, George Weigel, and Henry Olsen, "A Party of Ideas," Ethics & Public Policy Center, April 5, 2011, https://eppc.org/publications/a-party-of-ideas/.
21. All election data in this article are taken from Dave Leip's Atlas of U.S. Presidential Elections, https://uselectionatlas.org/RESULTS/.
22. David Wasserman, Sophie Andrews, Leo Saenger, Lev Cohen, Ally Flinn, and Griff Tatarsky, "2020 House Vote Tracker," *Cook Political Report,* https://cookpolitical.com/2020-house-vote-tracker. As of this writing, the race between Republican Claudia Tenney and Democrat Anthony Brindisi has not been resolved. That race will likely be determined by a few dozen votes one way or the other, and would not substantially affect this analysis.
23. Sean Trende, "What Redrawn Districts Could Mean for House Control in 2023," *RealClearPolitics*, November 12, 2020, https://www.realclearpolitics.com/articles/2020/11/12/what_redrawn_districts_could_mean_for_house_control_in_2023_144644.html.
24. David Axelrod, "The Obama Theory of Trump," *New York Times*, January 25, 2016, https://www.nytimes.com/2016/01/25/opinion/campaign-stops/the-obama-theory-of-trump.html.

Index

About the Contributors

Alan I. Abramowitz is the Alben W. Barkley Professor of Political Science at Emory University and a senior columnist for *Sabato's Crystal Ball.* His most recent book is *The Great Alignment: Race, Party Transformation, and the Rise of Donald Trump.*

David Byler is a data analyst and political columnist for the *Washington Post* Opinions Section. He was previously the Chief Elections Analyst at the *Weekly Standard* and an elections analyst at *RealClearPolitics*.

J. Miles Coleman is associate editor of *Sabato's Crystal Ball*, the University of Virginia Center for Politics' nonpartisan newsletter on American campaigns and elections. A political cartographer with a portfolio of thousands of maps, he's studied American electoral geography for over a decade.

Rhodes Cook was a political reporter for *Congressional Quarterly* for more than two decades and a senior columnist at *Sabato's Crystal Ball.* He is the author of *The Presidential Nominating Process: A Place for Us?*, which was published by Rowman & Littlefield.

Theodore R. Johnson is a senior fellow and director of the fellows program at the Brennan Center for Justice. He's written on black political behavior for the *New York Times Magazine*, *The Atlantic*, and the *Washington Post*, among other national publications. Previously, he was a fellow at New America and a naval officer.

Kyle Kondik is managing editor of *Sabato's Crystal Ball*, the University of Virginia Center for Politics' nonpartisan newsletter on American campaigns and elections. He is the author of *The Bellwether,* a history of Ohio's presidential voting, and is working on a second book, *The Long Red Thread*, a history of modern U.S. House elections.

Mary Frances McGowan is the gubernatorial and state legislative elections reporter for *National Journal.* Prior to joining *National Journal*, she was a Tim Russert Fellow with *Meet the Press* and a researcher at NBC's Washington Bureau.

Diana Owen is Associate Professor of Political Science at Georgetown University and teaches in the Communication, Culture, and Technology graduate program, and he has served as director of the American Studies Program. She is the author of *Media Messages in American Presidential Elections; New Media and American Politics* (with Richard Davis); and *American Government and Politics in the Information Age* (with David Paletz and Timothy Cook).

Grace Panetta is a senior politics reporter at *Business Insider* covering politics with a focus on elections, voting rights, and election administration. Grace closely covered voting during the COVID-19 pandemic, and played a leading role in *Business Insider*'s live results coverage of all of 2020's elections in partnership with Decision Desk HQ.

Madelaine Pisani has covered politics for *National Journal*'s *Hotline* team since 2018, working on both the Senate and gubernatorial beats.

Larry J. Sabato is the Robert Kent Gooch Professor of Politics at the University of Virginia and director of its Center for Politics. He is the author or editor of more than 20 books on American politics and elections.

Michael E. Toner is former chairman of the Federal Election Commission and is chair of the Election Law and Government Ethics Practice Group at Wiley LLP in Washington, DC.

Karen E. Trainer served in the FEC's Reports Analysis Division and is a senior reporting specialist at Wiley LLP.

Sean Trende is the senior elections analyst for *RealClearPolitics*. He is the author of *The Lost Majority: Why the Future of Government Is Up for Grabs and Who Will Take It*, and he coauthored the *Almanac of American Politics 2014*.